CONTENTS

Preface

This Solutions Manual and Study Guide has been developed to accompany the text, <u>Business Statistics:</u> <u>Contemporary Decision Making</u>, 3rd Edition. All materials in this manual have been developed by Ken Black to assure that topics considered and presented here are consistent with the manner of presentation in the main text. This manual has been organized to parallel the eighteen chapters of the main text. Each of the chapters in the manual contains six parts: chapter objectives, chapter outline, key words, study questions, answers to study questions, and solutions to the odd-numbered problems in the main text.

The study questions have been prepared in such a way as to guide you, the student, through the chapter. This is accomplished by asking questions about key words and concepts presented in the chapter. Also, additional problems have been created and presented in the study question section to afford you the opportunity for further practice. These problems cover most of the major topics in each chapter. Problem scenarios have been kept to a minimum to allow you to focus on data manipulation and computation. The answers to each of these study questions is given in the next section of the chapter to allow you to evaluate your progress in mastering the chapter material.

Section six of each chapter contains the solutions to the odd-numbered problems from the main text chapter. I have made an attempt to provide you with the maximum amount of detailed information on each problem. I find in teaching statistics that a lot of learning goes on between the student and the solutions manual in wrestling with the whys and wherefores of the printed solution.

I hope that you find this solutions manual and study guide to be an integral part of your learning experience in this course. This book is intended to facilitate the creation of an optimal experience in studying statistics.

Finally, I wish you a successful journey into the world of statistics. Keep pushing on! In time, it will come together. I hope that this manual assists in making the course a successful one.

Chapter 1
Introduction to Statistics

LEARNING OBJECTIVES

The primary objective of chapter 1 is to introduce you to the world of statistics, enabling you to:

1. Define statistics.

2. Be aware of a wide range of applications of statistics in business.

3. Differentiate between descriptive and inferential statistics.

4. Classify numbers by level of data and understand why doing so is important.

CHAPTER OUTLINE

1.1   Statistics in Business

1.2   What is Statistics?

1.3   Descriptive Versus Inferential Statistics

1.4   Levels of Data Measurement

        Nominal Level

        Ordinal Level

        Interval Level

        Ratio Level

        Comparison of the Four Levels of Data

        Statistical Analysis Using the Computer: Excel and MINITAB

KEY WORDS

Census
Descriptive Statistics
Inferential Statistics
Interval Level Data
Metric Data
Nominal Level Data
Nonmetric Data
Nonparametric Statistics

Ordinal Level Data
Parameter
Parametric Statistics
Population
Ratio Level Data
Sample
Statistic
Statistics

STUDY QUESTIONS

1. A science dealing with the collection, analysis, interpretation, and presentation of numerical data is called _statistics_ .

2. One way to subdivide the field of statistics is into the two branches of _Descriptive_ statistics and _Inferential_ statistics.

3. A collection of persons, objects or items of interest is a _population_.

4. Data gathered from a whole population is called a _census_ .

5. If a population consists of all the radios produced today in the Akron facility and if a quality control inspector randomly selects forty of the ratios, the group of forty is referred to as _sample_ .

6. If data are used to reach conclusions only about the group from which the data are gathered, then the statistics are referred to as _descriptive_ statistics.

7. If data are gathered from a subgroup of a larger group and the data are used to reach conclusions about the larger group, then the statistics are said to be _inferential_ statistics.

8. Another name for inferential statistics is _Inductive_ statistics.

9. Descriptive measures which are usually denoted by Greek letters are called _Parameters_

10. The highest level of data measurement is _Ratio_ .

11. The level of data measurement used when ranking items is _Ordinal_ .

12. If a number represents the geographic location of a business, then the level of data represented by the number is probably _Nominal_ .

13. If the data being gathered are only ordinal level data, then the researcher should only use _Non parametec_ statistics to analyze the data.

For each of the following (14-25), the data gathered are most likely to be which level of data? Nominal, Ordinal, Interval, or Ratio?

14. The ages of managers of fast-food restaurants.

15. An employee's identification number.

16. The number of freight cars per train for five hundred trains.

17.   The elevation of a town.

18.   The number of feet it takes a car to stop going fifty miles per hour.

19.   The number of ounces of orange juice consumed by each Floridian in the morning.

20.   The volume of wheat in each silo in Nebraska in August.

21.   A rating scale of the productivity of each worker which has as its adjectives: very poor, poor, average, good, outstanding.

22.   A person's religious preference.

23.   Weights of statistics' textbooks.

24.   Years of experience on the job.

25.   Number representing a worker's assignment to the red team, blue team, or green team at work where the red team is considered the top workers and the green team is considered the least productive workers.

ANSWERS TO STUDY QUESTIONS

1. Statistics

2. Descriptive, Inferential

3. Population

4. Census

5. Sample

6. Descriptive

7. Inferential

8. Inductive

9. Parameters

10. Ratio

11. Ordinal

12. Nominal

13. Nonparametric

14. Ratio

15. Nominal

16. Ratio

17. Interval

18. Ratio

19. Ratio

20. Ratio

21. Ordinal

22. Nominal

23. Ratio

24. Ratio

25. Ordinal

SOLUTIONS TO PROBLEMS IN CHAPTER 1

1.1   Examples of data in functional areas:

accounting - cost of goods, salary expense, depreciation, utility costs, taxes, equipment inventory, etc.

finance - World bank bond rates, number of failed savings and loans, measured risk of common stocks, stock dividends, foreign exchange rate, liquidity rates for a single-family, etc.

human resources - salaries, size of engineering staff, years experience, age of employees, years of education, etc.

marketing - number of units sold, dollar sales volume, forecast sales, size of sales force, market share, measurement of consumer motivation, measurement of consumer frustration, measurement of brand preference, attitude measurement, measurement of consumer risk, etc.

information systems - c.p.u. time, size of memory, number of work stations, storage capacity, percent of professionals who are connected to a computer network, dollar assets of company computing, number of "hits" on the Internet, time spent on the Internet per day, percentage of people who use the Internet, retail dollars spent in e-commerce, etc.

production - number of production runs per day, weight of a product; assembly time, number of defects per run, temperature in the plant, amount of inventory, turnaround time, etc.

management - measurement of union participation, measurement of employer support, measurement of tendency to control, number of subordinates reporting to a manager, measurement of leadership style, etc.

1.3   Descriptive statistics in recorded music industry -

1)   RCA total sales of compact discs this week, number of artists under contract to a company at a given time.

2)   total dollars spent on advertising last month to promote an album.

3)   number of units produced in a day.

4)   number of retail outlets selling the company's products.

Inferential statistics in recorded music industry -

1)   measure the amount spent per month on recorded music for a few consumers then use that figure to infer the amount for the population.

2)   determination of market share for rap music by randomly selecting a sample of 500 purchasers of recorded music.

3)   Determination of top ten single records by sampling the number of requests at a few radio stations.

4)   Estimation of the average length of a single recording by taking a sample of records and measuring them.

The difference between descriptive and inferential statistics lies mainly in the usage of the data. These descriptive examples all gather data from every item in the population about which the description is being made. For example, RCA measures the sales on <u>all</u> its compact discs for a week and reports the total.

In each of the inferential statistics examples, a <u>sample</u> of the population is taken and the population value is estimated or inferred from the sample. For example, it may be practically impossible to determine the proportion of buyers who prefer rap music. However, a random sample of buyers can be contacted and interviewed for music preference. The results can be inferred to population market share.

1.5   a)   ratio
      b)   ratio
      c)   ordinal
      d)   nominal
      e)   ratio
      f)   ratio
      g)   nominal
      h)   ratio

1.7   a)   The population for this study is the 900 electric contractors who purchased Rathburn wire.

      b)   The sample is the randomly chosen group of thirty-five contractors.

      c)   The statistic is the average satisfaction score for the sample of thirty-five contractors.

      d)   The parameter is the average satisfaction score for all 900 electric contractors in the population.

Chapter 2
Charts and Graphs

The overall objective of chapter 2 is for you to master several techniques for summarizing and depicting data, thereby enabling you to:

1. Recognize the difference between grouped and ungrouped data.

2. Construct a frequency distribution.

3. Construct a histogram, a frequency polygon, an ogive, a pie chart, and a stem and leaf plot.

CHAPTER OUTLINE

2.1   Frequency Distributions

        Class Midpoint

        Relative Frequency

        Cumulative Frequency

2.2   Graphic Depiction of Data

        Histograms

        Frequency Polygons

        Ogives

        Pie Charts

        Stem and Leaf Plots

KEY TERMS

Class Mark
Class Midpoint
Cumulative Frequency
Frequency Distribution
Frequency Polygon
Grouped Data
Histogram

Ogive
Pie Chart
Range
Relative Frequency
Stem and Leaf Plot
Ungrouped Data

STUDY QUESTIONS

1. The following data represents the number of printer ribbons used by each of 28 departments in a company annually. This is an example of _ungrouped_ data.

   8   4   5   10   6   5   4   6   3   4   4   6   1   12
   2   11   2   5   3   2   6   7   6   12   7   1   8   9

2. Below is a frequency distribution of ages of managers with a large retail firm. This is an example of _grouped_ data.

Age	f
20-29	11
30-39	32
40-49	57
50-59	43
over 60	18

3. For best results, a frequency distribution should have between ___5___ and ___15___ classes.

4. The difference between the largest and smallest numbers is called the ___Range___.

5. Consider the values below. In constructing a frequency distribution, the lowest class beginning point should be at least as small as ___8___ and the highest class endpoint should be at least as large as ___34___.

   27 21 8 10 9 16 11 12 21 11 29 19 17 22 28 28 29 19 18 26 17 34 19 16 20

6. The class midpoint can be determined by ___Averaging the two class endpoints___

7-9 Examine the frequency distribution below:

class	frequency
5 - under 10	56
10 - under 15	43
15 - under 20	21
20 - under 25	11
25 - under 30	12
30 - under 35	8

   56, 43, 21, 11 } 131

   151

7. The relative frequency for the class 15 - under 20 is ___21/151 = .1391___

8. The cumulative frequency for the class 20 - under 25 is _____131_____.

9. The midpoint for the class 25 - under 30 is ___27.5___. $\dfrac{25+30}{2} = 27.5$

10. The graphical depiction in chapter two which is a type of vertical bar chart is a ___Histogram___.

11. The graphical depiction that utilizes cumulative frequencies is a ___Ogive___.

12. The graph shown below is an example of a ___Frequency Polygon___

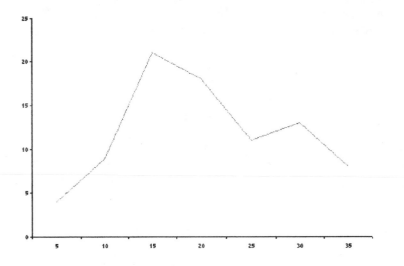

13. Consider the categories below and their relative amounts:

Category	Amount
A	112
B	319
C	57
D	148 —
E	202

    148/838 of 360°
    = 63.6°

    If you were to construct a Pie Chart to depict these categories, then you would allot _____ degrees to category D.

14. Given the values below, construct a stem and leaf plot using two digits for the stem.

    346 340 322 339 342 332 338
    357 328 329 346 341 321 332

ANSWERS TO STUDY QUESTIONS

1. Raw or Ungrouped

2. Grouped

3. 5, 15

4. Range

5. 8, 34

6. Averaging the two class endpoints

7. 21/151 = .1391

8. 131

9. 27.5

10. Histogram

11. Ogive

12. Frequency Polygon

13. 148/838 of 360° = 63.6°

14.
32	1 2 8 9
33	2 2 8 9
34	0 1 2 6 6
35	7

SOLUTIONS TO ODD-NUMBERED PROBLEMS IN CHAPTER 2

2.1 a)   One possible 5 class frequency distribution:

Class Interval	Frequency
10 - under 25	9
25 - under 40	13
40 - under 55	11
55 - under 70	9
70 - under 85	8
	50

b)   One possible 10 class frequency distribution:

Class Interval	Frequency
10 - under 18	7
18 - under 26	3
26 - under 34	5
34 - under 42	9
42 - under 50	7
50 - under 58	3
58 - under 66	6
66 - under 74	4
74 - under 82	4
82 - under 90	2

c)   The ten class frequency distribution gives a more detailed breakdown of temperatures, pointing out the smaller frequencies for the higher temperature intervals. The five class distribution collapses the intervals into broader classes making it appear that there are nearly equal frequencies in each class.

2.3

Class Interval	Frequency	Class Midpoint	Relative Frequency	Cumulative Frequency
0 - 5	6	2.5	6/86 = .0698	6
5 - 10	8	7.5	.0930	14
10 - 15	17	12.5	.1977	31
15 - 20	23	17.5	.2674	54
20 - 25	18	22.5	.2093	72
25 - 30	10	27.5	.1163	82
30 - 35	4	32.5	.0465	86
TOTAL	86		1.0000	

The relative frequency tells us that it is most probable that a customer is in the 15 - 20 category (.2674). Over two thirds (.6744) of the customers are between 10 and 25 years of age.

2.5   Some examples of cumulative frequencies in business:

sales for the fiscal year,

costs for the fiscal year,

spending for the fiscal year,

inventory build-up,

accumulation of workers during a hiring buildup,

production output over a time period.

2.7 Histogram

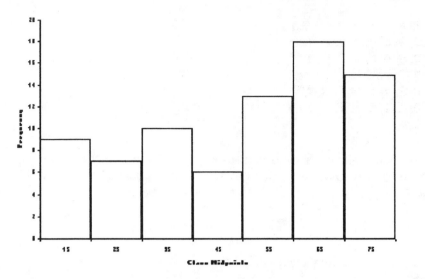

Frequency Polygon

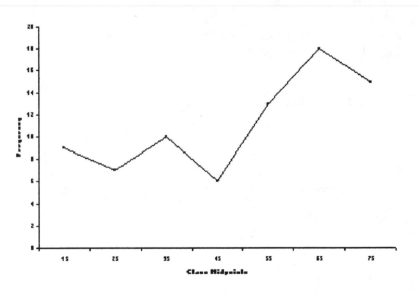

2.9

STEM	LEAF
21	2, 8, 8, 9
22	0, 1, 2, 4, 6, 6, 7, 9, 9
23	0, 0, 4, 5, 8, 8, 9, 9, 9, 9
24	0, 0, 3, 6, 9, 9, 9
25	0, 3, 4, 5, 5, 7, 7, 8, 9
26	0, 1, 1, 2, 3, 3, 5, 6
27	0, 1,

2. 11

Company	Proportion	Degrees
Delta	.27	97
United	.22	79
American	.21	76
US Airways	.15	54
Southwest	.15	54
TOTAL	1.00	360

Leading U.S. Airlines

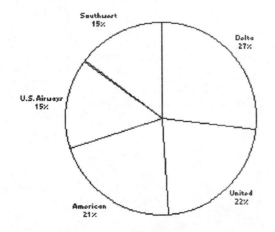

2.13

STEM	LEAF
1	3, 6, 7, 7, 7, 9, 9, 9
2	0, 3, 3, 5, 7, 8, 9, 9
3	2, 3, 4, 5, 7, 8, 8
4	1, 4, 5, 6, 6, 7, 7, 8, 8, 9
5	0, 1, 2, 2, 7, 8, 9
6	0, 1, 4, 5, 6, 7, 9
7	0, 7
8	0

The stem and leaf plot shows that the number of passengers per flight were relatively evenly distributed between the high teens through the sixties. Rarely was there a flight with at least 70 passengers. The category of 40's contained the most flights (10).

2.15

Class Interval	Frequency	Midpoint	Rel.Freq.	Cum.Freq.
20 - under 25	17	22.5	.207	.207
25 - under 30	20	27.5	.244	.451
30 - under 35	16	32.5	.195	.646
35 - under 40	15	37.5	.183	.829
40 - under 45	8	42.5	.098	.927
45 - under 50	6	47.5	.073	1.000

2.17

Label	Value	Proportion	Degrees
A	55	.180	65
B	121	.397	143
C	83	.272	98
D	46	.151	54
TOTAL	305	1.000	360

Pie Chart

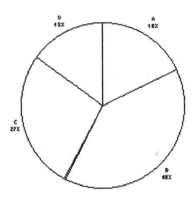

2.19 Olson Company

Frequency distribution

Class Interval	Frequency
32 - under 37	1
37 - under 42	4
42 - under 47	12
47 - under 52	11
52 - under 57	14
57 - under 62	5
62 - under 67	2
67 - under 72	1
TOTAL	50

2.21 Frequency Distribution:

Class Interval	Frequency
10 - under 20	2
20 - under 30	3
30 - under 40	9
40 - under 50	7
50 - under 60	12
60 - under 70	9
70 - under 80	6
80 - under 90	2
	50

Histogram

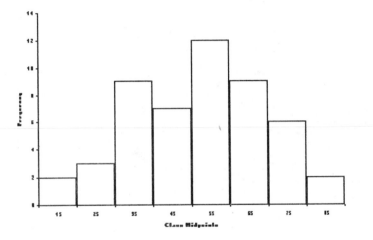

Frequency Polygon

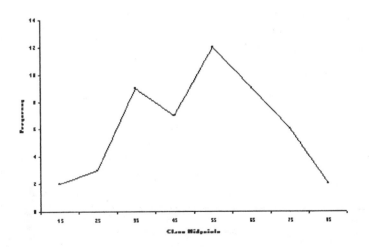

The normal distribution appears to peak near the center and diminish towards the end intervals.

2.23

Asking Price	Frequency	Cumulative Frequency
$ 60,000 - under $ 70,000	21	21
$ 70,000 - under $ 80,000	27	48
$ 80,000 - under $ 90,000	18	66
$ 90,000 - under $100,000	11	77
$100,000 - under $110,000	6	83
$110,000 - under $120,000	3	86
	86	

Histogram

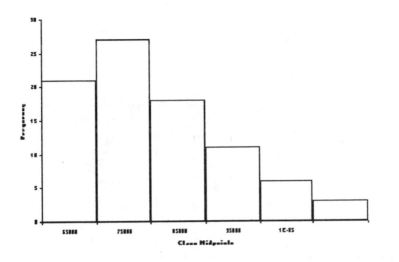

Frequency Polygon

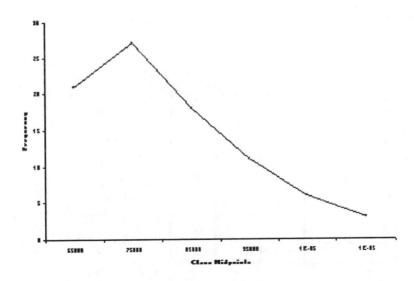

Ogive

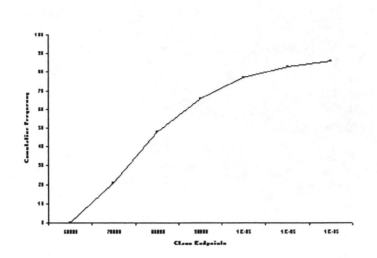

2.25

Price	Frequency	Cumulative Frequency
$1.75 - under $1.90	9	9
$1.90 - under $2.05	14	23
$2.05 - under $2.20	17	40
$2.20 - under $2.35	16	56
$2.35 - under $2.50	18	74
$2.50 - under $2.65	8	82
$2.65 - under $2.80	5	87
	87	

Histogram

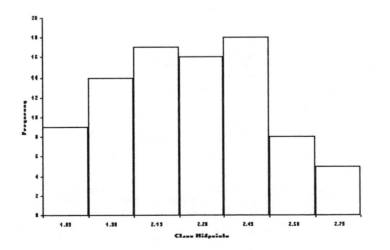

Frequency Polygon

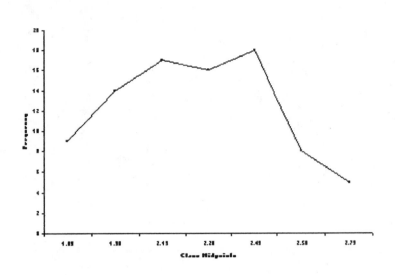

Ogive

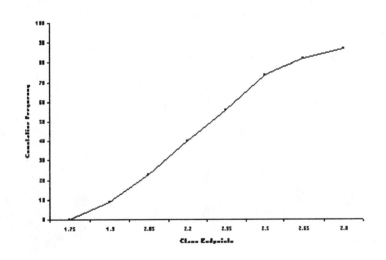

2.27

Industry	Total Release	Proportion	Degrees
Chemicals	785,178,163	.38	137
Primary metals	564,535,183	.27	97
Paper	227,563,372	.11	40
Plastics	116,409,291	.06	22
Transportation Equipment	111,352,769	.05	18
Fabricated Metals	90,254,367	.04	14
Food	83,303,395	.04	14
Petroleum	68,887,258	.03	11
Electrical Equipment	41,765,377	.02	7
TOTAL		1.00360	

Pie Chart

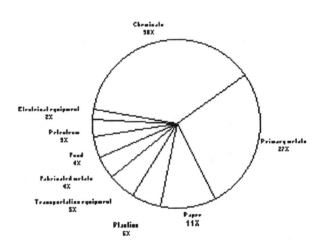

2.29

STEM	LEAF
22	00, 68
23	01, 37, 44, 75
24	05, 37, 48, 60, 68
25	24, 55
26	02, 56, 70, 77
27	42, 60, 64
28	14, 30
29	22, 61, 75, 76, 90, 96
30	02, 10

2.31 The distribution of household income is bell-shaped with an average of about $ 90,000 and a range of from $ 30,000 to $ 140,000.

2.33 The fewest number of audits is 12 and the most is 42. More companies (8) performed 27 audits than any other number. Thirty-five companies performed between 12 and 19 audits. Only 7 companies performed 40 or more audits.

Chapter 3
Descriptive Statistics

LEARNING OBJECTIVES

The focus of Chapter 3 is on the use of statistical techniques to describe data, thereby enabling you to:

1. Distinguish between measures of central tendency, measures of variability, and measures of shape.

2. Understand conceptually the meanings of mean, median, mode, quartile, percentile, and range.

3. Compute mean, median, mode, percentile, quartile, range, variance, standard deviation, and mean absolute deviation on ungrouped data.

4. Differentiate between sample and population variance and standard deviation.

5. Understand the meaning of standard deviation as it is applied using the empirical rule and Chebyshev's theorem.

6. Compute the mean, median, standard deviation, and variance on grouped data.

7. Understand box and whisker plots, skewness, and kurtosis.

CHAPTER OUTLINE

→ (3.1) Measures of Central Tendency: Ungrouped Data

Mode — Value w/ highest frequency

50% above
50% below — Median

Mean — Average

Percentiles — pth percentile is a number such that p% of the data lie below it and 100 - p% above. 50th percentile is the median.

(median) Q₁ is 25th percentile
Q₂ is 50th percentile — Quartiles
Q₃ is 75th percentile

(3.2) Measures of Variability - Ungrouped Data

Range — largest observation – smallest observation

(IQR) Interquartile Range — Q₃ – Q₁

Mean Absolute Deviation, Variance, and Standard Deviation

Mean Absolute Deviation

Variance

Standard Deviation

(p.5?)

68%   95%   99.7   Meaning of Standard Deviation

Empirical Rule

μ±1σ   μ±2σ   μ±3σ   Chebyshev's Theorem

Population Versus Sample Variance and Standard Deviation

Computational Formulas for Variance and Standard Deviation

Z Scores

Coefficient of Variation

mean - For ungrouped data, the mean is computed by summing & dividing. With grouped data, the specific values are unknown. The midpoint of each class interval is used to represent all the values in a class interval. The midpoint is weighted by the frequency of values in that class interval. The mean for grouped data is then computed by summing

(p.63)

3.3 Measures of Central Tendency and Variability - Grouped Data

Measures of Location

Mean

Median

Mode

Measures of Variability

3.4 Measures of Shape

Skewness

Skewness and the Relationship of the Mean, Median, and Mode

Coefficient of Skewness

Kurtosis

3.5 Descriptive Statistics on the Computer

KEY WORDS

Arithmetic Mean	Measures of Variability
Bimodal	Median
Box and Whisker Plot	Mesokurtic
Chebyshev's Theorem	Mode
Coefficient of Skewness	Multimodal
Coefficient of Variation	Percentiles
Deviations from the Mean	Platykurtic
Empirical Rule	Quartiles
Interquartile Range	Range
Kurtosis	Skewness
Leptokurtic	Standard Deviation
Mean Absolute Deviation	Sum of Squares of X
Measures of Central Tendency	Variance
Measures of Shape	Z Score

STUDY QUESTIONS

(handwritten: ok) 1. Statistical measures used to yield information about the center or middle part of a group of numbers are called __*measures of central tendency*__

(handwritten: ok) 2. The "average" is the __*mean*__.

(handwritten: ok) 3. The value occurring most often in a group of numbers is called __*mode*__.

(handwritten: ok) 4. In a set of 110 numbers arranged in order, the median is located at the __*55.5*__ position.

(handwritten margin:
$$\begin{array}{r} 55.\\ 2\overline{)110}\\ \underline{10}\\ 10\\ \underline{10}\\ 0 \end{array}$$
)

(handwritten: ok) 5. If a set of data has an odd number of values arranged in ascending order, the median is the __*middle*__ value.

Consider the data: 5, 4, 6, 6, 4, 5, 3, 2, 6, 4, 6, 3, 5 $= \dfrac{59}{13} =$
Answer questions 6-8 using this data.

(handwritten margin list:
$$\begin{array}{r} 2\\ 3\\ 3\\ 4\\ 4\\ \textcircled{5}\\ 5\\ 5\\ 6\\ 6\\ 6\\ 6\\ \hline 13 \end{array}$$
)

(handwritten: ok) 6. The mode is __*6*__.

(handwritten: ok) 7. The median is __*5*__.

(handwritten: ok) 8. The mean is __*4.54*__. $\dfrac{59}{13} = 4.54$

(handwritten: ok) 9. If a set of values is a population, then the mean is denoted by __μ__.

(handwritten: ok) 10. In computing a mean for grouped data, the __*class midpoint*__ is used to represent all data in a given class interval.

(handwritten: ok) 11. The mean for the data given below is _____.

(handwritten left:
$50 + 53/2 = 51.5$
$53 + 56/2 = 54.5$
$56 + 59/2 = 57.5$
$59 + 62/2 = 60.5$
$62 + 65/2 = 63.5$
)

Class Interval	Frequency	midpoint	fm
50 - under 53	14	51.50	721
53 - under 56	17	54.50	926.50
56 - under 59	29	57.50	1667.50
59 - under 62	31	60.50	1875.50
62 - under 65	18	63.50	1143.
	109		6333.50

(handwritten: ok)

12. Measures of variability describe the _____ of a set of data.

(handwritten: ok) __*spread or dispersion*__

(handwritten: $\dfrac{6333.50}{109} = 58.1$ *)*

19
20
27
28
31
—— a_1 $\dfrac{31+34}{2} = 32.5$
34

37

43

43

44 Q_2 $\dfrac{44+47}{2}$

47

48 $= 45.5$

49

50

52 Q_3 $\dfrac{52+58}{2}$

58

61 $=$

61

65

91

—— $20 = n$

$\dfrac{n+1}{4} = \dfrac{21}{4} = 5.25$

Use the following data for Questions 13-17:

27 65 28 61 34 91 61 37 58 31
43 47 44 20 48 50 49 43 19 52

largest value - smallest

13. The range of the data is ___ $91 - 19 = 72$ ___ $\dfrac{44+47}{2} = 2$ $3\left(\dfrac{n+1}{4}\right) = 3\left(\dfrac{21}{4}\right) =$

14. The value of Q_1 is ___ 32.5 ___, Q_2 is ___ 45.5 ___, and Q_3 is ___ 55 ___.   oh

mean

15. The interquartile range is ___ $55 - 32.5 = 22.50$ ___

16. The value of the 34th percentile is _____.

17. The value of the Pearsonian coefficient of skewness for these data is

_____.

18. The Mean Absolute Deviation is computed by averaging the ___ Absolute Value ___ of deviations around the mean.

19. Subtracting each value of a set of data from the mean produces ___ Deviations ___ from the mean.

20. The sum of the deviations from the mean is always ___ Zero ___.

21. The variance is the ___ Square ___ of the standard deviation.

22. The population variance is computed by using ___ N ___ in the denominator. Whereas, the sample variance is computed by using ___ $n-1$ ___ in the denominator.

23. If the sample standard deviation is 9, then the sample variance is ___ $9^2 = 81$ ___.

Consider the data below and answer questions 24-26 using the data:

2, 3, 6, 12

24. The mean absolute deviation for this data is _____.

25. The sample variance for this data is _____.

26. The population standard deviation for this data is ___ 3.89 ___.

27. In estimating what proportion of values fall within so many standard deviations of the mean, a researcher should use _____ if the shape of the distribution of numbers is unknown.

28. Suppose a distribution of numbers is mound shaped with a mean of 150 and a variance of 225. Approximately _____ percent of the values fall between 120 and 180. Between _____ and _____ fall 99.7% of these values.

29. The shape of a distribution of numbers is unknown. The distribution has a mean of 275 and a standard deviation of 12. The value of k for 299 is _____. At least _____ percent of the values fall between 251 and 299.

30. Suppose data are normally distributed with a mean of 36 and a standard deviation of 4.8. The Z score for 30 is _____. The Z score for 40 is

   _____.

31. A normal distribution of values has a mean of 74 and a standard deviation of 21. The coefficient of variation for this distribution is _____?

   Consider the data below and use the data to answer questions 32-35.

Class Interval	Frequency
2- 4	5
4- 6	12
6- 8	14
8-10	15
10-12	8
12-14	4

32. The sample variance for the data above is _____.

33. The population standard deviation for the data above is _____.

34. The median of the data is _____.

35. The mode of the data is _____.

36. The distribution _____ is _____.

37. If a unimodal distribution has a mean of 50, a median of 48, and a mode of 47, the distribution is skewed _____.

38. If the value of S_k is positive, then it may be said that the distribution is _____ skewed.

39. The peakedness of a distribution is called _____.

40. If a distribution is flat and spread out, then it is referred to as _____; if it is "normal" in shape, then it is referred to as _____; if it is high and thin, then it is referred to as

   _____.

41. In a box plot, the inner fences are computed by _____ and _____. The outer fences are computed by _____ and _____.

42. Data values that lie outside the mainstream of values in a distribution are referred to as _____.

ANSWERS TO STUDY QUESTIONS

1. Measures of Central Tendency
2. Mean
3. Mode
4. 55.5^{th}
5. Middle
6. 6
7. 5
8. 4.54
9. μ
10. Class Midpoint
11. 58.11
12. Spread or Dispersion
13. 72
14. $Q_1 = 32.5$, $Q_2 = 45.5$, $Q_3 = 55$
15. $IQR = 22.5$
16. $P_{34} = 37$
17. $S_k = -0.018$

18. Absolute Value
19. Deviations
20. Zero
21. Square
22. N, n - 1
23. 81
24. 3.25
25. 20.25
26. 3.897
27. Chebyshev's Theorem
28. 95, 105, and 195
29. 2, 75
30. -1.25, 0.83
31. 28.38%
32. 7.54
33. 2.72
34. 7.7143

35. 9

36. Skewed Left

37. Right

38. Positively

39. Kurtosis

40. Platykurtic, Mesokurtic, Leptokurtic

41. $Q_1 - 1.5$ IQR and $Q_3 + 1.5$ IQR
    $Q_1 - 3.0$ IQR and $Q_3 + 3.0$ IQR

42. Outliers

SOLUTIONS TO ODD-NUMBERED PROBLEMS IN CHAPTER 3

3.1 **Mode**

2, 2, 3, 3, 4, 4, 4, 4, 5, 6, 7, 8, 8, 8, 9
The mode = **4**
4 is the most frequently occurring value

3.3 **Median**
Arrange terms in ascending order:
073, 167, 199, 213, 243, 345, 444, 524, 609, 682
There are 10 terms.
Since there are an even number of terms, the median is the average of the two middle terms:

$$\text{Median} = \frac{243 + 345}{2} = \frac{588}{2} = 294$$

Using the formula, the median is located at the $\frac{n + 1}{2}$ th term.

n = 10 therefore $\frac{10 + 1}{2} = \frac{11}{2} = 5.5^{th}$ term.

The median is located halfway between the 5th and 6th terms.
     5th term = 243 6th term = 345
Halfway between 243 and 345 is the median = **294**

3.5   Mean

       7
     -2
      5                $\mu = \Sigma X/N = -12/12 = \mathbf{-1}$
      9
      0
     -3
     -6 $\overline{X} = \Sigma X/n = -12/12 = \mathbf{-1}$
     -7
     -4
     -5
      2
     -8   (It is not stated in the problem whether the
$\Sigma X = -12$ data represent a population or a sample).

3.7   Rearranging the data in ascending order:

80, 94, 97, 105, 107, 112, 116, 116, 118, 119, 120, 127,

128, 138, 138, 139, 142, 143, 144, 145, 150, 162, 171, 172

n = 24

$$i = \frac{20}{100}(24) = 4.8$$

P_{20} is located at the $4 + 1 = 5^{th}$ term

$P_{20} = \mathbf{107}$

$$i = \frac{47}{100}(24) = 11.28$$

P_{47} is located at the $11 + 1 = 12^{th}$ term

$P_{47} = \mathbf{127}$

$$i = \frac{83}{100}(24) = 19.92$$

P_{83} is located at the $19 + 1 = 20^{th}$ term

$P_{83} = \mathbf{145}$

$Q_1 = P_{25}$

$$i = \frac{25}{100}(24) = 6$$

Q_1 is located at the 6.5^{th} term

$Q_1 = (112 + 116)/ 2 = $ **114**

$Q_2 = $ Median

The median is located at the:

$$\left(\frac{24+1}{2}\right)^{th} = 12.5^{th}\, term$$

$Q_2 = (127 + 128)/ 2 = $ **127.5**

$Q_3 = P_{75}$

$$i = \frac{75}{100}(24) = 18$$

Q_3 is located at the 18.5^{th} term

$Q_3 = (143 + 144)/ 2 = $ **143.5**

3.9   The median is located at the $\left(\frac{10+1}{2}\right)^{th} = 5.5^{th}$ position

The median $= (595 + 653)/2 = $ **624**

$Q_3 = P_{75}$: $i = \frac{75}{100}(10) = 7.5$

P_{75} is located at the $7+1 = 8^{th}$ term

$Q_3 = $ **751**

For P_{20}:

$$i = \frac{20}{100}(10) = 2$$

P_{20} is located at the 2.5^{th} term

$P_{20} = (483 + 489)/2 = \mathbf{486}$

For P_{60}:

$$i = \frac{60}{100}(10) = 6$$

P_{60} is located at the 6.5^{th} term

$P_{60} = (653 + 701)/2 = \mathbf{677}$

For P_{80}:

$$i = \frac{80}{100}(10) = 8$$

P_{80} is located at the 8.5^{th} term

$P_{80} = (751 + 800)/2 = \mathbf{775.5}$

For P_{93}:

$$i = \frac{93}{100}(10) = 9.3$$

P_{93} is located at the $9+1 = 10^{\text{th}}$ term

$P_{93} = \mathbf{1096}$

3.11

X	X -μ	(X-μ)²
6	6-4.2857 = 1.7143	2.9388
2	2.2857	5.2244
4	0.2857	.0816
9	4.7143	22.2246
1	3.2857	10.7958
3	1.2857	1.6530
5	0.7143	.5102
$\Sigma X = 30$	$\Sigma\lvert X\text{-}\mu\rvert = 14.2857$	$\Sigma(X\text{ -}\mu)^2 = 43.4284$

$$\mu = \frac{\Sigma X}{N} = \frac{30}{7} = 4.2857$$

a.) Range = 9 - 1 = **8**

b.) M.A.D. $= \dfrac{\Sigma\lvert X - \mu\rvert}{N} = \dfrac{14.2857}{7} = $ **2.041**

c.) $\sigma^2 = \dfrac{\Sigma(X - \mu)^2}{N} = \dfrac{43.4284}{7} = $ **6.204**

d.) $\sigma = \sqrt{\dfrac{\Sigma(X - \mu)^2}{N}} = \sqrt{6.204} = $ **2.491**

e.) 1, 2, 3, 4, 5, 6, 9

$Q_1 = P_{25}$

$$i = \frac{25}{100}(7) = 1.75$$

Q_1 is located at the $1 + 1 = 2^{th}$ term, $Q_1 = $ **2**

$Q_3 = P_{75}$:

$$i = \frac{75}{100}(7) = 5.25$$

Q_3 is located at the $5 + 1 = 6^{th}$ term, $Q_3 = $ **6**

$$IQR = Q_3 - Q_1 = 6 - 2 = \ \mathbf{4}$$

f.) $\quad Z = \dfrac{6 - 4.2857}{2.491} = \mathbf{0.69}$

$\qquad Z = \dfrac{2 - 4.2857}{2.491} = \mathbf{-0.92}$

$\qquad Z = \dfrac{4 - 4.2857}{2.491} = \mathbf{-0.11}$

$\qquad Z = \dfrac{9 - 4.2857}{2.491} = \mathbf{1.89}$

$\qquad Z = \dfrac{1 - 4.2857}{2.491} = \mathbf{-1.32}$

$\qquad Z = \dfrac{3 - 4.2857}{2.491} = \mathbf{-0.52}$

$\qquad Z = \dfrac{5 - 4.2857}{2.491} = \mathbf{0.29}$

3.13 a.)

X	(X-μ)	(X -μ)^2
12	12-21.167= -9.167	84.034
23	1.833	3.360
19	-2.167	4.696
26	4.833	23.358
24	2.833	8.026
23	1.833	3.360
ΣX = 127	Σ(X -μ) = -0.002	Σ(X -μ)^2 = 126.834

$$\mu = \frac{\Sigma X}{N} = \frac{127}{6} = 21.167$$

$$\sigma = \sqrt{\frac{\Sigma (X - \mu)^2}{N}} = \sqrt{\frac{126.834}{6}} = \sqrt{21.139} = \mathbf{4.598} \quad \underline{\textbf{ORIGINAL FORMULA}}$$

b.)

X	X^2
12	144
23	529
19	361
26	676
24	576
23	529
$\Sigma X = 127$	$\Sigma X^2 = 2815$

$$\sigma = \sqrt{\dfrac{\Sigma X^2 - \dfrac{(\Sigma X)^2}{N}}{N}} = \sqrt{\dfrac{2815 - \dfrac{(127)^2}{6}}{6}} = \sqrt{\dfrac{126.83}{6}} = \sqrt{21.138}$$

= **4.598**   <u>SHORT-CUT FORMULA</u>

The short-cut formula is faster.

3.15

$\sigma^2 = 58,631.359$

$\sigma = 242.139$

$\Sigma X = 6886$

$\Sigma X^2 = 3,901,664$

$n = 16$

$\mu = 430.375$

3.17

a) $1 - \dfrac{1}{2^2} = 1 - \dfrac{1}{4} = \dfrac{3}{4} = .75$

b) $1 - \dfrac{1}{2.5^2} = 1 - \dfrac{1}{6.25} = .84$

c) $1 - \dfrac{1}{1.6^2} = 1 - \dfrac{1}{2.56} = .609$

d) $1 - \dfrac{1}{3.2^2} = 1 - \dfrac{1}{10.24} = .902$

3.19

$\overline{X}$	$\left| X - \overline{X} \right|$	$(X - \overline{X})^2$
7	1.833	3.361
5	3.833	14.694
10	1.167	1.361
12	3.167	10.028
9	0.167	0.028
8	0.833	0.694
14	5.167	26.694
3	5.833	34.028
11	2.167	4.694
13	4.167	17.361
8	0.833	0.694
6	2.833	8.028
106	32.000	121.665

$$\overline{X} = \frac{\Sigma X}{n} = \frac{106}{12} = 8.833$$

a) $\text{MAD} = \dfrac{\Sigma \left| X - \overline{X} \right|}{n} = \dfrac{32}{12} = \mathbf{2.667}$

b) $S^2 = \dfrac{\Sigma (X - \overline{X})^2}{n-1} = \dfrac{121.665}{11} = \mathbf{11.06}$

c) $S = \sqrt{S^2} = \sqrt{11.06} = \mathbf{3.326}$

d)   Rearranging terms in order:

3 5 6 7 8 8 9 10 11 12 13 14

$Q_1 = P_{25}$: $i = (.25)(12) = 3$

Q_1 = the average of the 3rd and 4th terms:

$Q_1 = (6 + 7)/2 = 6.5$

$Q_3 = P_{75}$: $i = (.75)(12) = 9$

Q_3 = the average of the 9th and 10th terms:

$Q_3 = (11 + 12)/2 = 11.5$

$IQR = Q_3 - Q_1 = 11.5 - 9 = $ **2.5**

e.) $Z = \dfrac{6 - 8.833}{3.326} = $ **- 0.85**

f.) $CV = \dfrac{(3.326)(100)}{8.833} = $ **37.65%**

3.21 $\mu = 125$ $\sigma = 12$

68% of the values fall within:

$\mu \pm 1 = 125 \pm 1(12) = 125 \pm 12$

between 113 and 137

95% of the values fall within:

$\mu \pm 2 = 125 \pm 2(12) = 125 \pm 24$

between 101 and 149

99.7% of the values fall within:

$\mu \pm 3 = 125 \pm 3(12) = 125 \pm 36$

between 89 and 161

3.23 $1 - \dfrac{1}{K^2} = .80$

$1 - .80 = \dfrac{1}{K^2}$

$.20 = \dfrac{1}{K^2}$

$.20K^2 = 1$

$K^2 = 5$ and $K = 2.236$

2.236 standard deviations

3.25 $\mu = 29$ $\sigma = 4$

$X_1 - \mu = 21 - 29 = -8$
$X_2 - \mu = 37 - 29 = +8$

$\dfrac{X_1 - \mu}{\sigma} = \dfrac{-8}{4} = -2$ Standard Deviations

$\dfrac{X_2 - \mu}{\sigma} = \dfrac{8}{4} = 2$ Standard Deviations

Since the distribution is normal, the empirical rule states that 95% of the values fall within $\mu \pm 2\sigma$.

Exceed 37 days:

Since 95% fall between 21 and 37 days, 5% fall outside this range. Since the normal distribution is symmetrical 2½% fall below 21 and above 37.

Thus, 2½% lie above the value of 37.

Exceed 41 days:

$$\frac{X - \mu}{\sigma} = \frac{41 - 29}{4} = \frac{12}{4} = 3 \text{ Standard deviations}$$

The empirical rule states that 99.7% of the values fall within $\mu \pm 3 = 29 \pm 3(4) = 29 \pm 12$

between 17 and 41, 99.7% of the values will fall.

0.3% will fall outside this range.

Half of this or .15% will lie above 41.

Less than 25: $\mu = 29$ $\sigma = 4$

$$\frac{X - \mu}{\sigma} = \frac{25 - 29}{4} = \frac{-4}{4} = -1 \text{ Standard Deviation}$$

According to the empirical rule:

$\mu \pm 1$ contains 68% of the values

$29 \pm 1(4) = 29 \pm 4$

from 25 to 33.

32% lie outside this range with $\frac{1}{2}(32\%) =$ **16% less than 25.**

3.27   Mean

Class	f	M	fM
0 - 2	39	1	39
2 - 4	27	3	81
4 - 6	16	5	80
6 - 8	15	7	105
8 - 10	10	9	90
10 - 12	8	11	88
12 - 14	6	13	78
	Σf=121		ΣfM=561

$$\mu = \frac{\Sigma fM}{\Sigma f} = \frac{561}{121} = \textbf{4.64}$$

$$\text{Median} = 2 + \frac{60.5 - 39}{27}(2) = \textbf{3.5926}$$

Mode: The modal class is $0 - 2$.
         The midpoint of the modal class = the mode = **1**

3.29

Class	f	M	fM
20-30	7	25	175
30-40	11	35	385
40-50	18	45	810
50-60	13	55	715
60-70	6	65	390
70-80	4	75	300
Total	59		2775

$$\mu = \frac{\Sigma fM}{\Sigma f} = \frac{2775}{59} = \textbf{47.034}$$

M - μ	(M - μ)^2	f(M - μ)^2
-22.0339	485.4927	3398.449
-12.0339	144.8147	1592.962
- 2.0339	4.1367	74.462
7.9661	63.4588	824.964
17.9661	322.7808	1936.685
27.9661	782.1028	3128.411
	Total	10,955.933

$$\sigma^2 = \frac{\Sigma f (M - \mu)^2}{\Sigma f} = \frac{10,955.93}{59} = \mathbf{185.694}$$

$$\sigma = \sqrt{185.694} = \mathbf{13.627}$$

3.31

Class	f	M	fM	fM^2
18 - 24	17	21	357	7,497
24 - 30	22	27	594	16,038
30 - 36	26	33	858	28,314
36 - 42	35	39	1,365	53,235
42 - 48	33	45	1,485	66,825
48 - 54	30	51	1,530	78,030
54 - 60	32	57	1,824	103,968
60 - 66	21	63	1,323	83,349
66 - 72	15	69	1,035	71,415
	Σf= 231		ΣfM= 10,371	ΣfM^2= 508,671

a.) Mean: $\overline{X} = \dfrac{\Sigma fM}{n} = \dfrac{\Sigma fM}{\Sigma f} = \dfrac{10,371}{231} = \mathbf{44.9}$

b.) Median: $\dfrac{n}{2} = \dfrac{231}{2} = 115.5^{\text{th}}$ term

Median $= 42 + \dfrac{115.5 - 100}{33}(6) = \mathbf{44.818}$

c.) Mode. The Modal Class = 36-42. The mode is the class midpoint = **39**

d.) $S^2 = \dfrac{\Sigma fM^2 - \dfrac{(\Sigma fM)^2}{n}}{n-1} = \dfrac{508,671 - \dfrac{(10,371)^2}{231}}{230} = \dfrac{43,053.5}{230} = \mathbf{187.2}$

e.) $S = \sqrt{187.2} = \mathbf{13.7}$

3.33

	f	M	fM	fM²
20-30	8	25	200	5000
30-40	7	35	245	8575
40-50	1	45	45	2025
50-60	0	55	0	0
60-70	3	65	195	12675
70-80	1	75	75	5625
	$\Sigma f = 20$		$\Sigma fM = 760$	$\Sigma fM^2 = 33900$

a.) Mean:

$$\mu \; = \; \frac{\Sigma fM}{\Sigma f} = \frac{760}{20} \; = \; \mathbf{38}$$

b.) Median.   Located at $(n/2)^{th} = (20/2)^{th} = 10^{th}$ term

$$\text{Median} \; = \; 30 + \frac{10-8}{7}(10) \; = \; \mathbf{32.857}$$

c.) Mode. The Modal Class = 20-30. The mode is the midpoint of this class = **25**.

d.) Variance:

$$\sigma^2 \; = \; \frac{\Sigma fM^2 - \dfrac{(\Sigma fM)^2}{N}}{N} = \frac{33{,}900 - \dfrac{(760)^2}{20}}{20} \; = \; \mathbf{251}$$

e.) Standard Deviation:

$$\sigma \; = \; \sqrt{\sigma^2} = \sqrt{251} \; = \; \mathbf{15.843}$$

3.35   mean = \$35
       median = \$33
       mode = \$21

The stock prices are skewed to the right. While many of the stock prices are at the cheaper end, a few extreme prices at the higher end pull the mean.

3.37 $S_k = \dfrac{3(\mu - M_d)}{\sigma} = \dfrac{3(5.51 - 3.19)}{9.59} = \mathbf{0.726}$

3.39 $Q_1 = 500.$ Median = 558.5. $Q_3 = 589.$

IQR = 589 - 500 = 89

Inner Fences: Q_1 - 1.5 IQR = 500 - 1.5 (89) = 366.5

                and Q_3 + 1.5 IQR = 589 + 1.5 (89) = 722.5

Outer Fences: Q_1 - 3.0 IQR = 500 - 3 (89) = 233

                and Q_3 + 3.0 IQR = 589 + 3 (89) = 856

The distribution is negatively skewed. There are no mild or extreme outliers.

3.41   Arranging the values in an ordered array:

1, 1, 1, 1, 1, 1, 1, 1, 2, 2, 2, 2, 2, 2, 2, 2, 2, 2, 2,
3, 3, 3, 3, 3, 3, 4, 4, 5, 6, 8

Mean: $\overline{X} = \dfrac{\Sigma X}{n} = \dfrac{75}{30} = \mathbf{2.5}$

Mode = **2** (There are eleven 2's)

Median: There are n = 30 terms.

The median is located at $\dfrac{n+1}{2}^{th} = \dfrac{30+1}{2} = \dfrac{21}{2} = 15.5^{th}$ position.

Median is the average of the 15th and 16th value.

However, since these are both 2, the median is **2**.

Range = 8 - 1 = **7**

$Q_1 = P_{25}$:

$$i = \frac{25}{100}(30) = 7.5$$

Q_1 is the 8th term =   **1**

$Q_3 = P_{75}$:

$$i = \frac{75}{100}(30) = 22.5$$

Q_3 is the 23rd term =   **3**

IQR = Q_3 - Q_1 = 3 - 1 = **2**

3.43 $\mu = \dfrac{\Sigma X}{N} = \dfrac{126{,}904}{20} = $ **6345.2**

The median is located at the (n+1)/2 th value = 21/2 = 10.5th value

The median is the average of 5414 and 5563 = **5488.5**

P_{30}: i = (.30)(20) = 6

P_{30} is located at the average of the 6th and 7th terms

P_{30} = (4507+4541)/2 = **4524**

P_{60}: i = (.60)(20) = 12

P_{60} is located at the average of the 12th and 13th terms

$P_{60} = (6101+6498)/2 = \mathbf{6299.5}$

P_{90}: $i = (.90)(20) = 18$

P_{90} is located at the average of the 18th and 19th terms

$P_{90} = (9863+11,019)/2 = 10,441$

$Q_1 = P_{25}$: $i = (.25)(20) = 5$

Q_1 is located at the average of the 5th and 6th terms

$Q_1 = (4464+4507)/2 = \mathbf{4485.5}$

$Q_3 = P_{75}$: $i = (.75)(20) = 15$

Q_3 is located at the average of the 15th and 16th terms

$Q_3 = (6796+8687)/2 = \mathbf{7741.5}$

Range = 11,388 - 3619 = **7769**

IQR = $Q_3 - Q_1 = 7741.5 - 4485.5 = \mathbf{3256}$

3.45

a.) $\mu = (X)/N = 26,945/12 = \mathbf{2245.42}$

Median = (1965+1970)/2 = **1967.5**

b.)   Range = 4273 - 1092 = **3181**

$Q_3 = 2652$

$Q_1 = 1536$ IQR = $Q_3 - Q_1 = \mathbf{1116}$

c.)   Variance:

$$\sigma^2 = \frac{\Sigma X^2 - \frac{(\Sigma X)^2}{N}}{N} = \frac{70,787,611 - \frac{(26,945)^2}{12}}{12} = \mathbf{857,071.58}$$

d.)   Texaco:

$$Z = \frac{X - \mu}{\sigma} = \frac{1532 - 2245.42}{925.78} = \textbf{-0.77}$$

Mobil:

$$Z = \frac{X - \mu}{\sigma} = \frac{2297 - 2245.42}{925.78} = \textbf{0.06}$$

e.) Skewness:

$$S_k = \frac{3(\mu - M_d)}{\sigma} = \frac{3(2245.42 - 1967.5)}{925.78} = \textbf{0.90}$$

3.47

	f	M	fM	fM²
15-20	9	17.5	157.5	2756.25
20-25	16	22.5	360.0	8100.00
25-30	27	27.5	742.5	20418.75
30-35	44	32.5	1430.0	46475.00
35-40	42	37.5	1575.0	59062.50
40-45	23	42.5	977.5	41543.75
45-50	7	47.5	332.5	15793.75
50-55	2	52.5	105.0	5512.50

$\Sigma f = 170$ $\Sigma fM = 5680.0$ $\Sigma fM^2 = 199662.50$

a.)   Mean:

$$\mu = \frac{\Sigma fM}{\Sigma f} = \frac{5680}{170} = \textbf{33.412}$$

Median: The median is located at the $\frac{n^{th}}{2} = \frac{170^{th}}{2} = $ 85th term

$$Median = 30 + \frac{85 - 52}{44}(5) = \textbf{33.75}$$

Mode: The Modal Class is 30-35. The class midpoint is the mode = **32.5**.

b.)   Variance:

$$\sigma^2 = \frac{\Sigma fM^2 - \dfrac{(\Sigma fM)^2}{N}}{N} = \frac{199{,}662.5 - \dfrac{(5680)^2}{170}}{170} = \mathbf{58.139}$$

Standard Deviation:

$$\sigma = \sqrt{\sigma^2} = \sqrt{58.139} = \mathbf{7.625}$$

3.49 $CV_x = \dfrac{\sigma_x}{\mu_x}(100\%) = \dfrac{3.45}{32}(100\%) = \mathbf{10.78\%}$

$CV_Y = \dfrac{\sigma_y}{\mu_y}(100\%) = \dfrac{5.40}{84}(100\%) = \mathbf{6.43\%}$

Stock X has a greater relative variability.

3.51 $\mu = 419$, $\sigma = 27$

a.) 68%: $\mu \pm 1\sigma$ 419 ± 27 **392 to 446**

95%: $\mu \pm 2\sigma$ $419 \pm 2(27)$ **365 to 473**

99.7%: $\mu \pm 3\sigma$ $419 \pm 3(27)$ **338 to 500**

b.) Use Chebyshev's:

The distance from 359 to 479 is 120

$\mu = 419$ The distance from the mean to the limit is 60.

k = (distance from the mean)/σ = 60/27 = 2.22

Proportion = 1 - 1/k^2 = 1 - 1/$(2.22)^2$ = .797 = **79.7%**

c.) X = 400. $Z = \dfrac{400 - 419}{27} = \mathbf{-0.704}$. This worker is in the lower half of workers but within one standard deviation of the mean.

3.53   Mean $35,748
       Median $31,369
       Mode $29,500

Since these three measures are not equal, the distribution is skewed. The
distribution is skewed to the right. Often, the median is preferred in reporting
income data because it yields information about the middle of the data while
ignoring extremes.

3.55   Paris: $1 - 1/k^2 = .53$ $k = 1.459$

The distance from $\mu = 349$ to $X = 381$ is 32

$1.459\sigma = 32$

$\sigma = \mathbf{21.93}$

Moscow: $1 - 1/k^2 = .83$ $k = 2.425$

The distance from $\mu = 415$ to $X = 459$ is 44

$2.425\sigma = 44$

$\sigma = \mathbf{18.14}$

Chapter 4
Probability

LEARNING OBJECTIVES

The main objective of Chapter 4 is to help you understand the basic principles of probability, specifically enabling you to

1.   Comprehend the different ways of assigning probability.

2.   Understand and apply marginal, union, joint, and conditional probabilities.

3.   Select the appropriate law of probability to use in solving problems.

4.   Solve problems using the laws of probability, including the law of addition, the law of multiplication, and the law of conditional probability.

5.   Revise probabilities using Bayes' rule.

CHAPTER OUTLINE

4.1   Introduction to Probability

4.2   Methods of Assigning Probabilities

      Classical Method of Assigning Probabilities

      Relative Frequency of Occurrence

      Subjective Probability

4.3   Structure of Probability

      Experiment

      Event

      Elementary Events

      Sample Space

      Unions and Intersections

      Mutually Exclusive Events

      Independent Events

      Collectively Exhaustive Events

      Complimentary Events

      Counting the Possibilities

            The mn Counting Rule

            Sampling from a Population with Replacement

            Combinations: Sampling from a Population Without Replacement

4.4   Marginal, Union, Joint, and Conditional Probabilities

KEY WORDS

A Priori
Bayes' Rule
Classical Method of Assigning Probabilities
Collectively Exhaustive Events
Combinations
Complement of a Union
Complementary Events
Conditional Probability
Elementary Events
Event
Experiment
Independent Events

Intersection
Joint Probability
Law of Conditional Probability
Marginal Probability
mn Counting Rule
Mutually Exclusive Events
Relative Frequency of Occurrence
Sample Space
Set Notation
Subjective Probability
Union
Union Probability

STUDY QUESTIONS

1. The _____ method of assigning probabilities relies on the insight or feelings of the person determining the probabilities.

2. If probabilities are determined "a priori" to an experiment using rules and laws, then the _____ method of assigning probabilities is being used.

3. The range of possibilities for probability values is from _____ to _____.

4. Suppose a technician keeps track of all defects in raw materials for a single day and uses this information to determine the probability of finding a defect in raw materials the next day. She is using the _____ method of assigning probabilities.

5. The outcome of an experiment is called a(n) _____. If these outcomes cannot be decomposed further, then they are referred to as _____ _____.

6. A computer hardware retailer allows you to order your own computer monitor. The store carries five different brands of monitors. Each brand comes in 14", 15" or 17" models. In addition, you can purchase either the deluxe model or the regular model in each brand and in each size. How many different types of monitors are available considering all the factors? _____ You probably used the _____ rule to solve this.

7. Suppose you are playing the Lotto game and you are trying to "pick" three numbers. For each of the three numbers, any of the digits 0 through 9 are possible (with replacement). How many different sets of numbers are available? _____

8. A population consists of the odd numbers between 1 and 9 inclusive. If a researcher randomly samples numbers from the population three at a time, the sample space is _____. Using combinations, how could we have determined ahead of time how many elementary events would be in the sample space? _____

9. Let A = {2,3,5,6,7,9} and B = {1,3,4,6,7,9}

   $A \cup B =$ 12345679   and $A \cap B =$ 3, 6, 7, 9 .

10. If the occurrence of one event does not affect the occurrence of the other event, then the events are said to be _____.

11. The outcome of the roll of one die is said to be _____ of the outcome of the roll of another die.

12. The event of rolling a three on a die and the event of rolling an even number on the same roll with the same die are _____.

13. If the probability of the intersection of two events is zero, then the events are said to be
     _____.

14. If three objects are selected from a bin, one at a time with replacement, the outcomes of
     each selection are _____.

15. Suppose a population consists of a manufacturing facility's 1600 workers. Suppose an
     experiment is conducted in which a worker is randomly selected. If an event is the selection
     of a worker over 40 years old, then the event of selecting a worker 40 years or younger is
     called the _____ of the first event.

16. The probability of selecting X given that Y has occurred is called a _____
     probability.

17. The probability of X is called a _____ probability.

18. The probability of X or Y occurring is called a _____ probability.

19. The probability of X and Y occurring is called a _____ probability.

20. Only one of the four types of probability does not use the total possible outcomes in the
     denominator when calculating the probability. This type of probability is called
     _____ probability.

21. If the $P(A \mid B) = P(A)$, then the events A, B are _____ events.

22. If the $P(X) = .53$, the $P(Y) = .12$, and the $P(X \cap Y) = .07$, then $P(X \cup Y)$ = _____.

23. If the $P(X) = .26$, the $P(Y) = .31$, and X, Y are mutually exclusive, then $P(X \cup Y)$ =
     _____.

24. In a company, 47% of the employees wear glasses, 60% of the employees are women, and
     28% of the employees are women and wear glasses. Complete the probability matrix below
     for this problem.

		Wear Glasses?	
		Yes	No
Gender	Men		
	Women		

25. Suppose that in another company, 40% of the workers are part time and 80% of the part
     time workers are men. The probability of randomly selecting a company worker who is
     both part time and a man is _____.

26. The probability of tossing three coins in a row and getting all tails is _____.
     This is an application of the _____ law of multiplication because each toss is
     _____.

27.   Suppose 70% of all cars purchased in America are U.S.A. made and that 18% of all cars purchased in America are both U.S.A. made and are red. The probability that a randomly selected car purchased in America is red given that it is U.S.A. made is _____.

Use the matrix below to answer questions 28-37:

	C	D	
A	.35	.31	.66
B	.14	.20	.34
	.49	.51	1.00

28.   The probability of A and C occurring is _____.

29.   The probability of A or D occurring is _____.

30.   The probability of D occurring is _____.

31.   The probability of B occurring given C is _____.

32.   The probability of B and D occurring is _____.

33.   The probability of C and D occurring is _____.

34.   The probability of C or D occurring is _____.

35.   The probability of C occurring given D is _____.

36.   The probability of C occurring given A is _____.

37.   The probability of C or B occurring is _____.

38.   Suppose 42% of all people in a county have characteristic X. Suppose 17% of all people in this county have characteristic X and characteristic Y. If a person is randomly selected from the county who is known to have characteristic X, then the probability that they have characteristic Y is _____.

39.   Suppose 22% of all parts produced at a plant have flaw X and 37% have flaw Y. In addition, suppose 53% of the parts with flaw X have flaw Y. If a part is randomly selected, the probability that it has flaw X or flaw Y is _____.

40.   Another name for revision of probabilities is _____.

41.   Suppose the prior probabilities of A and B are .57 and .43 respectively. Suppose that $P(E \mid A) = .24$ and $P(E \mid B) = .56$. If E is known to have occurred, then the revised probability of A occurring is _____ and of B occurring is _____.

ANSWERS TO STUDY QUESTIONS

1. Subjective

2. Classical

3. 0, 1

4. Relative Frequency

5. Event, Elementary Events

6. 30, mn counting rule

7. $10^3 = 1000$ numbers

8. {(1,3,5), (1,3,7), (1,3,9), (1,5,7), (1,5,9), (1,7,9), (3,5,7), (3,5,9), (3,7,9), (5,7,9)}, $_5C_3 = 10$

9. {1,2,3,4,5,6,7,9}, {3,6,7,9}

10. Independent

11. Independent

12. Mutually Exclusive

13. Mutually Exclusive

14. Independent

15. Complement

16. Conditional

17. Marginal

18. Union

19. Joint or Intersection

20. Conditional

21. Independent

22. .58

23. .57

24.

	Wear Glasses		
	Yes	No	
Men	.19	.21	.40
Women	.28	.32	.60
	.47	.53	1.00

25. .32

26. $1/8 = .125$, Special, Independent

27. .2571

28. .35

29. .86

30. .51

31. .2857

32. .20

33. .0000

34. 1.00

35. .0000

36. .5303

37. .69

38. .4048

39. .4646

40. Bayes' Rule

41. .3623, .6377

SOLUTIONS TO ODD-NUMBERED PROBLEMS IN CHAPTER 4

4.1   Enumeration of the six parts: $D_1, D_2, D_3, A_4, A_5, A_6$
                   D = Defective part
                   A = Acceptable part

Sample Space:

$$D_1 D_2, \quad D_2 D_3, \quad D_3 A_5$$
$$D_1 D_3, \quad D_2 A_4, \quad D_3 A_6$$
$$D_1 A_4, \quad D_2 A_5, \quad A_4 A_5$$
$$D_1 A_5, \quad D_2 A_6, \quad A_4 A_6$$
$$D_1 A_6, \quad D_3 A_4, \quad A_5 A_6$$

There are 15 members of the sample space

The probability of selecting exactly one defect out of
two is:

$$9/15 = .60$$

4.3   If A = {2, 6, 12, 24} and the population is the positive even numbers through 30,

A' = {4, 8, 10, 14, 16, 18, 20, 22, 26, 28, 30}

4.5   Enumeration of the six parts: $D_1, D_2, A_1, A_2, A_3, A_4$
                   D = Defective part
                   A = Acceptable part

Sample Space:

$$D_1 D_2 A_1, \quad D_1 D_2 A_2, \quad D_1 D_2 A_3,$$
$$D_1 D_2 A_4, \quad D_1 A_1 A_2, \quad D_1 A_1 A_3,$$
$$D_1 A_1 A_4, \quad D_1 A_2 A_3, \quad D_1 A_2 A_4,$$
$$D_1 A_3 A_4, \quad D_2 A_1 A_2, \quad D_2 A_1 A_3,$$
$$D_2 A_1 A_4, \quad D_2 A_2 A_3, \quad D_2 A_2 A_4,$$
$$D_2 A_3 A_4, \quad A_1 A_2 A_3, \quad A_1 A_2 A_4,$$
$$A_1 A_3 A_4, \quad A_2 A_3 A_4$$

Combinations are used to counting the sample space because sampling is done without replacement.

$$_6C_3 = \frac{6!}{3!3!} = 20$$

Probability that one of three is defective is:

12/20 = 3/5   **.60**

There are 20 members of the sample space and 12 of them have 1 defective part.

4.7 $$_{20}C_6 = \frac{20!}{6!14!} = \mathbf{38,760}$$

It is assumed here that 6 different (without replacement) employees are to be selected.

4.9

	D	E	F	
A	5	8	12	25
B	10	6	4	20
C	8	2	5	15
	23	16	21	60

a) $P(A \cup D) = P(A) + P(D) - P(A \cap D) =$ 25/60 + 23/60 - 5/60 = 43/60 = **.7167**

b) $P(E \cup B) = P(E) + P(B) - P(E \cap B) =$ 16/60 + 20/60 - 6/60 = 30/60 = **.5000**

c) $P(D \cup E) = P(D) + P(E) = 23/60 + 16/60 = 39/60 =$ **.6500**

d) $P(C \cup F) = P(C) + P(F) - P(C \cap F) =$ 15/60 + 21/60 - 5/60 = 31/60 = **.5167**

4.11   A = event - flown in an airplane at least once
        T = event - ridden in a train at least once

$$P(A) = .47 \qquad P(T) = .28$$

P (ridden either a train or an airplane) =

$$P(A \cup T) = P(A) + P(T) - P(A \cap T) = .47 + .28 - P(A \cap T)$$

Cannot solve this problem without knowing the probability of the intersection.
We need to know the probability of the intersection of A and T, the proportion
who have ridden both.

4.13   Let C = have cable TV
        Let T = have 2 or more TV sets

$$P(C) = .67, \; P(T) = .74, \; P(C \; T) = .55$$

a) $P(C \cup T) = P(C) + P(T) - P(C \cap T) = .67 + .74 - .55 = \mathbf{.86}$

b) $P(C \cup T \text{ but not both}) = P(C \cup T) - P(C \cap T) = .86 - .55 = \mathbf{.31}$

c) $P(NC \cap NT) = 1 - P(C \cup T) = 1 - .86 = \mathbf{.14}$

d) The special law of addition does not apply because $P(C \cap T)$ is not .0000.
    Possession of cable TV and 2 or more TV sets are not mutually exclusive.

4.15

	C	D	E	F	
A	5	11	16	8	40
B	2	3	5	7	17
	7	14	21	15	57

a) $P(A \cap E) = 16/57 = $ **.2807**

b) $P(D \cap B) = 3/57 = $ **.0526**

c) $P(D \cap E) = $ **.0000**

d) $P(A \cap B) = $ **.0000**

4.17   Let D = Defective part

a) (without replacement)

$$P(D_1 \cap D_2) = P(D_1) \cdot P(D_2 \mid D_1) = \frac{6}{50} \cdot \frac{5}{49} = \frac{30}{2450} = \textbf{.0122}$$

b) (with replacement)

$$P(D_1 \cap D_2) = P(D_1) \cdot P(D_2) = \frac{6}{50} \cdot \frac{6}{50} = \frac{36}{2500} = \textbf{.0144}$$

4.19   Let S = stockholder
Let C = college

$P(S) = .43$ $P(C) = .37$ $P(C \mid S) = .75$

a) $P(NS) = 1 - .43 = $ **.57**

b) $P(S \cap C) = P(S) \cdot P(C \mid S) = (.43)(.75) = $ **.3225**

c) $P(S \cup C) = P(S) + P(C) - P(S \cap C) = .43 + .37 - .3225 = $ **.4775**

d) $P(NS \cap NC) = 1 - P(S \cup C) = 1 - .4775 = $ **.5225**

e) $P(NS \cup NC) = P(NS) + P(NC) - P(NS \cap NC) = .57 + .63 - .5225 = $ **.6775**

f) $P(C \cap NS) = P(C) - P(C \cap S) = .37 - .3225 = $ **.0475**

4.21   Let S = safety
       Let A = age

$P(S) = .30$ $P(A) = .39$ $P(A \mid S) = .87$

a) $P(S \cap NA) = P(S) \cdot P(NA \mid S)$

   but $P(NA \mid S) = 1 - P(A \mid S) = 1 - .87 = .13$

   $P(S \cap NA) = (.30)(.13) = \mathbf{.039}$

b) $P(NS \cap NA) = 1 - P(S \cup A) = 1 - [P(S) + P(A) - P(S \cap A)]$

   but $P(S \cap A) = P(S) \cdot P(A \mid S) = (.30)(.87) = .261$

   $P(NS \cap NA) = 1 - (.30 + .39 - .261) = \mathbf{.571}$

c) $P(NS \cap A) = P(NS) - P(NS \cap NA)$

   but $P(NS) = 1 - P(S) = 1 - .30 = .70$

   $P(NS \cap A) = .70 - 571 = \mathbf{.129}$

4.23

	E	F	G	
A	15	12	8	35
B	11	17	19	47
C	21	32	27	80
D	18	13	12	43
	65	74	66	205

a) $P(G \mid A) = 8/35 = \mathbf{.2286}$

b) $P(B \mid F) = 17/74 = \mathbf{.2297}$

c) $P(C \mid E) = 21/65 = \mathbf{.3231}$

d) $P(E \mid G) = \mathbf{.0000}$

4.25

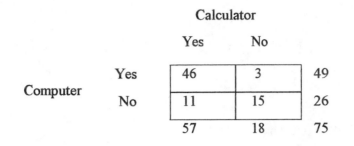

Calculator

		Yes	No	
	Yes	46	3	49
Computer	No	11	15	26
		57	18	75

Select a category from each variable and test

$$P(V_1 | V_2) = P(V_1).$$

For example,   P(Yes Computer | Yes Calculator) = P(Yes Computer)?

$$\frac{46}{57} = \frac{49}{75}?$$

$$.8070 \neq .6533$$

Variable of Computer not independent of Variable of Calculator.

4.27   Let E = Economy
        Let Q = Qualified

P(E) = .46   P(Q) = .37 $P(E \cap Q) = .15$

a) $P(E | Q) = P(E \cap Q)/P(Q) = .15/.37 = $ **.4054**

b) $P(Q | E) = P(E \cap Q)/P(E) = .15/.46 = $ **.3261**

c) $P(Q | NE) = P(Q \cap NE)/P(NE)$

   but $P(Q \cap NE) = P(Q) - P(Q \cap E) = .37 - .15 = .22$

   $P(NE) = 1 - P(E) = 1 - .46 = .54$

   $P(Q | NE) = .22/.54 = $ **.4074**

d) $P(NE \cap NQ) = 1 - P(E \cup Q) = 1 - [P(E) + P(Q) - P(E \cap Q)]$

   $= 1 - [.46 + .37 + .15] = 1 - (.68) = $ **.32**

4.29   Let H = hardware
        Let S = software

$P(H) = .37 \qquad P(S) = .54 \qquad P(S \mid H) = .97$

a) $P(NS \mid H) = 1 - P(S \mid H) = 1 - .97 = \textbf{.03}$

b) $P(S \mid NH) = P(S \cap NH)/P(NH)$

   but $P(H \cap S) = P(H) \cdot P(S \mid H) = (.37)(.97) = .3589$

   so $P(NH \cap S) = P(S) - P(H \cap S) = .54 - .3589 = .1811$

   $P(NH) = 1 - P(H) = 1 - .37 = .63$

   $P(S \mid NH) = (.1811)/(.63) = \textbf{.2875}$

c) $P(NH \mid S) = P(NH \cap S)/P(S) = .1811//54 = \textbf{.3354}$

d) $P(NH \mid NS) = P(NH \cap NS)/P(NS)$

   but $P(NH \cap NS) = P(NH) - P(NH \cap S) = .63 - .1811 = .4489$

   and $P(NS) = 1 - P(S) = 1 - .54 = .46$

   $P(NH \mid NS) = .4489/.46 = \textbf{.9759}$

4.31   Let: A = Alex fills the order
                     B = Alicia fills the order
                     C = Juan fills the order
                     I = order filled incorrectly
                     K = order filled correctly

$P(A) = .30 \qquad P(B) = .45 \qquad P(C) = .25$
$P(I \mid A) = .20 \quad P(I \mid B) = .12 \quad P(I \mid C) = .05$
$P(K \mid A) = .80 \quad P(K \mid B) = .88 \quad P(K \mid C) = .95$

a) $P(B) = .45$

b) $P(K \mid C) = 1 - P(I \mid C) = 1 - .05 = .95$

c)

Event	Prior	Conditional	Joint	Revised
	$P(E_i)$	$P(I \mid E_i)$	$P(I \cap E_i)$	$P(E_i \mid I)$
A	.30	.20	.0600	.0600/.1265=**.4743**
B	.45	.12	.0540	.0540/.1265=**.4269**
C	.25	.05	.0125	.0125/.1265=**.0988**
			P(I)=.1265	

Revised: $P(A \mid I) = .0600/.1265 = \mathbf{.4743}$

$P(B \mid I) = .0540/.1265 = \mathbf{.4269}$

$P(C \mid I) = .0125/.1265 = \mathbf{.0988}$

d)

Event	Prior	Conditional	Joint	Revised
	$P(E_i)$	$P(K \mid E_i)$	$P(K \cap E_i)$	$P(E_i \mid K)$
A	.30	.80	.2400	.2400/.8735=**.2748**
B	.45	.88	.3960	.3960/.8735=**.4533**
C	.25	.95	.2375	.2375/.8735=**.2719**
			P(K)=.8735	

4.33   Let T = training
Let S = small

P(T) = .65
$P(S \mid T) = .18$ $P(NS \mid T) = .82$
$P(S \mid NT) = .75$ $P(NS \mid NT) = .25$

Event	Prior	Conditional	Joint	Revised
	$P(E_i)$	$P(NS \mid E_i)$	$P(NS \cap E_i)$	$P(E_i \mid NS)$
T	.65	.82	.5330	.5330/.6205=**.8590**
NT	.35	.25	.0875	.0875/.6205=.1410
			P(NS)=**.6205**	

4.35

	D	E	F	G	
A	3	9	7	12	31
B	8	4	6	4	22
C	10	5	3	7	25
	21	18	16	23	78

a) $P(F \cap A) = 7/78 = .08974$

b) $P(A \mid B) = \dfrac{P(A \cap B)}{P(B)} = \dfrac{.0000}{22/78} = .0000$

c) $P(B) = 22/78 = .28205$

d) $P(E \cap F) = .0000$ **Mutually Exclusive**

e) $P(D \mid B) = 8/22 = .36364$

f) $P(B \mid D) = 8/21 = .38095$

g) $P(D \cup C) = 21/78 + 25/78 = 46/78 = .5897$

h) $P(F) = 16/78 = .20513$

4.37   Let T = thoroughness
Let K = knowledge

$P(T) = .78$ $P(K) = .40$ $P(T \cap K) = .27$

a) $P(T \cup K) = P(T) + P(K) - P(T \cap K) =$

 $.78 + .40 - .27 = .91$

b) $P(NT \cap NK) = 1 - P(T \cup K) = 1 - .91 = .09$

c) $P(K \mid T) = P(K \cap T)/P(T) = .27/.78 = .3462$

d) $P(NT \cap K) = P(NT) - P(NT \cap NK)$

 but $P(NT) = 1 - P(T) = .22$

 $P(NT \cap K) = .22 - .09 = .13$

4.39 $P(T) = .16$ $P(T|W) = .20$ $P(T|NE) = .17$ $P(W) = .21$ $P(NE) = .20$

    a) $P(W \cap T) = P(W) \cdot P(T|W) = (.21)(.20) = \textbf{.042}$

    b) $P(NE \cap T) = P(NE) \cdot P(T|NE) = (.20)(.17) = \textbf{.034}$

    c) $P(W|T) = P(W \cap T)/P(T) = (.042)/(.16) = \textbf{.2625}$

    d) $P(NE|NT) = P(NE \cap NT)/P(NT) = \{P(NE) \cdot P(NT|NE)\}/P(NT)$

        but $P(NT|NE) = 1 - P(T|NE) = 1 - .17 = .83$ and

        $P(NT) = 1 - P(T) = 1 - .16 = .84$

        Therefore, $P(NE|NT) = \{P(NE) \cdot P(NT|NE)\}/P(NT) =$

        $\{(.20)(.83)\}/(.84) = \textbf{.1976}$

    e) $P(\text{not } W \cap \text{not } NE | T) = P(\text{not } W \cap \text{not } NE \cap T)/P(T)$

        but $P(\text{not } W \cap \text{not } NE \cap T) =$

        $.16 - P(W \cap T) - P(NE \cap T) = .16 - .042 - .034 = .084$

        $P(\text{not } W \cap \text{not } NE \cap T)/P(T) = (.084)/(.16) = \textbf{.525}$

4.41   Let S = believe SS secure
       N = don't believe SS will be secure
       <45 = under 45 years old
       $\geq$45 = 45 or more years old

       $P(N) = .51$
       Therefore, $P(S) = 1 - .51 = .49$

       $P(S|\geq 45) = .70$
       Therefore, $P(N|\geq 45) = 1 - P(S|\geq 45) = 1 - .70 = .30$

       $P(<45) = .57$

    a) $P(\geq 45) = 1 - P(<45) = 1 - .57 = \textbf{.43}$

b) $P(\geq 45 \cap S) = P(\geq 45) \cdot P(S \mid \geq 45) = (.57)(.70) = .301$

   $P(<45 \cap S) = P(S) - P(\geq 45 \cap S) = .49 - .301 = \mathbf{.189}$

c) $P(\geq 45 \mid S) = P(\geq 45 \cap S)/P(S) = P(\geq 45) \cdot P(S \mid \geq 45)/P(S) =$

   $(.43)(.70)/.49 = \mathbf{.6143}$

d) $(<45 \cup N) = P(<45) + P(N) - P(<45 \cap N) =$

   but $P(<45 \cap N) = P(<45) - P(<45 \cap S) =$

   $.57 - .189 = .381$

   so $P(<45 \cup N) = .57 + .51 - .381 = \mathbf{.699}$

Probability Matrix Solution for Problem 4.41:

	S	N	
<45	.189	.381	.57
>45	.301	.129	.43
	.490	.510	1.00

4.43   Let R = read
   Let B = checked in the with boss

   $P(R) = .40 \qquad P(B) = .34 \qquad P(B \mid R) = .78$

a) $P(B \cap R) = P(R) \cdot P(B \mid R) = (.40)(.78) = \mathbf{.312}$

b) $P(NR \cap NB) = 1 - P(R \cup B)$

   but $P(R \cup B) = P(R) + P(B) - P(R \cap B) =$

   $.40 + .34 - .312 = .428$

   $P(NR \cap NB) = 1 - .428 = \mathbf{.572}$

c) $P(R \mid B) = P(R \cap B)/P(B) = (.312)/(.34) = \mathbf{.9176}$

d) $P(NB|R) = 1 - P(B|R) = 1 - .78 = .22$

e) $P(NB|NR) = P(NB \cap NR)/P(NR)$

but $P(NR) = 1 - P(R) = 1 - .40 = .60$

$P(NB|NR) = .572/.60 = .9533$

f) Probability matrix for problem 4.43:

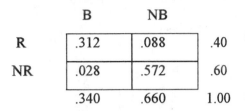

	B	NB	
R	.312	.088	.40
NR	.028	.572	.60
	.340	.660	1.00

4.45   Let R = retention
Let P = process

$P(R) = .56 \qquad P(P \cap R) = .36 \qquad P(R|P) = .90$

a) $P(R \cap NP) = P(R) - P(P \cap R) = .56 - .36 = .20$

b) $P(P|R) = P(P \cap R)/P(R) = .36/.56 = .6429$

c) $P(P) = ??$

$P(R|P) = P(R \cap P)/P(P)$

so $P(P) = P(R \cap P)/P(R|P) = .36/.90 = .40$

d) $P(R \cup P) = P(R) + P(P) - P(R \cap P) =$

$.56 + .40 - .36 = .60$

e) $P(NR \cap NP) = 1 - P(R \cup P) = 1 - .60 = .40$

f) $P(R|NP) = P(R \cap NP)/P(NP)$

but $P(NP) = 1 - P(P) = 1 - .40 = .60$

$P(R|NP) = .20/.60 = .33$

4.47   Let S = Sarabia
        T = Tran
        J = Jackson
        B = blood test

$P(S) = .41$ $P(T) = .32$ $P(J) = .27$
$P(B\ S) = .05$ $P(B\ T) = .08$ $P(B\ J) = .06$

Event	Prior $P(E_i)$	Conditional $P(B\mid E_i)$	Joint $P(B \cap E_i)$	Revised $P(B_i \mid NS)$
S	.41	.05	.0205	**.329**
T	.32	.08	.0256	.411
J	.27	.06	.0162	.260
			$P(B)=.0623$	

4.49

Event	Prior $P(E_i)$	Conditional $P(NS \mid E_i)$	Joint $P(NS \cap E_i)$	Revised $P(E_i \mid NS)$
Soup	.60	.73	.4380	**.8456**
Breakfast Meats	.35	.17	.0595	**.1149**
Hot Dogs	.05	.41	.0205	**.0396**
			.5180	

Chapter 5
Discrete Distributions

LEARNING OBJECTIVES

The overall learning objective of Chapter 5 is to help you understand a category of probability distributions that produces only discrete outcomes, thereby enabling you to:

1. Distinguish between discrete random variables and continuous random variables.

2. Know how to determine the mean and variance of a discrete distribution.

3. Identify the type of statistical experiments that can be described by the binomial distribution and know how to work such problems.

4. Decide when to use the Poisson distribution in analyzing statistical experiments and know how to work such problems.

5. Decide when binomial distribution problems can be approximated by the Poisson distribution and know how to work such problems.

6. Decide when to use the hypergeometric distribution and know how to work such problems

CHAPTER OUTLINE

5.1   Discrete Versus Continuous Distributions

5.2   Describing a Discrete Distribution

      Mean, Variance, and Standard Deviation of Discrete Distributions

          Mean or Expected Value

          Variance and Standard Deviation of a Discrete Distribution

5.3   Binomial Distribution

      Solving a Binomial Problem

      Using the Binomial Table

      Using the Computer to Produce a Binomial Distribution

      Mean and Standard Deviation of the Binomial Distribution

      Graphing Binomial Distributions

5.4   Poisson Distribution

      Working Poisson Problems by Formula

      Using the Poisson Tables

      Mean and Standard Deviation of a Poisson Distribution

      Graphing Poisson Distributions

      Using the Computer to Generate Poisson Distributions

      Approximating Binomial Problems by the Poisson Distribution

5.5   Hypergeometric Distribution

      Using the Computer to Solve for Hypergeometric Distribution
      Probabilities

KEY WORDS

Binomial Distribution	Hypergeometric Distribution
Continuous Distributions	Lambda
Continuous Random Variables	Mean, or Expected Value
Discrete Distributions	Poisson Distribution
Discrete Random Variables	Random Variable

STUDY QUESTIONS

1. Variables that take on values at every point over a given interval are called
   _____ _____ variables.

2. If the set of all possible values of a variable is at most finite or a countably infinite number of
   possible values, then the variable is called a _____ _____ variable.

3. An experiment in which a die is rolled six times will likely produce values of a
   _____ random variable.

4. An experiment in which a researcher counts the number of customers arriving at a
   supermarket checkout counter every two minutes produces values of a _____
   random variable.

5. An experiment in which the time it takes to assemble a product is measured is likely to
   produce values of a _____ random variable.

6. A binomial distribution is an example of a _____ distribution.

7. The normal distribution is an example of a _____ distribution.

8. The long-run average of a discrete distribution is called the _____ or
   _____.

Use the following discrete distribution to answer 9 and 10

X	P(X)
1	.435
2	.241
3	.216
4	.108

9. The mean of the discrete distribution above is _____.

10. The variance of the discrete distribution above is _____.

11.   On any one trial of a binomial experiment, there can be only _____ possible outcomes.

12.   Suppose the probability that a given part is defective is .10. If four such parts are randomly drawn from a large population, the probability that exactly two parts are defective is _____.

13.   Suppose the probability that a given part is defective is .04. If thirteen such parts are randomly drawn from a large population, the expected value or mean of the binomial distribution that describes this experiment is _____.

14.   Suppose a binomial experiment is conducted by randomly selecting 20 items where p = .30. The standard deviation of the binomial distribution is _____.

15.   Suppose forty-seven percent of the workers in a large corporation are under thirty-five years of age. If fifteen workers are randomly selected from this corporation, the probability of selecting exactly ten who are under thirty-five years of age is _____.

16.   Suppose that twenty-three percent of all adult Americans fly at least once a year. If twelve adult Americans are randomly selected, the probability that exactly four have flown at least once last year is _____.

17.   Suppose that sixty percent of all voters support the President of the United States at this time. If twenty voters are randomly selected, the probability that at least eleven support the President is _____.

18.   The Poisson distribution was named after the French mathematician _____.

19.   The Poisson distribution focuses on the number of discrete occurrences per _____.

20.   The Poisson distribution tends to describe _____ occurrences.

21.   The long-run average or mean of a Poisson distribution is _____.

22.   The variance of a Poisson distribution is equal to _____.

23.   If Lambda is 2.6 occurrences over an interval of five minutes, the probability of getting six occurrences over one five minute interval is _____.

24.   Suppose that in the long-run a company determines that there are 1.2 flaws per every twenty pages of typing paper produced. If ten pages of typing paper are randomly selected, the probability that more than two flaws are found is _____.

25.   If Lambda is 1.8 for a four minute interval, an adjusted new Lambda of _____ would be used to analyze the number of occurrences for a twelve minute interval.

26.   Suppose a binomial distribution problem has an n = 200 and a p = .03. If this problem is worked using the Poisson distribution, the value of Lambda is _____.

27. The hypergeometric distribution should be used when a binomial type experiment is being conducted without replacement and the sample size is greater than or equal to _____% of the population.

28. Suppose a population contains sixteen items of which seven are X and nine are Y. If a random sample of five of these population items is selected, the probability that exactly three of the five are X is _____.

29. Suppose a population contains twenty people of which eight are members of the Catholic church. If a sample of four of the population is taken, the probability that at least three of the four are members of the Catholic church is _____.

30. Suppose a lot of fifteen personal computer printers contains two defective printers. If three of the fifteen printers are randomly selected for testing, the probability that no defective printers are selected is _____.

ANSWERS TO STUDY QUESTIONS

1. Continuous Random	16. .1712
2. Discrete Random	17. .755
3. Discrete	18. Poisson
4. Discrete	19. Interval
5. Continuous	20. Rare
6. Discrete	21. Lambda
7. Continuous	22. Lambda
8. Mean, Expected Value	23. .0319
9. 1.997	24. .0232
10. 1.083	25. 5.4
11. Two	26. 6.0
12. .0486	27. 5
13. 0.52	28. .2885
14. 2.049	29. .1531
15. .0661	30. .6286

SOLUTIONS TO PROBLEMS IN CHAPTER 5

5.1

$\underline{X}$	$\underline{P(X)}$	$\underline{X \cdot P(X)}$	$\underline{(X-\mu)^2}$	$\underline{(X-\mu)^2 \cdot P(X)}$
1	.238	.238	2.775556	0.6605823
2	.290	.580	0.443556	0.1286312
3	.177	.531	0.111556	0.0197454
4	.158	.632	1.779556	0.2811700
5	.137	.685	5.447556	0.7463152

$\mu = [X \cdot P(X)] = \mathbf{2.666}$ $\sigma^2 = (X-\mu)^2 \cdot P(X) = \mathbf{1.836444}$

$\sigma = \sqrt{1.836444} = \mathbf{1.355155}$

5.3

$\underline{X}$	$\underline{P(X)}$	$\underline{X \cdot P(X)}$	$\underline{(X-\mu)^2}$	$\underline{(X-\mu)^2 \cdot P(X)}$
0	.461	.000	0.913936	0.421324
1	.285	.285	0.001936	0.000552
2	.129	.258	1.089936	0.140602
3	.087	.261	4.177936	0.363480
4	.038	.152	9.265936	0.352106

$E(X) = \mu = [X \cdot P(X)] = \mathbf{0.956}$ $\sigma^2 = (X-\mu)^2 \cdot P(X) = \mathbf{1.278064}$

$\sigma = \sqrt{1.278064} = \mathbf{1.1305}$

5.5   **a)** $n = 4$ $p = .10$ $q = .90$

$P(X=3) = {}_4C_3(.10)^3(.90)^1 = 4(.001)(.90) = \mathbf{.0036}$

b) $n = 7$ $p = .80$ $q = .20$

$P(X=4) = {}_7C_4(.80)^4(.20)^3 = 35(.4096)(.008) = \mathbf{.1147}$

c) $n = 10$ $p = .60$ $q = .40$

$P(X \geq 7) = P(X=7) + P(X=8) + P(X=9) + P(X=10) =$

$_{10}C_7(.60)^7(.40)^3 + _{10}C_8(.60)^8(.40)^2 + _{10}C_9(.60)^9(.40)^1 + _{10}C_{10}(.60)^{10}(.40)^0 =$

$120(.0280)(.064) + 45(.0168)(.16) + 10(.0101)(.40) + 1(.0060)(1) =$

$.2150 + .1209 + .0403 + .0060 = \textbf{.3822}$

d) $n = 12$ $p = .45 \; q = .55$

$P(5 \leq X \leq 7) = P(X=5) + P(X=6) + P(X=7) =$

$_{12}C_5(.45)^5(.55)^7 + _{12}C_6(.45)^6(.55)^6 + _{12}C_7(.45)^7(.55)^5 =$

$792(.0185)(.0152) + 924(.0083)(.0277) + 792(.0037)(.0503) =$

$.2225 + .2124 + .1489 = \textbf{.5838}$

5.7   a) $n = 20$ $p = .70$ $q = .30$

$\mu = n \cdot p = 20(.70) = \textbf{14}$

$\sigma = \sqrt{n \cdot p \cdot q} = \sqrt{20(.70)(.30)} = \sqrt{4.2} = \textbf{2.05}$

b) $n = 70$ $p = .35$ $q = .65$

$\mu = n \cdot p = 70(.35) = \textbf{24.5}$

$\sigma = \sqrt{n \cdot p \cdot q} = \sqrt{70(.35)(.65)} = \sqrt{15.925} = \textbf{3.99}$

c) $n = 100 \; p = .50$ $q = .50$

$\mu = n \cdot p = 100(.50) = \textbf{50}$

$\sigma = \sqrt{n \cdot p \cdot q} = \sqrt{100(.50)(.50)} = \sqrt{25} = \textbf{5}$

5.9   a) $n = 20$ $p = .78$ $X = 14$

$_{20}C_{14} (.78)^{14}(.22)^6 = 38,760(.030855)(.00011338) = \mathbf{.1356}$

b) $n = 20$ $p = .75$ $X = 20$

$_{20}C_{20} (.75)^{20}(.25)^0 = (1)(.0031712)(1) = \mathbf{.0032}$

c) $n = 20$ $p = .70$ $X < 12$

Use table A.2:

$P(X=0) + P(X=1) + \ldots + P(X=11) =$

$.000 + .000 + .000 + .000 + .000 + .000 + .000 +$

$.001 + .004 + .012 + .031 + .065 = \mathbf{.113}$

5.11 $n = 25$ $P = .60$

a) $X \geq 15$

$P(X \geq 15) = P(X = 15) + P(X = 16) + \cdots + P(X = 25)$

Using Table A.2 $n = 25$, $p = .80$

X	Prob
15	.161
16	.151
17	.120
18	.080
19	.044
20	.020
21	.007
22	.002

.585

b) X > 20

from a): P(X > 20) = P(X = 21) + P(X = 22) + P(X = 23) +

P(X = 24) + P(X = 25) =

.007 + .002 + .000 + .000 + .000 = **.009**

c) P(X < 10)

from Table A.2,

X	Prob.
9	.009
8	.003
7	.001
$\leq$6	.000
	.013

5.13   n = 15   p = .20

a) P(X = 5) = $_{15}C_5(.20)^5(.80)^{10}$ =

3003(.00032)(.1073742) = **.1032**

b) P(X > 9): Using Table A.2

P(X = 10) + P(X = 11) + . . . + P(X = 15) =

.000 + .000 + . . . + .000 = **.000**

c) P(X = 0) = $_{15}C_0(.20)^0(.80)^{15}$ =

(1)(1)(.035184) = **.0352**

d) P(4 $\leq$ X $\leq$ 7): Using Table A.2

P(X = 4) + P(X = 5) + P(X = 6) + P(X = 7) =

.188 + .103 + .043 + .014 = **.348**

e)

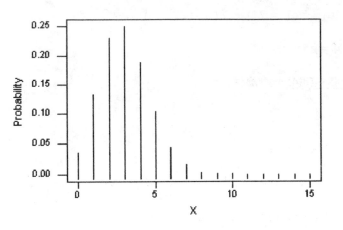

Binomial Distribution for n=15 and p=.20

5.15   a) Prob(X=5 | $\lambda = 2.3$)=

$$\frac{(2.3^5)(e^{-2.3})}{5!} = \frac{(64.36343)(.1002588)}{(120)} = \ \mathbf{.0538}$$

b) Prob(X=2 | $\lambda = 3.9$) =

$$\frac{(3.9^2)(e^{-3.9})}{2!} = \frac{(15.21)(.02024)}{(2)} = \ \mathbf{.1539}$$

c) Prob(X $\leq$ 3 | $\lambda = 4.1$) =

Prob(X=3) + Prob(X=2) + Prob(X=1) + Prob(X=0) =

$$\frac{(4.1^3)(e^{-4.1})}{3!} = \frac{(68.921)(.016574)}{6} = .1904$$

$$+ \frac{(4.1^2)(e^{-4.1})}{2!} = \frac{(16.81)(.016573)}{2} = .1393$$

$$+ \frac{(4.1^1)(e^{-4.1})}{1!} = \frac{(4.1)(.016573)}{1} = .0679$$

$$+ \frac{(4.1^0)(e^{-4.1})}{0!} = \frac{(1)(.016573)}{1} = .0166$$

.1904 + .1393 + .0679 + .0166 = **.4142**

d) $\text{Prob}(X=0 \mid \lambda = 2.7) =$

$$\frac{(2.7^0)(e^{-2.7})}{0!} = \frac{(1)(.0672)}{1} = \mathbf{.0672}$$

e) $\text{Prob}(X=1 \mid \lambda = 5.4) =$

$$\frac{(5.4^1)(e^{-5.4})}{1!} = \frac{(5.4)(.0045)}{1} = \mathbf{.0244}$$

f) $\text{Prob}(4 < X < 8 \mid \lambda = 4.4) =$

$\text{Prob}(X=5 \mid \lambda = 4.4) + \text{Prob}(X=6 \mid \lambda = 4.4) + \text{Prob}(X=7 \mid \lambda = 4.4) =$

$$\frac{(4.4^5)(e^{-4.4})}{5!} + \frac{(4.4^6)(e^{-4.4})}{6!} + \frac{(4.4^7)(e^{-4.4})}{7!} =$$

$$\frac{(1649.162)(.012277)}{120} + \frac{(7256.314)(.012277)}{720} + \frac{(31927.781)(.012277)}{5040}$$

$$= .1687 + .1237 + .0778 = \mathbf{.3702}$$

5.17 a) $\lambda = 6.3$ mean = **6.3**   Standard deviation = $\sqrt{6.3} = \mathbf{2.51}$

X	Prob
0	.0018
1	.0116
2	.0364
3	.0765
4	.1205
5	.1519
6	.1595
7	.1435
8	.1130
9	.0791
10	.0498
11	.0285
12	.0150
13	.0073
14	.0033
15	.0014
16	.0005
17	.0002
18	.0001
19	.0000

Poisson Distribution with Lambda = 6.3

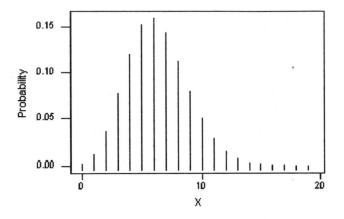

b) $\lambda = 1.3$ mean = **1.3**   standard deviation = $\sqrt{1.3}$ = **1.14**

X	Prob
0	.2725
1	.3542
2	.2303
3	.0998
4	.0324
5	.0084
6	.0018
7	.0003
8	.0001
9	.0000

Poisson Distribution with Lambda = 1.3

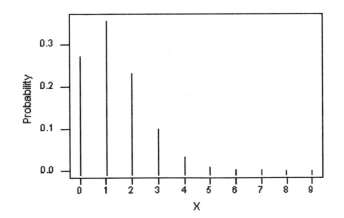

c) $\lambda = 8.9$ mean = **8.9**   standard deviation = $\sqrt{8.9} = $ **2.98**

X	Prob
0	.0001
1	.0012
2	.0054
3	.0160
4	.0357
5	.0635
6	.0941
7	.1197
8	.1332
9	.1317
10	.1172
11	.0948
12	.0703
13	.0481
14	.0306
15	.0182
16	.0101
17	.0053
18	.0026
19	.0012
20	.0005
21	.0002
22	.0001

Poisson Distribution with Lambda = 8.9

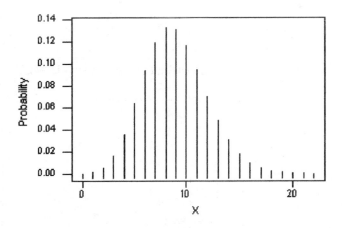

d) $\lambda = 0.6$ mean = **0.6**   standard deviation = $\sqrt{0.6} = .775$

X	Prob
0	.5488
1	.3293
2	.0988
3	.0198
4	.0030
5	.0004
6	.0000

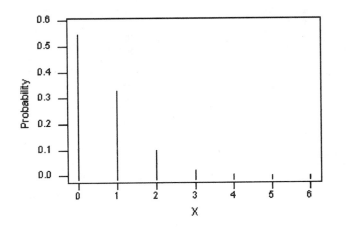

Poisson Distribution with Lambda = 0.6

5.19 $\lambda = \Sigma X/n = 126/36 = 3.5$

Using Table A.3

a) $P(X = 0) = \textbf{.0302}$

b) $P(X \geq 6) = P(X = 6) + P(X = 7) + \ldots =$

$.0771 + .0385 + .0169 + .0066 + .0023 +$

$.0007 + .0002 + .0001 = \textbf{.1424}$

c) $P(X < 4 \mid 10$ minutes$)$

$\lambda = 7.0 \mid 10$ minutes

$P(X < 4) = P(X = 0) + P(X = 1) + P(X = 2) + P(X = 3) =$

$.0009 + .0064 + .0223 + .0521 = \textbf{.0817}$

d) $P(3 \leq X \leq 6 \mid 10$ minutes$)$

$\lambda = 7.0 \mid 10$ minutes

$P(3 \leq X \leq 6) = P(X = 3) + P(X = 4) + P(X = 5) + P(X = 6)$

$= .0521 + .0912 + .1277 + .1490 = \textbf{.42}$

e) $P(X = 8 \mid 15$ minutes$)$

$\lambda = 10.5 \mid 15$ minutes

$P(X = 8 \mid 15 \text{ minutes}) = \dfrac{\lambda^{X} \cdot e^{-\lambda}}{X!} = \dfrac{(10.5^{8})(e^{-10.5})}{8!} = \textbf{.1009}$

5.21 $\lambda = 0.6$ trips $|$ 1 year

   a)   Prob(X=0 $|$ $\lambda = 0.6$):

   from Table A.3 = **.5488**

   b)   Prob(X=1 $|$ $\lambda = 0.6$):

   from Table A.3 = **.3293**

   c)   Prob(X $\geq$ 2 $|$ $\lambda = 0.6$):

   from Table A.3

X	Prob.
2	.0988
3	.0198
4	.0030
5	.0004
6	.0000
X $\geq$ 2	**.1220**

   d)   Prob(X $\leq$ 3 $|$ 3 year period):

   The interval length has been increased (3 times)

   New Lambda = λ = 1.8 trips $|$ 3 years

   Prob(X $\leq$ 3 $|$ $\lambda = 1.8$):

   from Table A.3

X	Prob.
0	.1653
1	.2975
2	.2678
3	.1607
X $\leq$ 3	**.8913**

   e)   Prob(X=4 $|$ 6 years):

   The interval has been increased (6 times)

   New Lambda = λ = 3.6 trips $|$ 6 years

   Prob(X=4 $|$ $\lambda = 3.6$):

   from Table A.3 = **.1912**

5.23 $\lambda = 1.2$ pens|carton

a) Prob(X=0 | $\lambda = 1.2$):

from Table A.3 = **.3012**

b) Prob(X $\geq$ 8 | $\lambda = 1.2$):

from Table A.3 = **.0000**

c) Prob(X > 3 | $\lambda = 1.2$):

from Table A.3

X	Prob.
4	.0260
5	.0062
6	.0012
7	.0002
8	.0000
X > 3	**.0336**

5.25   p = .009   n = 200

Use the Poisson Distribution:

$\lambda = n \cdot p = 200(.009) = 1.8$

P(X $\geq$ 6) from Table A.3 =

P(X = 6) + P(X = 7) + P(X = 8) + P(X = 9) + . . . =

.0078 + .0020 + .0005 + .0001 = **.0104**

P(X > 10) = **.0000**

P(X = 0) = **.1653**

P(X < 5) = P(X = 0) + P(X = 1) + P(X = 2) + P(X = 3) + P(X = 4) =

.1653 + .2975 + .2678 + .1607 + .0723 = **.9636**

5.27   a) $\text{Prob}(x = 3 \mid N = 11, A = 8, n = 4)$

$$\frac{_8C_3 \, _3C_1}{_{11}C_4} = \frac{(56)(3)}{330} = \mathbf{.5091}$$

b) $\text{Prob}(x < 2) \mid N = 15, A = 5, n = 6)$

$\text{Prob}(x = 1) + \text{Prob}(x = 0) =$

$$\frac{_5C_1 \, _{10}C_5}{_{15}C_6} + \frac{_5C_0 \, _{10}C_6}{_{15}C_6} = \frac{(5)(252)}{5005} + \frac{(1)(210)}{5005} =$$

$.2517 + .0420 = \mathbf{.2937}$

c) $\text{Prob}(x=0 \mid N = 9, A = 2, n = 3)$

$$\frac{_2C_0 \, _7C_3}{_9C_3} = \frac{(1)(35)}{84} = \mathbf{.4167}$$

d) $\text{Prob}(x > 4 \mid N = 20, A = 5, n = 7) =$

$\text{Prob}(x = 5) + \text{Prob}(x = 6) + \text{Prob}(x = 7) =$

$$\frac{_5C_5 \, _{15}C_2}{_{20}C_7} + \frac{_5C_6 \, _{15}C_1}{_{20}C_7} + \frac{_5C_7 \, _{15}C_0}{_{20}C_7} =$$

$$\frac{(1)(105)}{77520} + {}_5C_6 \,(\text{impossible}) + {}_5C_7(\text{impossible}) = \mathbf{.0014}$$

5.29 $N = 17$ $A = 8$ $n = 4$

a) $P(X = 0) = (_8C_0 \, _9C_4)/_{17}C_4 = [(1)(126)]/2380 = \mathbf{.0529}$

b) $P(X = 4) = (_8C_4 \, _9C_0)/_{17}C_4 = [(70)(1)]/2380 = \mathbf{.0294}$

c) $P(X = 2 \text{ non computer}) = (_9C_2 \, _8C_2)/_{17}C_4 = [(36)(28)]/2380 = \mathbf{.4235}$

5.31 $N = 10$ $n = 4$

a) $A = 3$ $X = 2$

$(_3C_2 \; _7C_2)/_{10}C_4 = [(3)(21)]/210 = \mathbf{.30}$

b) $A = 5$ $X = 0$

$(_5C_0 \; _5C_4)/_{10}C_4 = [(1)(5)]/210 = \mathbf{.0238}$

c) $A = 5$ $X = 3$

$(_5C_3 \; _5C_1)/_{10}C_4 = [(10)(5)]/210 = \mathbf{.2381}$

5.33 $N = 18$ $A = 11$ Hispanic $n = 5$

$\text{Prob}(X \leq 1) = \text{Prob}(1) + \text{Prob}(0) =$

$$\frac{_{11}C_1 \, _7C_4}{_{18}C_5} + \frac{_{11}C_0 \, _7C_5}{_{18}C_5} = \frac{(11)(35)}{8568} + \frac{(1)(21)}{8568} =$$

$.0449 + .0025 = \mathbf{.0474}$

It is fairly unlikely that these results occur by chance. A researcher might investigate further the causes of this result. Were officers selected based on leadership, years of service, dedication, prejudice, or what?

5.35   a) $\text{Prob}(X = 14 \mid n = 20 \text{ and } p = .60) = $ **.124**

b) $\text{Prob}(X < 5 \mid n = 10 \text{ and } p = .30) = $

$\text{Prob}(X = 4) + \text{Prob}(X = 3) + \text{Prob}(X = 2) + \text{Prob}(X = 1) + \text{Prob}(X = 0) = $

X	Prob.
0	.028
1	.121
2	.233
3	.267
4	.200

$X < 5$ **.849**

c) $\text{Prob}(X \geq 12 \mid n = 15 \text{ and } p = .60) = $

$\text{Prob}(X = 12) + \text{Prob}(X = 13) + \text{Prob}(X = 14) + \text{Prob}(X = 15)$

X	Prob.
12	.063
13	.022
14	.005
15	.000

$X \geq 12$ **.090**

d) $\text{Prob}(X > 20 \mid n = 25 \text{ and } p = .40) = \text{Prob}(X = 21) + \text{Prob}(X = 22) + $

$\text{Prob}(X = 23) + \text{Prob}(X = 24) + \text{Prob}(X = 25) = $

X	Prob.
21	.000
22	.000
23	.000
24	.000
25	.000

$X > 20$ **.000**

5.37   a) Prob(X = 3 | λ = 1.8) = **.1607**

b) Prob(X < 5 | λ = 3.3) =

Prob(X = 4) + Prob(X = 3) + Prob(X = 2) + Prob(X = 1) + Prob(X = 0) =

X	Prob.
0	.0369
1	.1217
2	.2008
3	.2209
4	.1823

X < 5   **.7626**

c) Prob(X ≥ 3 | λ = 2.1) =

X	Prob.
3	.1890
4	.0992
5	.0417
6	.0146
7	.0044
8	.0011
9	.0003
10	.0001
11	.0000

X ≥ 5   **.3504**

d) Prob(2 < X ≤ 5 | λ = 4.2) = Prob(x=3) + Prob(x=4) + Prob(x=5) =

X	Prob.
3	.1852
4	.1944
5	.1633

2 < X ≤ 5   **.5429**

5.39 $n = 25$ $p = .20$ retired

from Table A.2: $P(X = 7) = .111$

$P(X \geq 10)$: $P(X = 10) + P(X = 11) + \ldots + P(X = 25) =$

$.012 + .004 + .001 = .017$

Expected Value $= \mu = n \cdot p = 25(.20) = 5$

$n = 20$ $p = .40$ mutual funds

$P(X = 8) = .180$

$P(X < 6) = P(X = 0) + P(X = 1) + \ldots + P(X = 5) =$

$.000 + .000 + .003 + .012 + .035 + .075 = .125$

$P(X = 0) = .000$

$P(X \geq 12) = P(X = 12) + P(X = 13) + \ldots + P(X = 20) =$

$.035 + .015 + .005 + .001 = .056$

$X = 8$

Expected Number $= \mu = n\,p = 20(.40) = 8$

5.41 $N = 32$ $A = 10$ $n = 12$

a) $P(X = 3) = ({}_{10}C_3\ {}_{22}C_9)/{}_{32}C_{12} =$

$[(120)(497,420)]/225,792,840 = .2644$

b) $P(X = 6) = ({}_{10}C_6\ {}_{22}C_6)/{}_{32}C_{12} =$

$[(210)(74,613)]/225,792,840 = .0694$

c) $P(X = 0) = ({}_{10}C_0\ {}_{22}C_{12})/{}_{32}C_{12} =$

$[(1)(646,646)]/225,792,840 = .0029$

d) $A = 22$

$P(7 \leq X \leq 9) =$

$(_{22}C_7 \, _{10}C_5)/_{32}C_{12} + (_{22}C_8 \, _{10}C_4)/_{32}C_{12} + (_{22}C_9 \, _{10}C_3)/_{32}C_{12} =$

$[(170,544)(252)]/225,792,840 + [(319,770)(210)]/225,792,840 +$

$[(497,420)(120)]/225,792,840 = .1903 + .2974 + .2644 = \textbf{.7521}$

5.43   a) $n = 20$ and $p = .25$

The expected number $= \mu = n \cdot p = (20)(.25) = \textbf{5.00}$

b) $\text{Prob}(X \leq 1 \mid n = 20 \text{ and } p = .25) =$

$\text{Prob}(X = 1) + \text{Prob}(X = 0) = {}_{20}C_1(.25)^1(.75)^{19} + {}_{20}C_0(.25)^0(.75)^{20}$

$= (20)(.25)(.00423) + (1)(1)(.0032) = .0212 + .0032 = \textbf{.0244}$

Since the probability is so low, the population of your state may have a lower percentage of chronic heart conditions than those of other states.

5.45 $n = 12$

a.) $\text{Prob}(X = 0 \text{ long hours})$:

$p = .20 \qquad {}_{12}C_0(.20)^0(.80)^{12} = \textbf{.0687}$

b.) $\text{Prob}(X \geq 6)$ long hours):

$p = .20$

Using Table A.2: $.016 + .003 + .001 = \textbf{.020}$

c) $\text{Prob}(X = 5 \text{ good financing})$:

$p = .25, \quad {}_{12}C_5(.25)^5(.75)^7 = \textbf{.1032}$

d.) $p = .19$ (good plan), expected number $= \mu = n(p) = 12(.19) = \textbf{2.28}$

5.47   Prob($X \leq 3$) $|$ n = 8 and p = .60) =   (from Table A.2)

X	Prob.
0	.001
1	.008
2	.041
3	.124
$X \leq 3$	**.174**

17.4% of the time in a sample of eight, three or fewer customers are walk-ins by chance. Other reasons for such a low number of walk-ins might be that she is retaining more old customers than before or perhaps a new competitor is attracting walk-ins away from her.

5.49 λ = 0.6 flats $|$ 2000 miles

Prob($X = 0 \mid \lambda = 0.6$) =   (from Table A.3)   **.5488**

Prob($X \geq 3 \mid \lambda = 0.6$) =   (from Table A.3)

X	Prob.
3	.0198
4	.0030
5	.0004
$X \geq 3$	**.0232**

One trip is independent of the other.

Let F = flat tire and NF = no flat tire

$P(NF_1 \cap NF_2) = P(NF_1) \cdot P(NF_2)$

$P(NF) = .5488$

$P(NF_1 \cap NF_2) = (.5488)(.5488) =$ **.3012**

5.51 $N = 24$ $n = 6$ $A = 8$

a) $P(X = 6) = ({}_8C_6\ {}_{16}C_0)/{}_{24}C_6 = [(28)(1)]/134,596 = \mathbf{.0002}$

b) $P(X = 0) = ({}_8C_0\ {}_{16}C_6)/{}_{24}C_6 = [(1)(8008)]/134,596 = \mathbf{.0595}$

d) $A = 16$ East Side

  $P(X = 3) = ({}_{16}C_3\ {}_8C_3)/{}_{24}C_6 = [(560)(56)]/134,596 = \mathbf{.2330}$

5.53 $\lambda = 2.4$ calls $|$ 1 minute

a) $\text{Prob}(X = 0\ |\ \lambda = 2.4) = $ (from Table A.3) $\mathbf{.0907}$

b) Can handle $X \leq 5$ calls   Cannot handle $X > 5$ calls

  $\text{Prob}(X > 5\ |\ \lambda = 2.4) = $ (from Table A.3)

X	Prob.
6	.0241
7	.0083
8	.0025
9	.0007
10	.0002
11	.0000
$X > 5$	**.0358**

c) $\text{Prob}(X = 3$ calls $|$ 2 minutes$)$

  The interval has been increased 2 times.

  New Lambda $= \lambda = 4.8$ calls $|$ 2 minutes.

  from Table A.3: $\mathbf{.1517}$

d) Prob(X ≤ 1 calls | 15 seconds):

The interval has been decreased by ¼.

New Lambda = λ = 0.6 calls | 15 seconds.

Prob(X ≤ 1 | λ = 0.6) =   (from Table A.3)

Prob(X = 1) =   .3293
Prob(X = 0) =   .5488
Prob(X ≤ 1) =   **.8781**

5.55   p = .005   n = 1,000

λ = n·p = (1,000)(.005) = 5

a) P(X < 4) = P(X = 0) + P(X = 1) + P(X = 2) + P(X = 3) =

.0067 + .0337 + .0842 + .1404 = **.265**

b) P(X > 10) = P(X = 11) + P(X = 12) + ... =

.0082 + .0034 + .0013 + .0005 + .0002 = **.0136**

c) P(X = 0) = **.0067**

5.57   N = 26

a) n = 5 $X = 3$ A = 510

$(_{10}C_3 \, _{16}C_2)/_{26}C_5$ = [(120)(120)]/65,780 = **.2189**

b) n = 8 $X \le 2$ A = 6

$(_6C_0 \, _{20}C_8)/_{26}C_8 + (_6C_1 \, _{20}C_7)/_{26}C_8 + (_6C_2 \, _{20}C_6)/_{26}C_8$ =

[(1)(125,970)]/1,562,275 + [(6)(77,520)]/1,562,275 +

[(15)(38,760)]/1,562,275 = .0806 + .2977 + .3721 = **.7504**

c) $n = 5$ $X = 2$ $p = 3/26 = .1154$

$_5C_2(.1154)^2(.8846)^3 = (10)(.013317)(.692215) = \mathbf{.0922}$

5.59   a) $\lambda = 3.84 \,|\, 1,000$

$$P(X = 0) = \frac{3.84^0 \cdot e^{-3.84}}{0!} = \mathbf{.0215}$$

b) $\lambda = 7.68 \,|\, 2,000$

$$P(X = 6) = \frac{7.68^6 \cdot e^{-7.68}}{6!} = \frac{(205,195.258)(.000461975)}{720} = \mathbf{.1317}$$

c) $\lambda = 1.6 \,|\, 1,000$ and $\lambda = 4.8 \,|\, 3,000$

from Table A.3:

$P(X < 7) = P(X = 0) + P(X = 1) + \ldots + P(X = 6) =$

$.0082 + .0395 + .0948 + .1517 + .1820 + .1747 + .1398 = \mathbf{.7907}$

5.61   This printout contains the probabilities for various values of X from zero to eleven from a Poisson distribution with $\lambda = 2.78$. Note that the highest probabilities are at $X = 2$ and $X = 3$ which are near the mean. The probability is slightly higher at $X = 2$ than at $X = 3$ even though $X = 3$ is nearer to the mean because of the "piling up" effect of $X = 0$.

5.63   This is the graph of a Poisson Distribution with $\lambda = 1.784$. Note the high probabilities at $X = 1$ and $X = 2$ which are nearest to the mean. Note also that the probabilities for values of $X \geq 8$ are near to zero because they are so far away from the mean or expected value.

Ch 5 focused on discrete distributions
Ch 6 concentrates on continuous distributions –
constructed from continuous random variables
in which values are taken for every point on
a given interval and are usually generated from
experiments in which things are "measured"
as opposed to "counted"

With continuous distributions, probabilities of outcomes
occurring between particular points are determined
by calculating the area under the curve between those pts.

Chapter 6
Continuous Distributions

The entire area under the whole curve is 1.

LEARNING OBJECTIVES

The primary objective of Chapter 6 is to help you understand continuous distributions, thereby enabling you to:

1. Understand concepts of the uniform distribution.

2. Appreciate the importance of the normal distribution.

3. Recognize normal distribution problems and know how to solve such problems.

4. Decide when to use the normal distribution to approximately binomial distribution problems and know how to work such problems.

5. Decide when to use the exponential distribution to solve problems in business and know how to work such problems.

DISC 3331
6.1 The Uniform Distribution
6.2 The Normal Distribution

With discrete distributions, the probability function yields the value of the probability. For contin

CHAPTER OUTLINE

6.1   The Uniform Distribution

Determining Probabilities in a Uniform Distribution

Using the Computer to Solve for Uniform Distribution Probabilities

6.2   Normal Distribution

History of the Normal Distribution

Probability Density Function of the Normal Distribution

Standardized Normal Distribution

Working Normal Curve Problems

Using the Computer to Solve for Normal Distribution Probabilities

6.3   Using the Normal Curve to Work Binomial Distribution Problems

Correcting for Continuity

6.4   Exponential Distribution

Probabilities of the Exponential Distribution

Using the Computer to Determine Exponential Distribution Probabilities

KEY WORDS

Correction for Continuity
Exponential Distribution
Normal Distribution
Rectangular Distribution

Standardized Normal Distribution
Uniform Distribution
Z Distribution
Z Score

Continuous distribution in which the same height or $f(x)$ is obtained over a range of values.

$$f(x) = \begin{cases} \frac{1}{b-a} & \text{for } a \leq x \leq b \\ 0 & \text{for all other values} \end{cases}$$

STUDY QUESTIONS

mean

$$\mu = \frac{a+b}{2}$$

6.1

1. The uniform distribution is sometimes referred to as the __Rectangular__ distribution.

std dev

$$\sigma = \frac{b-a}{\sqrt{12}}$$

$$\sigma = \frac{13-5}{\sqrt{12}}$$

$$= \frac{8}{3.464}$$

$$= 2.3094$$

6.1

2. Suppose a set of data are uniformly distributed from X = 5 to X = 13. The height of the distribution is __⅛__ ? . The mean of this distribution is ___ . The standard deviation of this distribution is ___ .
    __2.3094__ .

    = 18   18/2 = mean = 9
    18/2 = 9
    $\frac{1}{13-5} = 1/8 =$ Height

6.1

3. Suppose a set of data are uniformly distributed from X = 27 to X = 44. The height of this distribution is __1/17__ . The mean of this distribution is ___ . 27+44=71/2 = 35.5 . The standard deviation of this distribution is ___ .
    __4.9075__ ←

    = 71   71/2 = 35.5
    $\frac{1}{44-27} = \frac{1}{17} =$ Height
    $\frac{44-27}{\sqrt{12}} = \frac{17}{3.464} = 4.9076$

4. A set of values is uniformly distributed from 84 to 98. The probability of a value occurring between 89 and 93 is _____ . The probability of a value occurring between 80 and 90 is _____ . The probability of a value occurring that is greater than 75 is _____ .

5. Probably the most widely known and used of all distributions is the __Normal__ distribution.

6. Many human characteristics can be described by the __Normal__ distribution.

7. The area under the curve of a normal distribution is _____ .

8. In working normal curve problems using the raw values of X, the mean, and the standard deviation, a problem can be converted to __Z__ scores.

9. A Z score value is the number of __standard__ __deviations__ a value is from the mean.

10. Within a range of Z scores of ± 1σ from the mean, fall __68__ % of the values of a normal distribution.

11. Suppose a population of values is normally distributed with a mean of 155 and a standard deviation of 12. The Z score for X = 170 is _____ .

12. Suppose a population of values is normally distributed with a mean of 76 and a standard deviation of 5.2. The Z score for X = 73 is _____ .

13. Suppose a population of values is normally distributed with a mean of 250 and a variance of 225. The Z score for X = 286 is _____ .

14. Suppose a population of values is normally distributed with a mean of 9.8 and a standard deviation of 2.5. The probability that a value is greater than 11 in the distribution is _____.

15. A population is normally distributed with a mean of 80 and a variance of 400. The probability that X lies between 50 and 100 is _____.

16. A population is normally distributed with a mean of 115 and a standard deviation of 13. The probability that a value is less than 85 is _____.

17. A population is normally distributed with a mean of 64. The probability that a value from this population is more than 70 is .0485. The standard deviation is _____.

18. A population is normally distributed with a mean of 90. 85.99% of the values in this population are greater than 75. The standard deviation of this population is _____.

19. A population is normally distributed with a standard deviation of 18.5. 69.85% of the values in this population are greater than 93. The mean of the population is _____.

20. A population is normally distributed with a variance of 50. 98.17% of the values of the population are less than 27. The mean of the population is _____.

21. A population is normally distributed with a mean of 340 and a standard deviation of 55. 10.93% of values in the population are less than _____.

22. In working a binomial distribution problem by using the normal distribution, the interval, _____, should lie between 0 and n.

23. A binomial distribution problem has an n of 10 and a p value of .20. This problem _____ be worked by the normal distribution because of the size of n and p.

24. A binomial distribution problem has an n of 15 and a p value of .60. This problem _____ be worked by the normal distribution because of the size of n and p.

25. A binomial distribution problem has an n of 30 and a p value of .35. A researcher wants to determine the probability of X being greater than 13 and to use the normal distribution to work the problem. After correcting for continuity, the value of X that he/she will be solving for is _____.

26. A binomial distribution problem has an n of 48 and a p value of .80. A researcher wants to determine the probability of X being less than or equal to 35 and wants to work the problem using the normal distribution. After correcting for continuity, the value of X that he/she will be solving for is _____.

27. A binomial distribution problem has an n of 60 and a p value of .72. A researcher wants to determine the probability of X being exactly 45 and use the normal distribution to work the problem. After correcting for continuity, he/she will be solving for the area between _____ and _____.

28.   A binomial distribution problem has an n of 27 and a p value of .53. If this problem were converted to a normal distribution problem, the mean of the distribution would be _____. The standard deviation of the distribution would be _____.

29.   A binomial distribution problem has an n of 113 and a p value of .29. If this problem were converted to a normal distribution problem, the mean of the distribution would be _____. The standard deviation of the distribution would be _____.

30.   A binomial distribution problem is to determine the probability that X is less than 22 when the sample size is 40 and the value of p is .50. Using the normal distribution to work this problem produces a probability of _____.

31.   A binomial distribution problem is to determine the probability that X is exactly 14 when the sample size is 20 and the value of p is .60. Using the normal distribution to work this problem produces a probability of _____.

32.   A binomial distribution problem is to determine the probability that X is greater than or equal to 18 when the sample size is 30 and the value of p is .55. Using the normal distribution to work this problem produces a probability of _____.

33.   A binomial distribution problem is to determine the probability that X is greater than 10 when the sample size is 20 and the value of p is .60. Using the normal distribution to work this problem produces a probability of _____. If this problem had been worked using the binomial tables, the obtained probability would have been _____. The difference in answers using these two techniques is _____.

34.   The exponential distribution is a_____ distribution.

35.   The exponential distribution is closely related to the _____ distribution.

36.   The exponential distribution is skewed to the _____.

37.   Suppose random arrivals occur at a rate of 5 per minute. Assuming that random arrivals are Poisson distributed, the probability of there being at least 30 seconds between arrivals is _____.

38.   Suppose random arrivals occur at a rate of 1 per hour. Assuming that random arrivals are Poisson distributed, the probability of there being less than 2 hours between arrivals is _____.

39.   Suppose random arrivals occur at a rate of 1.6 every five minutes. Assuming that random arrivals are Poisson distributed, the probability of there being between three minutes and six minutes between arrivals is _____.

40.   Suppose that the mean time between arrivals is 40 seconds and that random arrivals are Poisson distributed. The probability that at least one minute passes between two arrivals is _____. The probability that at least two minutes pass between two arrivals is _____.

41.   Suppose that the mean time between arrivals is ten minutes and that random arrivals are Poisson distributed. The probability that no more than seven minutes pass between two arrivals is _____ .

42.   The mean of an exponential distribution equals _____ .

43.   Suppose that random arrivals are Poisson distributed with an average arrival of 2.4 per five minutes. The associated exponential distribution would have a mean of _____ and a standard deviation of _____ .

44.   An exponential distribution has an average interarrival time of 25 minutes. The standard deviation of this distribution is _____ .

ANSWERS TO STUDY QUESTIONS

1.	Rectangular	23.	Cannot
2.	1/8, 9, 2.3094	24.	Can
3.	1/17, 35.5, 4.9075	25.	≥ 13.5
4.	.2857, .7143, 1.000	26.	≤ 35.5
5.	Normal	27.	44.5, 45.5
6.	Normal	28.	14.31, 2.59
7.	1	29.	32.77, 4.82
8.	Z	30.	.6808
9.	Standard deviations	31.	.1212
10.	68%	32.	.3557
11.	1.25	33.	.7517, .7550, .0033
12.	-0.58	34.	Continuous
13.	2.40	35.	Poisson
14.	.3156	36.	Right
15.	.7745	37.	.0821
16.	.0104	38.	.8647
17.	3.614	39.	.2363
18.	13.89	40.	.2313, .0498
19.	102.62	41.	.5034
20.	12.22	42.	$1/\lambda$
21.	272.35	43.	2.08 Minutes, 2.08 Minutes
22.	$\mu \pm 3\sigma$	44.	25 Minutes

SOLUTIONS TO PROBLEMS IN CHAPTER 6

6.1 $a = 200$ $b = 240$

a) $f(X) = \dfrac{1}{b-a} = \dfrac{1}{240-200} = \dfrac{1}{40}$

b) $\mu = \dfrac{a+b}{2} = \dfrac{200+240}{2} = \mathbf{220}$

$\sigma = \dfrac{b-a}{\sqrt{12}} = \dfrac{240-200}{\sqrt{12}} = \dfrac{40}{\sqrt{12}} = \mathbf{11.547}$

c) $P(X > 230) = \dfrac{240-230}{240-200} = \dfrac{10}{40} = \mathbf{.250}$

d) $P(205 \le X \le 220) = \dfrac{220-205}{240-200} = \dfrac{15}{40} = \mathbf{.375}$

e) $P(X \le 225) = \dfrac{225-200}{240-200} = \dfrac{25}{40} = \mathbf{.625}$

6.3 $a = 2.80$ $b = 3.14$

$\mu = \dfrac{a+b}{2} = \dfrac{2.80-3.14}{2} = \mathbf{2.97}$

$\sigma = \dfrac{b-a}{\sqrt{12}} = \dfrac{3.14-2.80}{\sqrt{12}} = \mathbf{0.10}$

$P(3.00 < X < 3.10) = \dfrac{3.10-3.00}{3.14-2.80} = \mathbf{0.2941}$

6.5 $\mu = 2100$ $a = 400$ $b = 3800$

$$\sigma = \frac{b-a}{\sqrt{12}} = \frac{3800 - 400}{\sqrt{12}} = \textbf{981.5}$$

$$\text{Height} = \frac{1}{b-a} = \frac{3800 - 400}{\sqrt{12}} = \textbf{.000294}$$

$b-a = 3800 - 400 = 3400$

$$P(X > 3000) = \frac{3800 - 3000}{3800 - 400} = \frac{800}{3400} = \textbf{.2353}$$

$$P(X > 4000) = \textbf{.0000}$$

$$P(700 < X < 1500) = \frac{1500 - 700}{3800 - 400} = \frac{800}{3400} = \textbf{.2353}$$

6.7 a) $\text{Prob}(X \leq 635 \mid \mu = 604, \ \sigma = 56.8)$:

$$Z = \frac{X - \mu}{\sigma} = \frac{635 - 604}{56.8} = 0.55$$

Table A.5 value for $Z = 0.55$:   .2088

$\text{Prob}(X \leq 635) = .2088 + .5000 = \textbf{.7088}$

b) $\text{Prob}(X < 20 \mid \mu = 48, \ \sigma = 12)$:

$$Z = \frac{X - \mu}{\sigma} = \frac{20 - 48}{12} = -2.33$$

Table A.5 value for $Z = -2.33$:   .4901

$\text{Prob}(X < 20) = .5000 - .4901 = \textbf{.0099}$

c) $\text{Prob}(100 \leq X < 150 \mid \mu = 111, \ \sigma = 33.8)$:

$$Z = \frac{X - \mu}{\sigma} = \frac{150 - 111}{33.8} = 1.15$$

Table A.5 value for $Z = 1.15$:   .3749

$$Z = \frac{X - \mu}{\sigma} = \frac{100 - 111}{33.8} = -0.33$$

Table A.5 value for $Z = -0.33$:   .1293

$\text{Prob}(100 \leq X < 150) = .3749 + .1293 = $ **.5042**

d) $\text{Prob}(250 < X < 255 \mid \mu = 264, \sigma = 10.9)$:

$$Z = \frac{X - \mu}{\sigma} = \frac{250 - 264}{10.9} = -1.28$$

Table A.5 value for $Z = -1.28$:   .3997

$$Z = \frac{X - \mu}{\sigma} = \frac{255 - 264}{10.9} = =0.83$$

Table A.5 value for $Z = -0.83$:   .2967

$\text{Prob}(250 < X < 255) = .3997 - .2967 = $ **.1030**

e) $\text{Prob}(X > 35 \mid \mu = 37, \ \sigma = 4.35)$:

$$Z = \frac{X - \mu}{\sigma} = \frac{35 - 37}{4.35} = -0.46$$

Table A.5 value for $Z = -0.46$:   .1772

$\text{Prob}(X > 35) = .1772 + .5000 = $ **.6772**

f) $\text{Prob}(X \geq 170 \mid \mu = 156, \ \sigma = 11.4)$:

$$Z = \frac{X - \mu}{\sigma} = \frac{170 - 156}{11.4} = 1.23$$

Table A.5 value for $Z = 1.23$:   .3907

$\text{Prob}(X \geq 170) = .5000 - .3907 = \textbf{.1093}$

6.9 $\mu = 42.78$ $= 11.35$

a) $\text{Prob}(X > 67.75)$:

$$Z = \frac{X - \mu}{\sigma} = \frac{67.5 - 42.78}{11.35} = 2.20$$

from Table A.5, the value for $Z = 2.20$ is .4861

$\text{Prob}(X > 67.75) = .5000 - .4861 = \textbf{.0139}$

b) $\text{Prob}(30 < X < 50$:

$$Z = \frac{X - \mu}{\sigma} = \frac{30 - 42.78}{11.35} = -1.13$$

$$Z = \frac{X - \mu}{\sigma} = \frac{50 - 42.78}{11.35} = 0.64$$

from Table A.5, the value for $Z = -1.13$ is .3708

and for $Z = 0.64$ is .2389

$\text{Prob}(30 < X < 50) = .3708 + .2389 = \textbf{.6097}$

c) $\text{Prob}(X < 25)$:

$$Z = \frac{X - \mu}{\sigma} = \frac{25 - 42.78}{11.35} = -1.57$$

from Table A.5, the value for $Z = -1.57$ is .4418

$\text{Prob}(X < 25) = .5000 - .4418 = \textbf{.0582}$

d) Prob($45 \leq X \leq 55$):

$$Z = \frac{X - \mu}{\sigma} = \frac{55 - 42.78}{11.35} = 1.08$$

$$Z = \frac{X - \mu}{\sigma} = \frac{45 - 42.78}{11.35} = 0.20$$

from Table A.5, the value for Z = 1.08 is .3599

from Table A.5, the value for Z = 0.20 is .0793

Prob($45 \leq X \leq 55$) = .3599 - .0793 = **.2806**

6.11 μ = $30,000 σ = $9,000

a) Prob($15,000 $\leq$ X $\leq$ $45,000):

$$Z = \frac{X - \mu}{\sigma} = \frac{45,000 - 30,000}{9,000} = 1.67$$

From Table A.5, Z = 1.67 yields: .4525

$$Z = \frac{X - \mu}{\sigma} = \frac{15,000 - 30,000}{9,000} = -1.67$$

From Table A.5, Z = -1.67 yields: .4525

Prob($15,000 $\leq$ X $\leq$ $45,000) = .4525 + .4525 = **.9050**

b) Prob(X > $50,000):

$$Z = \frac{X - \mu}{\sigma} = \frac{50,000 - 30,000}{9,000} = 2.22$$

From Table A.5, Z = 2.22 yields: 4868

Prob(X > $50,000) = .5000 - .4868 = **.0132**

c) Prob($\$5,000 \leq X \leq \$20,000$):

$$Z = \frac{X - \mu}{\sigma} = \frac{5,000 - 30,000}{9,000} = -2.78$$

From Table A.5, Z = -2.78 yields: .4973

$$Z = \frac{X - \mu}{\sigma} = \frac{20,000 - 30,000}{9,000} = -1.11$$

From Table A.5, Z = -1.11 yields   .3665

Prob($\$5,000 \leq X \leq \$20,000$) = .4973 - .3665 = **.1308**

d) 90.82% of the values are greater than X = $7,000.
   Then X = $7,000 is in the lower half of the distribution and .9082 - .5000 =
   .4082 lie between X and μ.

   From Table A.5, Z = -1.33 is associated with an area of .4082.

   Solving for σ:

   $$Z = \frac{X - \mu}{\sigma}$$

   $$-1.33 = \frac{7,000 - 30,000}{\sigma}$$

   $$\sigma = \mathbf{17{,}293.23}$$

e) σ = $9,000. If 79.95% of the costs are less than $33,000, X = $33,000 is in
    the upper half of the distribution and   .7995 - .5000 = .2995 of the values lie
    between $33,000 and the mean.

    From Table A.5, an area of .2995 is associated with Z = 0.84

    Solving for μ:

    $$Z = \frac{X - \mu}{\sigma}$$

    $$0.84 = \frac{33,000 - \mu}{9,000}$$

    $$\mu = \mathbf{\$25{,}440}$$

6.13   a) $\sigma = 12.56$. If 71.97% of the values are greater than 56, then 21.97% of .2197 lie between 56 and the mean, μ. The Z value associated with .2197 is -0.58 since the 56 is below the mean.

Using Z = -0.58, X = 56, and μ = 12.56, μ can be solved for:

$$Z = \frac{X - \mu}{\sigma}$$

$$-0.58 = \frac{56 - \mu}{12.56}$$

$$\mu = \mathbf{63.285}$$

b) $\mu = 352$. Since only 13.35% of the values are less than X = 300, the X = 300 is at the lower end of the distribution. 36.65% (.5000 - .1335) lie between X = 300 and μ = 352. From Table A.5, a Z value of -1.11 is associated with .3665 area at the lower end of the distribution.

Using X = 300, μ = 352, and Z = -1.11, σ can be solved for:

$$Z = \frac{X - \mu}{\sigma}$$

$$-1.11 = \frac{300 - 352}{\sigma}$$

$$\sigma = \mathbf{46.85}$$

6.15 Prob($X < 20$) = .2900

X is less than μ because of the percentage. Between X and μ is .5000 - .2900 = .2100 of the area. The Z score associated with this area is -0.55. Solving for μ:

$$Z = \frac{X - \mu}{\sigma}$$

$$-0.55 = \frac{20 - \mu}{4}$$

$$\mu = \mathbf{22.20}$$

6.17   a) $P(X \leq 16 \mid n = 30$ and $p = .70)$

$\mu = n \cdot p = 30(.70) = 21$

$\sigma = \sqrt{n \cdot p \cdot q} = \sqrt{30(.70)(.30)} = 2.51$

$P(X \leq 16.5 \mid \mu = 21$ and $= 2.51)$

b) $P(10 < X \leq 20 \mid n = 25$ and $p = .50)$

$\mu = n \cdot p = 25(.50) = 12.5$

$\sigma = \sqrt{n \cdot p \cdot q} = \sqrt{25(.50)(.50)}$

$P(10.5 \leq X \leq 20.5 \mid \mu = 12.5$ and $= 2.5)$

c) $P(X = 22 \mid n = 40$ and $p = .60)$

$\mu = n \cdot p = 40(.60) = 24$

$\sigma = \sqrt{n \cdot p \cdot q} = \sqrt{40(.60)(.40)} = 3.10$

$P(21.5 \leq X \leq 22.5 \mid \mu = 24$ and $= 3.10)$

d) $P(X > 14$ $n = 16$ and $p = .45)$

$\mu = n \cdot p = 16(.45) = 7.2$

$\sigma = \sqrt{n \cdot p \cdot q} = \sqrt{16(.45)(.55)}$

$P(X \geq 14.5 \mid \mu = 7.2$ and $= 1.99)$

6.19   a) Prob(X = 8 | n = 25 and p = .40)

$\mu = n \cdot p = 25(.40) = 10$ $\sigma = \sqrt{n \cdot p \cdot q} = \sqrt{25(.40)(.60)}$

$\mu \pm 3\sigma = 10 \pm 3(2.449) = 10 \pm 7.347$

(2.653 to 17.347) lies between 0 and 25.
Approximation by the normal curve is sufficient.

Prob(7.5 ≤ X ≤ 8.5 | μ = 10 and = 2.449):

$Z = \dfrac{7.5 - 10}{2.449} = -1.02$

From Table A.5, area = .3461

$Z = \dfrac{8.5 - 10}{2.449} = -0.61$

From Table A.5, area = .2291

Prob(7.5 ≤ X ≤ 8.5) = .3461 - .2291 = **.1170**

From Table A.2 (binomial tables) = **.120**

b) Prob(X ≥ 13 | n = 20 and p = .60)

$\mu = n \cdot p = 20(.60) = 12$ $\sigma = \sqrt{n \cdot p \cdot q} = \sqrt{20(.60)(.40)} = 2.19$

$\mu \pm 3\sigma = 12 \pm 3(2.19) = 12 \pm 6.57$

(5.43 to 18.57) lies between 0 and 20.
Approximation by the normal curve is sufficient.

Prob(X ≤ 12.5 | μ = 12 and = 2.19):

$Z = \dfrac{X - \mu}{\sigma} = \dfrac{12.5 - 12}{2.19} = 0.23$

From Table A.5, area = .0910

Prob(X ≥ 12.5) = .5000 - .0910 = **.4090**

From Table A.2 (binomial tables) = **.415**

c) $Prob(X = 7 \mid n = 15 \text{ and } p = .50)$

$\mu = n \cdot p = 15(.50) = 7.5$

$\sigma = \sqrt{n \cdot p \cdot q} = \sqrt{15(.50)(.50)} = 1.9365$

$\mu \pm 3\sigma = 7.5 \pm 3(1.9365) = 7.5 \pm 5.81$

(1.69 to 13.31) lies between 0 and 15.
Approximation by the normal curve is sufficient.

$Prob(6.5 \leq X \leq 7.5 \mid \mu = 7.5 \text{ and } = 1.9365)$:

$Z = \dfrac{X - \mu}{\sigma} = \dfrac{6.5 - 7.5}{1.9365} = -0.52$

From Table A.5, area = **.1985**

From Table A.2 (binomial tables) = **.196**

d) $Prob(X < 3 \; n = 10 \text{ and } p = .70)$:

$\mu = n \cdot p = 10(.70) = 7$

$\sigma = \sqrt{n \cdot p \cdot q} = \sqrt{10(.70)(.30)}$

$\mu \pm 3\sigma = 7 \pm 3(1.449) = 7 \pm 4.347$

(2.653 to 11.347) does not lie between 0 and 10.
The normal curve is not a good approximation to this problem.

6.21   n = 70,   p = .59   Prob($X < 35$):

Converting to the normal dist.:

$\mu = n(p) = 70(.59) = 41.3$

$\sigma = \sqrt{n \cdot p \cdot q} = \sqrt{70(.59)(.41)} = 4.115$

Test for normalcy:

$0 \leq \mu \pm 3\sigma \leq n,   0 \leq 41.3 \pm 3(4.115) \leq 70$

$0 < 28.955$ to $53.645 < 70$, passes the test

correction for continuity, use $X = 34.5$

$Z = \dfrac{34.5 - 41.3}{4.115} = -1.65$

from table A.5, area = .4505

Prob($X < 35$) = .5000 - .4505 = **.0495**

6.23   p = .16   n = 130

Conversion to normal dist.: $\mu = n(p) = 130(.16) = 20.8$

$\sigma = \sqrt{n \cdot p \cdot q} = \sqrt{130(.16)(.84)} = 4.18$

a) Prob($X > 25$):

Correct for continuity: $X = 25.5$

$Z = \dfrac{25.5 - 20.8}{4.18} = 1.12$

from table A.5, area = .3686

Prob($X > 20$) = .5000 - .3686 = **.1314**

b) Prob($15 \leq X \leq 23$):

   Correct for continuity: 14.5 to 23.5

   $$Z = \frac{14.5 - 20.8}{4.18} = -1.51$$

   $$Z = \frac{23.5 - 20.8}{4.18} = 0.65$$

   from table A.5, area for Z = -1.51 is .4345
                     area for Z = 0.65 is .2422

   Prob($15 \leq X \leq 23$) = .4345 + .2422 = **.6767**

c) Prob($X < 12$):

   correct for continuity: $X = 11.5$

   $$Z = \frac{11.5 - 20.8}{4.18} = -2.22$$

   from table A.5, area for Z = -2.22 is .4868

   Prob($X < 12$) = .5000 - .4868 = **.0132**

d) Prob($X = 22$):

   correct for continuity: 21.5 to 22.5

   $$Z = \frac{21.5 - 20.8}{4.18} = 0.17$$

   $$Z = \frac{22.5 - 20.8}{4.18} = 0.41$$

   from table A.5, area for 0.17 = .0675
                     area for 0.41 = .1591

   Prob(X = 22) = .1591 - .0675 = **.0916**

6.25 a) $\lambda = 0.1$

$\underline{X_0}$	$\underline{Y}$
0	.1000
1	.0905
2	.0819
3	.0741
4	.0670
5	.0607
6	.0549
7	.0497
8	.0449
9	.0407
10	.0368

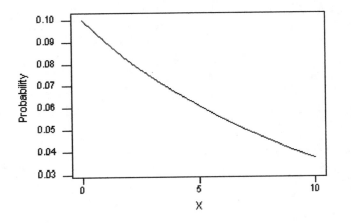

Exponential Distribution with Lambda=.1

b) $\lambda = 0.3$

$\underline{X_0}$	$\underline{Y}$
0	.3000
1	.2222
2	.1646
3	.1220
4	.0904
5	.0669
6	.0496
7	.0367
8	.0272
9	.0202

Exponential Distribution with Lambda=.3

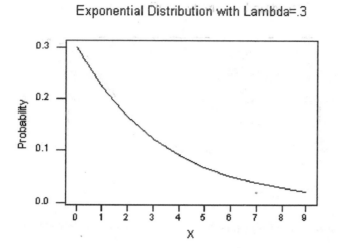

c) $\lambda = 0.8$

X_0	Y
0	.8000
1	.3595
2	.1615
3	.0726
4	.0326
5	.0147
6	.0066
7	.0030
8	.0013
9	.0006

Exponential Distribution with Lambda=.8

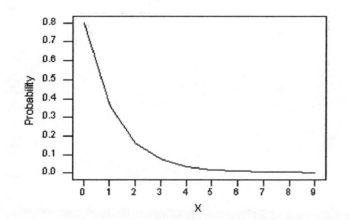

d) $\lambda = 3.0$

$\underline{X_0}$	$\underline{Y}$
0	3.0000
1	.1494
2	.0074
3	.0004
4	.0000
5	.0000

Exponential Distribution with Lambda=3

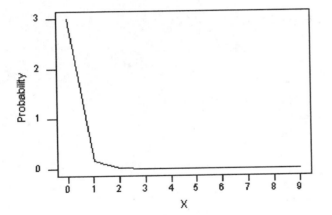

6.27   a) Prob$(X \geq 5 \mid \lambda = 1.35) =$

for $X_0 = 5$:   Prob$(X) = e^{-\lambda X} = e^{-1.35(5)} = e^{-6.75} = $ **.0012**

b) Prob$(X < 3 \mid \lambda = 0.68) = 1 - $ Prob$(X \leq 3 \mid \lambda = .68) =$

for $X_0 = 3$: $1 - e^{-\lambda X} = 1 - e^{-0.68(3)} = 1 - e^{-2.04} = 1 - .1300 = $ **.8700**

c) Prob$(X > 4 \mid \lambda = 1.7) =$

for $X_0 = 4$:   Prob$(X) = e^{-\lambda X} = e^{-1.7(4)} = e^{-6.8} = $ **.0011**

d) Prob$(X < 6 \mid \lambda = 0.80) = 1 - $ Prob$(X \geq 6 \mid \lambda = 0.80) =$

for $X_0 = 6$:   Prob$(X) = 1 - e^{-\lambda X} = 1 - e^{-0.80(6)} = 1 - e^{-4.8} = 1 - .0082$

$= $ **.9918**

6.29 $\lambda = 2.44/$min.

a) Prob$(X \geq 10$ min $\mid \lambda = 2.44/$min$) =$

Let $X_0 = 10$, $e^{-\lambda X} = e^{-2.44(10)} = e^{-24.4} = $ **.0000**

b) Prob$(X \geq 5$ min $\mid \lambda = 2.44/$min$) =$

Let $X_0 = 5$, $e^{-\lambda X} = e^{-2.44(5)} = e^{-12.20} = $ **.0000**

c) Prob$(X \geq 1$ min $\mid \lambda = 2.44/$min$) =$

Let $X_0 = 1$, $e^{-\lambda X} = e^{-2.44(1)} = e^{-2.44} = $ **.0872**

d) Expected time $= \mu = \dfrac{1}{\lambda} = \dfrac{1}{2.44}$ min. $= $ **.41 min = 24.6 sec.**

6.31 $\lambda = 3.39 / 1000$ passengers

$$\mu = \frac{1}{\lambda} = \frac{1}{3.39} = 0.295$$

$(0.295)(1,000) = \mathbf{295}$

Prob(X > 500):

Let $X_0 = 500/1,000$ passengers $= .5$

$e^{-\lambda X} = e^{-3.39(.5)} = e^{-1.695} = \mathbf{.1836}$

Prob(X < 200):

Let $X_0 = 200/1,000$ passengers $= .2$

$e^{-\lambda X} = e^{-3.39(.2)} = e^{-.678} = .5076$

Prob(X < 200) $= 1 - .5076 = \mathbf{.4924}$

6.33 $\lambda = 2/\text{month}$

Average number of time between rain $= \mu = \dfrac{1}{\lambda} = \dfrac{1}{2}$ month $= 15$ days

$\sigma = \mu = 15$ days

Prob(X $\leq$ 2 days $\mid \lambda = 2/\text{month}$

Change λ to days: $\lambda = \dfrac{2}{30} = .067/\text{day}$

Prob(X $\leq$ 2 days $\mid \lambda = .067/\text{day}) =$

$1 - \text{Prob}(X > 2 \text{ days} \mid \lambda = .067/\text{day})$

let $X_0 = 2,$ $1 - e^{-\lambda X} = 1 - e^{-.067(2)} = 1 - .8746 = \mathbf{.1254}$

6.35   a) Prob(X < 21 | $\mu = 25$ and $\sigma = 4$):

$$Z = \frac{X - \mu}{\sigma} = \frac{21 - 25}{4} = -1.00$$

From Table A.5, area = .3413

Prob(X < 21) = .5000 - .3413 = **.1587**

b) Prob(X ≥ 77 | $n = 50$ and $\sigma = 9$):

$$Z = \frac{X - \mu}{\sigma} = \frac{71 - 50}{9} = 3.00$$

From Table A.5, area = .4987

Prob(X ≥ 77) = .5000 - .4987 = **.0013**

c) Prob(X > 47 | $\mu = 50$ and $\sigma = 6$):

$$Z = \frac{X - \mu}{\sigma} = \frac{47 - 50}{6} = -0.50$$

From Table A.5, area = .1915

Prob(X > 47) = .5000 + .1915 = **.6915**

d) Prob(13 < X < 29 | $\mu = 23$ and $\sigma = 4$):

$$Z = \frac{X - \mu}{\sigma} = \frac{13 - 23}{4} = -2.50$$

From Table A.5, area = .4938

$$Z = \frac{X - \mu}{\sigma} = \frac{29 - 23}{4} = 1.50$$

From Table A.5, area = .4332

P(13 < X < 29) = .4938 + 4332 =   **.9270**

e) $Prob(X \geq 105 \mid \mu = 90$ and $\sigma = 2.86)$:

$$Z = \frac{X - \mu}{\sigma} = \frac{105 - 90}{2.86} = 5.24$$

From Table A.5, area = .5000

$P(X \geq 105) = .5000 - .5000 = $ **.0000**

6.37 a) $Prob(X \geq 3 \mid \lambda = 1.3)$:

let $x_0 = 3$

$Prob(X \geq 3 \mid \lambda = 1.3) = e^{-\lambda X} = e^{-1.3(3)} = e^{-3.9} = $ **.0202**

b) $Prob(X < 2 \mid \lambda = 2.0)$:

Let $x_0 = 2$

$Prob(X < 2 \mid \lambda = 2.0) = 1 - P(X \geq 2 \mid \lambda = 2.0) =$

$1 - e^{-\lambda X} = 1 - e^{-2(2)} = 1 - e^{-4} = 1 - .0183 = $ **.9817**

c) $Prob(1 \leq X \leq 3 \mid \lambda = 1.65)$:

$P(X \geq 1 \mid \lambda = 1.65)$:

Let $x_0 = 1$

$e^{-\lambda X} = e^{-1.65(1)} = e^{-1.65} = .1920$

$Prob(X \geq 3 \mid \lambda = 1.65)$:

Let $X_0 = 3$

$e^{-\lambda X} = e^{-1.65(3)} = e^{-4.95} = .0071$

$Prob(1 \leq X \leq 3) = Prob(X \geq 1) - P(X \geq 3) = .1920 - .0071 = $ **.1849**

d) $\text{Prob}(X > 2 \mid \lambda = 0.405)$:

Let $x_0 = 2$

$$e^{-\lambda X} = e^{-(.405)(2)} = e^{-.81} = \textbf{.4449}$$

6.39 $p = 1/5 = .20$ $n = 150$

$\text{Prob}(X > 50)$:

$\mu = 150(.20) = 30$

$\sigma = \sqrt{150(.20)(.80)} = 4.899$

$$Z = \frac{50.5 - 30}{4.899} = 4.18$$

Area associated with $Z = 4.18$ is .5000

$\text{Prob}(X > 50) = .5000 - .5000 = \textbf{.0000}$

6.41 $\mu = 90.28$ $\sigma = 8.53$

Prob(X < 80):

$$Z = \frac{80 - 90.28}{8.53} = -1.21$$

from Table A.5, area for Z = -1.21 is .3869

Prob(X < 80) = .5000 - .3869 = **.1131**

Prob(X > 95):

$$Z = \frac{95 - 90.28}{8.53} = 0.55$$

from Table A.5, area for Z = 0.55 is .2088

Prob(X > 95) = .5000 - .2088 = **.2912**

Prob(83 < X < 87):

$$Z = \frac{83 - 90.28}{8.53} = -0.85$$

$$Z = \frac{87 - 90.28}{8.53} = -0.38$$

from Table A.5, area for Z = -0.85 is .3023
                    area for Z = -0.38 is .1480

Prob(83 < X < 87) = .3023 - .1480 = **.1543**

6.43   a = 18   b = 65

$$\text{Prob}(25 < X < 50) = \frac{50-25}{65-18} = \frac{25}{47} = .5319$$

$$\mu = \frac{a+b}{2} = \frac{65+18}{2} = 41.5$$

$$f(X) = \frac{1}{b-a} = \frac{1}{65-18} = \frac{1}{47} = .0213$$

6.45   μ = 951   σ = 96

a) Prob(X ≥ 1000):

$$Z = \frac{x-\mu}{\sigma} = \frac{1000-951}{96} = 0.51$$

from Table A.5, the area for Z = 0.51 is .1950

Prob(X ≥ 1000) = .5000 - .1950 = **.3050**

b) Prob(900 < X < 1100):

$$Z = \frac{x-\mu}{\sigma} = \frac{900-951}{96} = -0.53$$

$$Z = \frac{x-\mu}{\sigma} = \frac{1100-951}{96} = 1.55$$

from Table A.5, the area for Z = -0.53 is .2019
the area for Z = 1.55 is .4394

Prob(900 < X < 1100) = .2019 + .4394 = **.6413**

c) Prob(825 < X < 925):

$$Z = \frac{x - \mu}{\sigma} = \frac{825 - 951}{96} = -1.31$$

$$Z = \frac{x - \mu}{\sigma} = \frac{925 - 951}{96} = -0.27$$

from Table A.5, the area for Z = -1.31 is .4049
           the area for Z = -0.27 is .1064

Prob(825 < X < 925) = .4049 - .1064 = **.2985**

d) Prob(X < 700):

$$Z = \frac{x - \mu}{\sigma} = \frac{700 - 951}{96} = -2.61$$

from Table A.5, the area for Z = -2.61 is .4955

Prob(X < 700) = .5000 - .4955 = **.0045**

6.47 $\mu = 34,383$ $\sigma = 4,097$

a) Prob(X > 40,000):

$$Z = \frac{x - \mu}{\sigma} = \frac{40,000 - 34,383}{4,097} = 1.37$$

from Table A.5, the area for Z = 1.37 is .4147

Prob(X > 40,000) = .5000 - .4147 = **.0853**

b) Prob(X < 30,000):

$$Z = \frac{x - \mu}{\sigma} = \frac{30,000 - 34,383}{4,097} = -1.07$$

from Table A.5, the area for Z = -1.07 is .3577

Prob(X < 30,000) = .5000 - .3577 = **.1423**

c) Prob(X > 20,000):

$$Z = \frac{x - \mu}{\sigma} = \frac{20,000 - 3,383}{4,097} = -3.51$$

from Table A.5, the area for Z = -3.51 is .4998

Prob(X > 20,000) = .5000 + .4998 = **.9998**

d) Prob(27,000 < X < 36,000):

$$Z = \frac{x - \mu}{\sigma} = \frac{27,000 - 34,383}{4,097} = -1.80$$

$$Z = \frac{x - \mu}{\sigma} = \frac{36,000 - 34,383}{4,097} = 0.39$$

from Table A.5, the area for Z = -1.80 is .4641
the area for Z = 0.39 is .1517

Prob(27,000 < X < 36,000) = .4641 + .1517 = **.6158**

6.49 $\mu = 88$ $\sigma = 6.4$

a) Prob(X < 70):

$$Z = \frac{x - \mu}{\sigma} = \frac{70 - 88}{6.4} = -2.81$$

From Table A.5, area = .4975

Prob(X < 70) = .5000 - .4975 = **.0025**

b) Prob(X > 80):

$$Z = \frac{x - \mu}{\sigma} = \frac{80 - 88}{6.4} = -1.25$$

From Table A.5, area = .3944

Prob(X > 80) = .5000 + .3944 = **.8944**

c) Prob($90 \leq X \leq 100$):

$$Z = \frac{x - \mu}{\sigma} = \frac{100 - 88}{6.4} = 1.88$$

From Table A.5, area = .4699

$$Z = \frac{x - \mu}{\sigma} = \frac{90 - 88}{6.4} = 0.31$$

From Table A.5, area = .1217

Prob($90 \leq X \leq 100$) = .4699 - .1217 = **.3482**

6.51   n = 150   p = .75

$$\mu = n{\cdot}p = 150(.75) = 112.5$$

$$\sigma = \sqrt{n \cdot p \cdot q} = \sqrt{150(.75)(.25)} = 5.3033$$

a) Prob(X < 105):

correcting for continuity: X = 104.5

$$Z = \frac{X - \mu}{\sigma} = \frac{104.5 - 112.5}{5.3033} = -1.51$$

from Table A.5, the area for Z = -1.51 is .4345

Prob(X < 105) = .5000 - .4345 = **.0655**

b) Prob($110 \le X \le 120$):

correcting for continuity: $X = 109.5$, $X = 120.5$

$$Z = \frac{109.5 - 112.5}{5.3033} = -0.57$$

$$Z = \frac{120.5 - 112.5}{5.3033} = 1.51$$

from Table A.5, the area for Z = -0.57 is .2157
the area for Z = 1.51 is .4345

Prob($110 \le X \le 120$) = .2157 + .4345 = **.6502**

c) Prob(X > 95):

correcting for continuity: $X = 95.5$

$$Z = \frac{95.5 - 112.5}{5.3033} = -3.21$$

from Table A.5, the area for -3.21 is .4993

Prob(X > 95) = .5000 + .4993 = **.9993**

6.53 $\mu = 70{,}400$

60% are between 61,200 and 79,600

79,600 - 70,400 = 9,200

70,400 - 61,200 = 9,200

The 60% can be split into 30% and 30% because the two X values are equal distance from the mean.

The Z value associated with .3000 area is 0.84

$$Z = \frac{X - \mu}{\sigma}$$

$$.84 = \frac{79{,}600 - 70{,}400}{\sigma}$$

$$\sigma = \mathbf{10{,}952.38}$$

6.55 $\lambda = 3$ hurricanes $|$ 5 months

Prob($X \geq 1$ month $|$ $\lambda = 3$ hurricanes per 5 months):

Since X and λ are for different intervals,

change Lambda $= \lambda = 3/$ 5 months $= 0.6$ month.

Prob($X \geq$ month $|$ $\lambda = 0.6$ per month):

Let $X_0 = 1$

Prob($X \geq 1$) $= e^{-\lambda X} = e^{-0.6(1)} = e^{-0.6} = $ **.5488**

Prob($X \leq 2$ weeks):   2 weeks $= 0.5$ month.

Prob($X \leq 0.5$ month $|$ $\lambda = 0.6$ per month) =

1 - Prob($X > 0.5$ month $|$ $\lambda = 0.6$ per month)

Prob($X > 0.5$ month $|$ $\lambda = 0.6$ per month):

Let $X_0 = 0.5$

Prob($X > 0.5$) $= e^{-\lambda X} = e^{-0.6(.5)} = e^{-0.30} = $ .7408

Prob($X \leq 0.5$ month) $= 1 - $ P($X > 0.5$ month) $= 1 - .7408 = $ **.2592**

Average time = Expected time $= \mu = 1/\lambda = $ **1.67 months**

6.57 $\mu = 2087$ $= 175$

If 20% are less, then 30% lie between X and μ.

$Z_{.30} = -.84$

$$Z = \frac{X - \mu}{\sigma}$$

$$-.84 = \frac{X - 2087}{175}$$

$$X = \mathbf{1940}$$

If 65% are more, then 15% lie between X and μ

$Z_{.15} = -0.39$

$$Z = \frac{X - \mu}{\sigma}$$

$$-.39 = \frac{X - 2087}{175}$$

$$X = \mathbf{2018.75}$$

If X is more than 85%, then 35% lie between X and μ.

$Z_{.35} = 1.03$

$$Z = \frac{X - \mu}{\sigma}$$

$$1.03 = \frac{X - 2087}{175}$$

$$X = \mathbf{2267.25}$$

6.59 $\mu = 1,774,880$ $\sigma = 50,940$

Prob(X > 1,850,000):

$$Z = \frac{1,850,000 - 1,774,880}{50,940} = 1.48$$

from table A.5 the area for Z = 1.48 is .4306

Prob(X > 1,850,000) = .5000 - .4306 = **.0694**

Prob(X < 1,620,000):

$$Z = \frac{1,620,000 - 1,774,880}{50,940} = -3.04$$

from table A.5 the area for Z = -3.04 is .4988

Prob(X < 1,620,000) = .5000 - .4988 = **.0012**

6.61   This is a uniform distribution with a = 11 and b = 32.

The mean is (11 + 32)/2 = 21.5 and the standard deviation is

(32 - 11)/ 12 = 6.06. Almost 81% of the time there are less than or equal to 28

sales associates working. One hundred percent of the time there are less than or

equal to 34 sales associates working and never more than 34. About 23.8% of

the time there are 16 or fewer sales associates working. There are 21 or fewer

sales associates working about 48% of the time.

6.63 The lengths of cell phone calls are normally distributed with a mean of 2.35 minutes and a standard deviation of .11 minutes. Almost 99% of the calls are less than or equal to 2.60 minutes, almost 82% are less than or equal to 2.45 minutes, over 32% are less than 2.3 minutes, and almost none are less than 2 minutes.

Chapter 7
Sampling and Sampling Distributions

LEARNING OBJECTIVES

The two main objectives for Chapter 7 are to give you an appreciation for the proper application of sampling techniques and an understanding of the sampling distributions of two statistics, thereby enabling you to:

1. Determine when to use sampling instead of a census.

2. Distinguish between random and nonrandom sampling.

3. Decide when and how to use various sampling techniques.

4. Be aware of the different types of error that can occur in a study.

5. Understand the impact of the central limit theorem on statistical analysis.

6. Use the sampling distributions of $\overline{X}$ and $\hat{p}$.

CHAPTER OUTLINE

7.1   Sampling

Reasons for Sampling

Reasons for Taking a Census

Frame

Random Versus Nonrandom Sampling

Random Sampling Techniques

Simple Random Sampling

Stratified Random Sampling

Systematic Sampling

Cluster or Area Sampling

Nonrandom Sampling

Convenience Sampling

Judgment Sampling

Quota Sampling

Snowball Sampling

Sampling Error

Nonsampling Errors

7.2   Sampling Distribution of $\overline{X}$

Sampling from a Finite Population

7.3   Sampling Distribution of $\hat{p}$

KEY WORDS

Central Limit Theorem
Cluster (or Area) Sampling
Convenience Sampling
Disproportionate Stratified Random Sampling
Finite Correction Factor
Frame
Judgment Sampling
Nonrandom Sampling
Nonrandom Sampling Techniques
Nonsampling Errors
Proportionate Stratified Random Sampling

Quota Sampling
Random Sampling
Sample Proportion
Sampling Error
Simple Random Sampling
Snowball Sampling
Standard Error of the Mean
Standard Error of the Proportion
Stratified Random Sampling
Systematic Sampling
Two-Stage Sampling

STUDY QUESTIONS

1. Saving time and money are reasons to take a _____ rather than a census.

2. If the research process is destructive, taking a _____ may be the only option in gathering data.

3. A researcher may opt to take a _____ to eliminate the possibility that by chance randomly selected items are not representative of the population.

4. The directory or map from which a sample is taken is called the _____.

5. If the population list from which the researcher takes the sample contains fewer units than the target population, then the list has _____.

6. There are two main types of sampling, _____ sampling and _____ sampling.

7. If every unit of the population does not have the same probability of being selected to the sample, then the researcher is probably conducting _____ sampling.

8. Nonrandom sampling is sometimes referred to as _____ sampling.

9. The most elementary type of random sampling is _____ random sampling.

10. In _____ random sampling, the population is divided into nonoverlapping subpopulations called strata.

11. Whenever the proportions of the strata in the sample are different than the proportions of the strata in the population, _____ _____ random sampling occurs.

12. With _____ random sampling, there is homogeneity within a subgroup or stratum.

13. If a researcher selects every kth item from a population of N items, then he/she is likely conducting _____ random sampling.

14. When the population is divided into nonoverlapping areas and then random samples are drawn from the areas, the researcher is likely conducting _____ or _____ sampling.

15. A nonrandom sampling technique in which elements are selected for the sample based on the convenience of the researcher is called _____ sampling.

16. A nonrandom sampling technique in which elements are selected for the sample based on the judgment of the researcher is called _____ sampling.

17. A nonrandom sampling technique which is similar to stratified random sampling is called _____ sampling.

18. A nonrandom sampling technique in which survey subjects are selected based on referral from other survey respondents is called _____ sampling.

19. _____ error occurs when, by chance, the sample is not representative of the population.

20. Missing data and recording errors are examples of _____ errors.

21. The central limit theorem states that if n is large enough, the sample means are _____ distributed regardless of the shape of the population.

22. According to the central limit theorem, the mean of the sample means for a given size of sample is equal to the _____ _____.

23. According to the central limit theorem, the standard deviation of sample means for a given size of sample equals _____.

24. If samples are being drawn from a known population size, the Z formula for sample means includes a _____ _____ factor.

25. Suppose a population has a mean of 90 and a standard deviation of 27. If a random sample of size 49 is drawn from the population, the probability of drawing a sample with a mean of more than 95 is _____.

26. Suppose a population has a mean of 455 and a variance of 900. If a random sample of size 65 is drawn from the population, the probability that the sample mean is between 448 and 453 is _____.

27. Suppose .60 of the population posses a given characteristic. If a random sample of size 300 is drawn from the population, then the probability that .53 or fewer of the sample possess the characteristic is _____.

28. Suppose .36 of a population posses a given characteristic. If a random sample of size 1200 is drawn from the population, then the probability that less than 480 posses that characteristic in the sample is _____.

ANSWERS TO STUDY QUESTIONS

1.   Sample

2.   Sample

3.   Census

4.   Frame

5.   Underregistration

6.   Random, Nonrandom

7.   Nonrandom

8.   Nonprobability

9.   Simple

10. Stratified

11. Disproportionate Stratified

12. Stratified

13. Systematic

14. Area, Cluster

15. Convenience

16. Judgment

17. Quota

18. Snowball

19. Sampling

20. Nonsampling

21. Normally

22. Population Mean

23. $\sigma/\sqrt{n}$

24. Finite Correction

25. .0968

26. .2645

27. .0068

28. .9981

SOLUTIONS TO PROBLEMS IN CHAPTER 7

7.1   a)   i.   A union membership list for the company.

                ii.   A list of all employees of the company.

        b)   i.   White pages of the telephone directory for Utica, New York.

                ii.   Utility company list of all customers.

        c)   i.   Airline company list of phone and mail purchasers of tickets from the airline during the past six months.

                ii.   A list of frequent flyer club members for the airline.

        d)   i.   List of boat manufacturer's employees.

                ii.   List of members of a boat owners association.

        e)   i.   Cable company telephone directory.

                ii.   Membership list of cable management association.

7.5   a)   Under 21 years of age, 21 to 39 years of age, 40 to 55 years of age, over 55 years of age.

        b)   Under $1,000,000 sales per year, $1,000,000 to $4,999,999 sales per year, $5,000,000 to $19,999,999 sales per year, $20,000,000 to $49,000,000 per year, $50,000,000 to $99,999,999 per year, over $100,000,000 per year.

        c)   Less than 2,000 sq. ft., 2,000 to 4,999 sq. ft., 5,000 to 9,999 sq. ft., over 10,000 sq. ft.

        d)   east, southeast, midwest, south, southwest, west, northwest.

        e)   Government worker, teacher, lawyer, physician, engineer, business person, police officer, fire fighter, computer worker.

        f)   Manufacturing, finance, communications, health care, retailing, chemical, transportation.

7.7 $N = n \cdot K =$ **825**

7.9   a)   i.   Counties
           ii.   Metropolitan areas

      b)   i.   States (beside which the oil wells lie)
           ii.   Companies that own the wells

      c)   i.   States
           ii.   Counties

7.11   Go to a conference where some of the <u>Fortune</u> 500 executives attend.
       Approach those executives who appear to be friendly and approachable.

7.13 $\mu = 50$, $\sigma = 10$, $n = 64$

a) Prob($\overline{X} > 52$):

$$Z = \frac{\overline{X} - \mu}{\frac{\sigma}{\sqrt{n}}} = \frac{52 - 50}{\frac{10}{\sqrt{64}}} = 1.6$$

from Table A.5 Prob. = .4452

Prob($\overline{X} > 52$) = .5000 - .4452 = **.0548**

b) Prob($\overline{X} < 51$):

$$Z = \frac{\overline{X} - \mu}{\frac{\sigma}{\sqrt{n}}} = \frac{51 - 50}{\frac{10}{\sqrt{64}}} = 0.80$$

from Table A.5   prob. = .2881

Prob($\overline{X} < 51$) = .5000 + .2881 = **.7881**

c) Prob($\overline{X} < 47$):

$$Z = \frac{\overline{X} - \mu}{\frac{\sigma}{\sqrt{n}}} = \frac{47 - 50}{\frac{10}{\sqrt{64}}} = -2.40$$

from Table A.5 prob. = .4918

Prob($\overline{X} < 47$) = .5000 - .4918 = **.0082**

d) Prob($48.5 \leq \overline{X} \leq 52.4$):

$$Z = \frac{\overline{X} - \mu}{\frac{\sigma}{\sqrt{n}}} = \frac{48.5 - 50}{\frac{10}{\sqrt{64}}} = -1.20$$

from Table A.5 prob. = .3849

$$Z = \frac{\overline{X} - \mu}{\frac{\sigma}{\sqrt{n}}} = \frac{52.4 - 50}{\frac{10}{\sqrt{64}}} = 1.92$$

from Table A.5 prob. = .4726

Prob($48.5 \leq \overline{X} \leq 52.4$) = .3849 + .4726 = **.8575**

e) Prob($50.6 \leq \overline{X} \leq 51.3$):

$$Z = \frac{\overline{X} - \mu}{\frac{\sigma}{\sqrt{n}}} = \frac{50.6 - 50}{\frac{10}{\sqrt{64}}} = 0.48$$

from Table A.5, prob. = .1844

$$Z = \frac{\overline{X} - \mu}{\frac{\sigma}{\sqrt{n}}} = \frac{51.3 - 50}{\frac{10}{\sqrt{64}}}$$

from Table A.5, prob. = .3508

Prob($50.6 \leq \overline{X} \leq 51.3$) = .3508 - .1844 = **.1644**

7.15 $n = 36$ $\mu = 278$

$P(\overline{X} < 280) = .86$

.3600 of the area lies between $\overline{X} = 280$ and $\mu = 278$. This probability is associated with $Z = 1.08$ from Table A.5. Solving for σ :

$$Z = \frac{\overline{X} - \mu}{\dfrac{\sigma}{\sqrt{n}}}$$

$$1.08 = \frac{280 - 278}{\dfrac{\sigma}{\sqrt{36}}}$$

$$1.08 \frac{\sigma}{6} = 2$$

$$1.08\sigma = 12$$

$$\sigma = \frac{12}{1.08} = \mathbf{11.11}$$

7.17 a) $N = 1,000$ $n = 60$ $\mu = 75$ $\sigma = 6$

Prob($\overline{X} < 76.5$):

$$Z = \frac{\overline{X} - \mu}{\dfrac{\sigma}{\sqrt{n}} \sqrt{\dfrac{N-n}{N-1}}} = \frac{76.5 - 75}{\dfrac{6}{\sqrt{60}} \sqrt{\dfrac{1000 - 60}{1000 - 1}}} = 2.00$$

from Table A.5,   prob. = .4772

Prob($\overline{X} < 76.5$) = .4772 + .5000 = **.9772**

b) $N = 90$ $n = 36$ $\mu = 108$ $\sigma = 3.46$

Prob$(107 < \overline{X} < 107.7)$:

$$Z = \frac{\overline{X} - \mu}{\dfrac{\sigma}{\sqrt{n}} \sqrt{\dfrac{N-n}{N-1}}} = \frac{107 - 108}{\dfrac{3.46}{\sqrt{36}} \sqrt{\dfrac{90 - 36}{90 - 1}}} = -2.23$$

from Table A.5, prob. = .4871

$$Z = \frac{\overline{X} - \mu}{\dfrac{\sigma}{\sqrt{n}} \sqrt{\dfrac{N-n}{N-1}}} = \frac{107.7 - 108}{\dfrac{3.46}{\sqrt{36}} \sqrt{\dfrac{90 - 36}{90 - 1}}} = -0.67$$

from Table A.5, prob. = .2486

Prob$(107 < \overline{X} < 107.7) = .4871 - .2486 =$ **.2385**

c) $N = 250$ $n = 100$ $\mu = 35.6$ $\sigma = 4.89$

Prob$(\overline{X} \geq 36)$:

$$Z = \frac{\overline{X} - \mu}{\dfrac{\sigma}{\sqrt{n}} \sqrt{\dfrac{N-n}{N-1}}} = \frac{36 - 35.6}{\dfrac{4.89}{\sqrt{100}} \sqrt{\dfrac{250 - 100}{250 - 1}}} = 1.05$$

from Table A.5, prob. = .3531

Prob$(\overline{X} \geq 36) = .5000 - .3531 =$ **.1469**

d) $N = 5000$ $n = 60$ $\mu = 125$ $\sigma = 13.4$

Prob$(\overline{X} \leq 123)$:

$$Z = \frac{\overline{X} - \mu}{\dfrac{\sigma}{\sqrt{n}} \sqrt{\dfrac{N-n}{N-1}}} = \frac{123 - 125}{\dfrac{13.4}{\sqrt{60}} \sqrt{\dfrac{5000 - 60}{5000 - 1}}} = -1.16$$

from Table A.5, prob. = .3770

Prob$(\overline{X} \leq 123) = .5000 - .3770 =$ **.1230**

7.19 $N = 1500$ $n = 100$ $\mu = 147{,}000$ $\sigma = 8{,}500$

Prob($\overline{X} > \$155{,}000$):

$$Z = \frac{\overline{X} - \mu}{\dfrac{\sigma}{\sqrt{n}}\sqrt{\dfrac{N-n}{N-1}}} = \frac{155{,}000 - 147{,}000}{\dfrac{8{,}500}{\sqrt{100}}\sqrt{\dfrac{1500-100}{1500-1}}} = 9.74$$

from Table A.5, prob. $= .5000$

Prob($\overline{X} > \$155{,}000$) $= .5000 - .5000 =$ **.0000**

7.21 $\mu = 50.4$ $\sigma = 11.8$ $n = 42$

a) Prob($\overline{X} > 52$):

$$Z = \frac{\overline{X} - \mu}{\dfrac{\sigma}{\sqrt{n}}} = \frac{52 - 50.4}{\dfrac{11.8}{\sqrt{42}}} = 0.88$$

from Table A.5, the area for $Z = 0.88$ is $.3106$

Prob($\overline{X} > 52$) $= .5000 - .3106 =$ **.1894**

b) Prob($\overline{X} < 47.5$):

$$Z = \frac{\overline{X} - \mu}{\dfrac{\sigma}{\sqrt{n}}} = \frac{47.5 - 50.4}{\dfrac{11.8}{\sqrt{42}}} = -1.59$$

from Table A.5, the area for $Z = -1.59$ is $.4441$

Prob($\overline{X} < 47.5$) $= .5000 - .4441 =$ **.0559**

c) Prob($\overline{X} < 40$):

$$Z = \frac{\overline{X} - \mu}{\frac{\sigma}{\sqrt{n}}} = \frac{40 - 50.4}{\frac{11.8}{\sqrt{42}}} = -5.71$$

from Table A.5, the area for Z = -5.71 is .5000

Prob($\overline{X} < 40$) = .5000 - .5000 = **.0000**

d) 71% of the values are greater than 49. Therefore, 21% are between the sample mean of 49 and the population mean, $\mu = 50.4$.

The Z value associated with the 21% of the area is -0.55

$Z_{.21} = -0.55$

$$Z = \frac{\overline{X} - \mu}{\frac{\sigma}{\sqrt{n}}}$$

$$-0.55 = \frac{49 - 50.4}{\frac{\sigma}{\sqrt{42}}}$$

$$\sigma = \textbf{16.4964}$$

7.23   P = .58   n = 660

a) Prob($\hat{p} > .60$):

$$Z = \frac{\hat{p} - P}{\sqrt{\frac{P \cdot Q}{n}}} = \frac{.60 - .58}{\sqrt{\frac{(.58)(.42)}{660}}} = 1.04$$

from table A.5, area = .3508

Prob($\hat{p} > .60$) = .5000 - .3508 = **.1492**

b) Prob$(.55 < \hat{p} < .65)$:

$$Z = \frac{\hat{p} - P}{\sqrt{\dfrac{P \cdot Q}{n}}} = \frac{.65 - .58}{\sqrt{\dfrac{(.58)(.42)}{660}}} = 3.64$$

from table A.5, area = .4998

$$Z = \frac{\hat{p} - P}{\sqrt{\dfrac{P \cdot Q}{n}}} = \frac{.55 - .58}{\sqrt{\dfrac{(.58)(.42)}{660}}} = 1.56$$

from table A.5, area = .4406

Prob$(.55 < \hat{p} < .65)$ = .4998 + .4406 = **.9404**

c) Prob$(\hat{p} > .57)$:

$$Z = \frac{\hat{p} - P}{\sqrt{\dfrac{P \cdot Q}{n}}} = \frac{.57 - .58}{\sqrt{\dfrac{(.58)(.42)}{660}}} = 0.52$$

from table A.5, area = **.1985**

d) Prob$(.53 \le \hat{p} \le .56)$:

$$Z = \frac{\hat{p} - P}{\sqrt{\dfrac{P \cdot Q}{n}}} = \frac{.56 - .58}{\sqrt{\dfrac{(.58)(.42)}{660}}} = 1.04$$

from table A.5, area = .3508

$$Z = \frac{\hat{p} - P}{\sqrt{\dfrac{P \cdot Q}{n}}} = \frac{.53 - .58}{\sqrt{\dfrac{(.58)(.42)}{660}}} = 2.60$$

from table A.5, area = .4953

Prob$(.53 \le \hat{p} \le .56)$ = .4953 - .3508 = **.1445**

e) Prob($\hat{p} < .48$):

$$Z = \frac{\hat{p} - P}{\sqrt{\dfrac{P \cdot Q}{n}}} = \frac{.48 - .58}{\sqrt{\dfrac{(.58)(.42)}{660}}} = 5.21$$

from table A.5, area = .5000

Prob($\hat{p} < .48$) = .5000 - .5000 = **.0000**

7.25   P = .28   n = 140 Prob($\hat{p} < \hat{p}_0$) = .3000

Prob($\hat{p} \leq \hat{p}_0 \leq .28$) = .5000 - .3000 = .2000

from Table A.5, $Z_{.2000}$ = -0.52

Solving for $\hat{p}_0$:

$$Z = \frac{\hat{p}_0 - P}{\sqrt{\dfrac{P \cdot Q}{n}}}$$

$$-0.52 = \frac{\hat{p}_0 - .28}{\sqrt{\dfrac{(.28)(.72)}{140}}}$$

$$-.02 = \hat{p}_0 - .28$$

$$\hat{p}_0 = .28 - .02 = \textbf{.26}$$

7.27   P = .39   n = 200

a) Prob(X < 70):

$$\hat{p} = \frac{70}{200} = .35$$

$$Z = \frac{\hat{p} - P}{\sqrt{\dfrac{P \cdot Q}{n}}} = \frac{.35 - .39}{\sqrt{\dfrac{(.39)(.61)}{200}}} = -1.16$$

from Table A.5, the area for Z = -1.16 is .3770

Prob(X < 70) = .5000 - .3770 = **.1230**

b) Prob(X > 90):

$$\hat{p} = \frac{90}{200} = .45$$

$$Z = \frac{\hat{p} - P}{\sqrt{\dfrac{P \cdot Q}{n}}} = \frac{.45 - .39}{\sqrt{\dfrac{(.39)(.61)}{200}}} = 1.74$$

from Table A.5, the area for Z = 1.74 is .4591

Prob(X > 90) = .5000 - .4591 = **.0409**

c) For not having a cell phone, P = .61

Prob(X > 65):

$$\hat{p} = \frac{65}{200} = .325$$

$$Z = \frac{\hat{p} - P}{\sqrt{\dfrac{P \cdot Q}{n}}} = \frac{.325 - .61}{\sqrt{\dfrac{(.39)(.61)}{200}}} = -8.26$$

from Table A.5, the area for Z = -8.26 is .5000

Prob(X > 65) = .5000 + .5000 = **1.0000**

7.29 $\mu = 76$, $\sigma = 14$

    a) n = 35,   Prob($\overline{X} \geq 79$):

$$Z = \frac{\overline{X} - \mu}{\frac{\sigma}{\sqrt{n}}} = \frac{79 - 76}{\frac{14}{\sqrt{35}}} = 1.27$$

    from table A.5, area = .3980

    Prob($\overline{X} \geq 79$) = .5000 - .3980 = **.1020**

    b) n = 140,   Prob($74 \leq \overline{X} \leq 77$):

$$Z = \frac{\overline{X} - \mu}{\frac{\sigma}{\sqrt{n}}} = \frac{74 - 76}{\frac{14}{\sqrt{140}}} = -1.69$$

    from table A.5, area = .4545

$$Z = \frac{\overline{X} - \mu}{\frac{\sigma}{\sqrt{n}}} = \frac{77 - 76}{\frac{14}{\sqrt{140}}} = 0.85$$

    from table A.5, area = .3023

    P($74 \leq \overline{X} \leq 77$) = .4545 + .3023 = **.7568**

    c) n = 219,   Prob($\overline{X} < 76.5$):

$$Z = \frac{\overline{X} - \mu}{\frac{\sigma}{\sqrt{n}}} = \frac{76.5 - 76}{\frac{14}{\sqrt{219}}} = 0.53$$

    from table A.5, area = .2019

    Prob($\overline{X} < 76.5$) = .5000 - .2019 = **.2981**

7.31

Under 18	250(.22) =	**55**
18 - 25	250(.18) =	**45**
26 - 50	250(.36) =	**90**
51 - 65	250(.10) =	**25**
over 65	250(.14) =	**35**
	n =	250

7.33 a) Roster of production employees secured from the human resources department of the company.

b) Alpha/Beta store records kept at the headquarters of their California division or merged files of store records from regional offices across the state.

c) Membership list of Maine lobster catchers association.

7.35   Number the employees from 0001 to 1250. Randomly sample from the random number table until 60 different usable numbers are obtained. You cannot use numbers from 1251 to 9999.

7.37 n = 1100

a) $X > 810$, $P = .73$

$$\hat{p} = \frac{x}{n} = \frac{810}{1100}$$

$$Z = \frac{\hat{p} - P}{\sqrt{\dfrac{P \cdot Q}{n}}} = \frac{.7364 - .73}{\sqrt{\dfrac{(.73)(.27)}{1100}}} = 0.48$$

from table A.5, area = .1844

Prob($X > 810$) = .5000 - .1844 = **.3156**

b) $X < 1030,$ $P = .96,$

$$\hat{p} = \frac{x}{n} = \frac{1030}{1100} = .9364$$

$$Z = \frac{\hat{p} - P}{\sqrt{\dfrac{P \cdot Q}{n}}} = \frac{.9364 - .96}{\sqrt{\dfrac{(.96)(.04)}{1100}}} = -3.99$$

from table A.5, area = .49997

Prob$(X < 1030) = .5000 - .49997 = $ **.00003**

c) $P = .85$

Prob$(.82 \leq \hat{p} \leq .84)$:

$$Z = \frac{\hat{p} - P}{\sqrt{\dfrac{P \cdot Q}{n}}} = \frac{.82 - .85}{\sqrt{\dfrac{(.85)(.15)}{1100}}} = -2.79$$

from table A.5, area = .4974

$$Z = \frac{\hat{p} - P}{\sqrt{\dfrac{P \cdot Q}{n}}} = \frac{.84 - .85}{\sqrt{\dfrac{(.85)(.15)}{1100}}} = -0.93$$

from table A.5, area = .3238

Prob$(.82 \leq \hat{p} \leq .84) = .4974 - .3238 = $ **.1736**

7.39   Divide the factories into geographic regions and select a few factories to represent those regional areas of the country. Take a random sample of employees from each selected factory. Do the same for distribution centers and retail outlets. Divide the United States into regions of areas. Select a few areas. Randomly sample from each of the selected area distribution centers and retail outlets.

7.41 $P = .54$ $n = 565$

a) Prob$(X \geq 339)$:

$$\hat{p} = \frac{x}{n} = \frac{339}{565} = .60$$

$$Z = \frac{\hat{p} - P}{\sqrt{\dfrac{P \cdot Q}{n}}} = \frac{.60 - .54}{\sqrt{\dfrac{(.54)(.46)}{565}}} = 2.86$$

from Table A.5, the area for $Z = 2.86$ is .4979

Prob$(X \geq 339) = .5000 - .4979 = $ **.0021**

b) Prob$(X \geq 288)$:

$$\hat{p} = \frac{x}{n} = \frac{288}{565} = .5097$$

$$Z = \frac{\hat{p} - P}{\sqrt{\dfrac{P \cdot Q}{n}}} = \frac{.5097 - .54}{\sqrt{\dfrac{(.54)(.46)}{565}}} = -1.45$$

from Table A.5, the area for $Z = -1.45$ is .4265

Prob$(X \geq 288) = .5000 + .4265 = $ **.9265**

c) Prob$(\hat{p} \leq .50)$:

$$Z = \frac{\hat{p} - P}{\sqrt{\dfrac{P \cdot Q}{n}}} = \frac{.50 - .54}{\sqrt{\dfrac{(.54)(.46)}{565}}} = -1.91$$

from Table A.5, the area for $Z = -1.91$ is .4719

Prob$(\hat{p} \leq .50) = .5000 - .4719 = $ **.0281**

7.43 $\mu = 56.8$ $n = 51$ $\sigma = 12.3$

a) Prob($\overline{X} > 60$):

$$Z = \frac{\overline{X} - \mu}{\frac{\sigma}{\sqrt{n}}} = \frac{60 - 56.8}{\frac{12.3}{\sqrt{51}}} = 1.86$$

from Table A.5, Prob. = .4686

Prob($\overline{X} > 60$) = .5000 - .4686 = **.0314**

b) Prob($\overline{X} > 58$):

$$Z = \frac{\overline{X} - \mu}{\frac{\sigma}{\sqrt{n}}} = \frac{58 - 56.8}{\frac{12.3}{\sqrt{51}}} = 0.70$$

from Table A.5, Prob.= .2580

Prob($\overline{X} > 58$) = .5000 - .2580 = **.2420**

c) Prob($56 < \overline{X} < 57$):

$$Z = \frac{\overline{X} - \mu}{\frac{\sigma}{\sqrt{n}}} = \frac{56 - 56.8}{\frac{12.3}{\sqrt{51}}} = -0.46$$

from Table A.5, Prob.= .1772

$$Z = \frac{\overline{X} - \mu}{\frac{\sigma}{\sqrt{n}}} = \frac{57 - 56.8}{\frac{12.3}{\sqrt{51}}} = 0.12$$

from Table A.5, Prob.= .0478

Prob($56 < \overline{X} < 57$) = .1772 + .0478 = **.2250**

d) Prob($\overline{X} < 55$):

$$Z = \frac{\overline{X} - \mu}{\dfrac{\sigma}{\sqrt{n}}} = \frac{55 - 56.8}{\dfrac{12.3}{\sqrt{51}}} = -1.05$$

from Table A.5, Prob.= .3531

Prob($\overline{X} < 55$) = .5000 - .3531 = **.1469**

e) Prob($\overline{X} < 50$):

$$Z = \frac{\overline{X} - \mu}{\dfrac{\sigma}{\sqrt{n}}} = \frac{50 - 56.8}{\dfrac{12.3}{\sqrt{51}}} = -3.95$$

from Table A.5, Prob.= .5000

Prob($\overline{X} < 50$) = .5000 - .5000 = **.0000**

7.45   P = .73   n = 300

a) Prob($210 \leq \overline{X} \leq 234$):

$$\hat{p}_1 = \frac{x}{n} = \frac{210}{300} = .70 \qquad\qquad \hat{p}_2 = \frac{x}{n} = \frac{234}{300} = .78$$

$$Z = \frac{\hat{p} - P}{\sqrt{\dfrac{PQ}{n}}} = \frac{.70 - .73}{\sqrt{\dfrac{(.73)(.27)}{300}}} = -1.17$$

$$Z = \frac{\hat{p} - P}{\sqrt{\dfrac{PQ}{n}}} = \frac{.78 - .73}{\sqrt{\dfrac{(.73)(.27)}{300}}} = 1.95$$

from Table A.5, the area for Z = -1.17 is .3790
the area for Z = 1.95 is .4744

Prob($210 \leq X \leq 234$) = .3790 + .4744 = **.8534**

b) Prob($\hat{p} \geq .78$):

$$Z = \frac{\hat{p} - P}{\sqrt{\dfrac{PQ}{n}}} = \frac{.78 - .73}{\sqrt{\dfrac{(.73)(.27)}{300}}} = 1.95$$

from Table A.5, the area for Z = 1.95 is .4744

Prob($\hat{p} \geq .78$) = .5000 - .4744 = **.0256**

c) P = .73   n = 800   Prob($\hat{p} \geq .78$):

$$Z = \frac{\hat{p} - P}{\sqrt{\dfrac{PQ}{n}}} = \frac{.78 - .73}{\sqrt{\dfrac{(.73)(.27)}{800}}} = 3.19$$

from Table A.5, the area for Z = 3.19 is .4993

Prob($\hat{p} \geq .78$) = .5000 - .4993 = **.0007**

7.47   By taking a sample, there is potential for more detailed information to be
obtained. More time can be spent with each employee. Probing questions can
be asked. There is more time for trust to be built between employee and
interviewer resulting in the potential for more honest, open answers.

With a census, data is usually more general and easier to analyze because it is in a
more standard format. Decision-makers are sometimes more comfortable with a
census because everyone is included and there is no sampling error. A census
appears to be a better political device because the CEO can claim that everyone in the
company has had input.

7.49 Switzerland: n = 40   μ = $ 28.34   σ = $ 3

Prob($28 \leq \overline{X} \leq 29$):

$$Z = \frac{\overline{X} - \mu}{\frac{\sigma}{\sqrt{n}}} = \frac{28 - 28.34}{\frac{3}{\sqrt{40}}} = -0.72$$

$$Z = \frac{\overline{X} - \mu}{\frac{\sigma}{\sqrt{n}}} = \frac{29 - 28.34}{\frac{3}{\sqrt{40}}} = 1.39$$

from Table A.5, the area for Z = -0.72 is .2642
                the area for Z = 1.39 is .4177

Prob($28 \leq \overline{X} \leq 29$) = .2642 + .4177 = **.6819**

Japan: n = 35   μ = $ 20.84   σ = $3

Prob($\overline{X} > 22$):

$$Z = \frac{\overline{X} - \mu}{\frac{\sigma}{\sqrt{n}}} = \frac{22 - 20.84}{\frac{3}{\sqrt{35}}} = 2.29$$

from Table A.5, the area for Z = 2.29 is .4890

P($\overline{X} > 22$) = .5000 - .4890 = **.0110**

U.S.: n = 50   μ = $ 17.70   σ = $ 3

Prob($\overline{X} < 16.50$):

$$Z = \frac{\overline{X} - \mu}{\frac{\sigma}{\sqrt{n}}} = \frac{16.50 - 17.70}{\frac{3}{\sqrt{50}}} = -2.83$$

from Table A.5, the area for Z = -2.83 is .4977

Prob($\overline{X} < 16.50$) = .5000 - .4977 = **.0023**

7.51 $\mu = \$281$ $n = 65$ $\sigma = \$47$

$P(\overline{X} > \$273)$:

$$Z = \frac{\overline{X} - \mu}{\frac{\sigma}{\sqrt{n}}} = \frac{273 - 281}{\frac{47}{\sqrt{65}}} = -1.37$$

from Table A.5 the area for $Z = -1.37$ is .4147

Prob.$(\overline{X} > \$273) = .5000 + .4147 = $ **.9147**

Chapter 8
Statistical Inference: Estimation for Single Populations

LEARNING OBJECTIVES

The overall learning objective of Chapter 8 is to help you understand estimating parameters of single populations, thereby enabling you to:

1. Know the difference between point and interval estimation.

2. Estimate a population mean from a sample mean for large sample sizes.

3. Estimate a population mean from a sample mean for small sample sizes.

4. Estimate a population proportion from a sample proportion.

5. Estimate the population variance from a sample variance.

6. Estimate the minimum sample size necessary to achieve given statistical goals.

CHAPTER OUTLINE

8.1   Estimating the Population Mean with Large Sample Sizes.

      Finite Correction Factor

      Confidence Interval to Estimate μ When σ is Unknown

8.2   Estimating the Population Mean: Small Sample Sizes, σ Unknown

      The t Distribution

      Robustness

      Characteristics of the t Distribution.

      Reading the t Distribution Table

      Confidence Intervals to Estimate μ When σ is Unknown and Sample Size is Small

      Using the Computer to Construct t Confidence Intervals for the Mean

8.3   Estimating the Population Proportion

      Using the Computer to Construct Intervals of the Population Proportion

8.4   Estimating the Population Variance

8.5   Estimating Sample Size

      Sample Size When Estimating μ

      Determing Sample Size When Estimating P

KEY WORDS

Bounds
Chi-square Distribution
Degrees of Freedom(df)
Error of Estimation
Interval Estimate

Point Estimate
Robust
Sample-Size Estimation
t Distribution
t Value

STUDY QUESTIONS

1. When a statistic taken from the sample is used to estimate a population parameter, it is called a(n) _____ estimate.

2. When a range of values is used to estimate a population parameter, it is called a(n) _____ estimate.

3. The Z value associated with a two-sided 90% confidence interval is _____.

4. The Z value associated with a two-sided 95% confidence interval is _____.

5. The Z value associated with a two-sided 80% confidence interval is _____.

6. Suppose a random sample of 40 is selected from a population with a standard deviation of 13. If the sample mean is 118, the 98% confidence interval to estimate the population mean is _____.

7. Suppose a random sample of size 75 is selected from a population. The sample yields a mean of 26 and a standard deviation of 6.4. From this information, the 90% confidence interval to estimate the population mean can be computed as _____.

8. The following random sample of numbers are drawn from a population: 45, 61, 55, 43, 49, 60, 62, 53, 57, 44, 39, 48, 57, 40, 61, 62, 45, 39, 38, 56, 55, 59, 63, 50, 41, 39, 45, 47, 56, 51, 61, 39, 36, 57. From this data, a 99% confidence interval to estimate the population mean can be computed as _____.

9. A random sample of 63 items is selected from a population of 400 items. The sample mean is 211 and the sample standard deviation is 48. From this data, a 95% confidence interval to estimate the population mean can be computed as _____.

10. Generally, _____ is considered the lower limit for large sample size.

11. The t test was developed by _____.

12. In order to find values in the t distribution table, you must convert the sample size or sizes to _____.

13. The table t value associated with 10 degrees of freedom and used to compute a 95% confidence interval is _____.

14.   The table t value associated with 18 degrees of freedom and used to compute a 99% confidence interval is _____.

15.   A researcher is interested in estimating the mean value for a population. She takes a random sample of 17 items and computes a sample mean of 224 and a sample standard deviation of 32. She decides to construct a 98% confidence interval to estimate the mean. The degrees of freedom associated with this problem are _____. It can be assumed that these values are normally distributed in the population.

16.   The table t value used to construct the confidence interval in question 15 is _____.

17.   The confidence interval resulting from the data in question 15 is _____.

18.   A researcher wants to estimate the proportion of the population which possesses a given characteristic. A random sample of size 800 is taken resulting in 380 items which possess the characteristic. The point estimate for this population proportion is _____.

19.   A researcher wants to estimate the proportion of a population which possesses a given characteristic. A random sample of size 1250 is taken and .67 of the sample possess the characteristic. The 90% confidence interval to estimate the population proportion is _____.

20.   A random sample of 255 items from a population results in 44% possessing a given characteristic. Using this information, the researcher constructs a 99% confidence interval to estimate the population proportion. The resulting confidence interval is _____.

21.   What proportion of a population possesses a given characteristic? To estimate this, a random sample of 1700 people are interviewed from the population. Seven hundred and fourteen of the people sampled posses the characteristic. Using this information, the researcher computes an 88% confidence interval to estimate the proportion of the population who posses the given characteristic. The resulting confidence interval is _____.

22.   A confidence interval to estimate the population variance can be constructed by using the sample variance and the _____ distribution.

23.   Suppose we want to construct a confidence interval to estimate a population variance. A sample variance is computed from a sample of 14 items. To construct a 95% confidence interval, the chi-square table values are _____ and _____.

24.   We want to estimate a population variance. A sample of 9 items produces a sample standard deviation of 4.29. The point estimate of the population variance is

_____.

25.   In an effort to estimate the population variance, a sample of 12 items is taken. The sample variance is 21.96. Using this information, it can be determined that the 90% confidence interval is _____.

26.   In estimating the sample size necessary to estimate μ, the error of estimation, E, is equal to _____.

27.   In estimating sample size, if the population standard deviation is unknown, it can be estimated by using _____.

28.   Suppose a researcher wants to conduct a study to estimate the population mean. He/she plans to use a 95% level of confidence to estimate the mean and the population standard deviation is approximately 34. The researcher wants the error to be no more than 4. The sample size should be at least _____.

29.   A researcher wants to determine the sample size necessary to adequately conduct a study to estimate the population mean to within 5 points. The range of population values is 80 and the researcher plans to use a 90% level of confidence. The sample size should be at least _____.

30.   A study is going to be conducted in which a population mean will be estimated using a 92% confidence interval. The estimate needs to be within 12 of the actual population mean. The population variance is estimated to be around 2200. The necessary sample size should be at least _____.

31.   In estimating the sample size necessary to estimate P, if there is no good approximation for the value of P available, the value of _____ should be used as an estimate of P in the formula.

32.   A researcher wants to estimate the population proportion with a 95% level of confidence. He/she estimates from previous studies that the population proportion is no more than .30. The researcher wants the estimate to have an error of no more than .02. The necessary sample size is at least _____.

33.   A study will be conducted to estimate the population proportion. A level of confidence of 99% will be used and an error of no more than .05 is desired. There is no knowledge as to what the population proportion will be. The size of sample should be at least _____.

34.   A researcher conducts a study to determine what the population proportion is for a given characteristic. Is it believed from previous studies that the proportion of the population will be at least .65. The researcher wants to use a 98% level of confidence. He/she also wants the error to be no more than .03. The sample size should be at least _____.

ANSWERS TO STUDY QUESTIONS

1. Point

2. Interval

3. 1.645

4. 1.96

5. 1.28

6. $113.2 \leq \mu \leq 122.8$

7. $24.8 \leq \mu \leq 27.2$

8. $46.6 \leq \mu \leq 54.2$

9. $200.1 \leq \mu \leq 221.9$

10. $n \geq 30$

11. William S. Gosset

12. Degrees of Freedom

13. 2.228

14. 2.878

15. 16

16. 2.583

17. $203.95 \leq \mu \leq 244.05$

18. .475

19. $.648 \leq P \leq .692$

20. $.36 \leq P \leq .52$

21. $.401 \leq P \leq .439$

22. Chi-square

23. 5.00874, 24.7356

24. $S^2 = 18.4041$

25. $12.277 \leq \sigma^2 \leq 52.802$

26. $\overline{X} - \mu$

27. ¼ Range

28. 278

29. 44

30. 47

31. .50

32. 2,017

33. 664

34. 1,373

SOLUTIONS TO ODD-NUMBERED PROBLEMS IN CHAPTER 8

8.1 a) $\overline{X} = 25$ $\sigma = 3.5$ n=60

95% Confidence $Z_{.025} = 1.96$

$$\overline{X} \pm Z\frac{\sigma}{\sqrt{n}} = 25 \pm 1.96\frac{3.5}{\sqrt{60}} = 25 \pm 0.89 = \mathbf{24.11 \leq \mu \leq 25.89}$$

b) $\overline{X} = 119.6$ S=23.89   n=75
98% Confidence $Z_{.01} = 2.33$

$$\overline{X} \pm Z\frac{S}{\sqrt{n}} = 119.6 \pm 2.33\frac{2.89}{\sqrt{75}} = 119.6 \pm 6.43 = \mathbf{113.17 \leq \mu \leq 126.03}$$

c) $\overline{X} = 3.419$ S=0.974   n=32
90% C.I. $Z_{.05} = 1.645$

$$\overline{X} \pm Z\frac{S}{\sqrt{n}} = 3.419 \pm 1.645\frac{0.974}{\sqrt{32}} = 3.419 \pm .283 = \mathbf{3.136 \leq \mu \leq 3.702}$$

d) $\overline{X} = 56.7$ $\sigma = 12.1$ N=500   n=47
80% C.I. $Z_{.10} = 1.28$

$$\overline{X} \pm Z\frac{\sigma}{\sqrt{n}}\sqrt{\frac{N-n}{N-1}} = 56.7 \pm 1.28\frac{12.1}{\sqrt{47}}\sqrt{\frac{500-47}{500-1}} = $$

$56.7 \pm 2.15 = \mathbf{54.55 \leq \mu \leq 58.85}$

8.3   n = 81 $\overline{X} = 47$ S=5.89
      90% C.I. $Z_{.05}$=1.645

$$\overline{X} \pm Z\frac{S}{\sqrt{n}} = 47 \pm 1.645\frac{5.89}{\sqrt{81}} = 47 \pm 1.08 = \mathbf{45.92 \leq \mu \leq 48.08}$$

8.5   n = 70 σ^2=49 $\overline{X} = 90.4$

$\overline{X} = \mathbf{90.4}$ **Point Estimate**

94% C.I. $Z_{.03} = 1.88$

$$\overline{X} \pm Z\frac{\sigma}{\sqrt{n}} = 90.4 \pm 1.88\frac{\sqrt{49}}{\sqrt{70}} = 90.4 \pm 1.57 = \mathbf{88.83 \leq \mu \leq 91.97}$$

8.7   n = 120 $\overline{X} = 18.72$ S = 0.8735
      99% C.I. $Z_{.005} = 2.575$

$\overline{X} = \mathbf{18.72}$ **Point Estimate**

$$\overline{X} \pm Z\frac{S}{\sqrt{n}} = 18.72 \pm 2.575\frac{0.8735}{\sqrt{120}} = 8.72 \pm .21 = \mathbf{18.51 \leq \mu \leq 18.93}$$

8.9   n = 32 $\overline{X} = 5.656$ S=3.229
      90% C.I. $Z_{.05} = 1.645$

$$\overline{X} \pm Z\frac{S}{\sqrt{n}} = 5.656 \pm 1.645\frac{3.229}{\sqrt{32}} = 5.656 \pm .939 = \mathbf{4.717 \leq \mu \leq 6.595}$$

8.11 $n = 48$ $\overline{X} = 7.68\%$ $S = 0.28\%$

a) $\overline{X} = 7.68\%$ **Point Estimate**

b) 98% C.I. $Z_{.01} = 2.33$

$$\overline{X} \pm Z\frac{S}{\sqrt{n}} = 7.68\% \pm 2.33\frac{.28\%}{\sqrt{48}} = 7.68\% \pm .09\% = \mathbf{7.59\% \le \mu \le 7.77\%}$$

8.13 $\mu = 27.4$ 95% confidence interval $n = 4$

Excel uses $\sigma = 5.1$

$\overline{X} = 25$ The error of the interval is 1.49

from data: $\Sigma X = 1104$ $\Sigma X^2 = 28{,}240$

$\overline{X} = 24.533$ $S = 5.1239$

$Z = \pm 1.96$

Confidence interval: $\overline{X} \pm Z\frac{S}{\sqrt{n}} = 24.533 \pm 1.96\frac{5.1239}{\sqrt{45}} =$

$24.533 \pm 1.497 = \mathbf{23.036 \le \mu \le 26.030}$

The error of the interval is 1.497 which is quite close to the Excel figure.

8.15 $n = 13$ $\overline{X} = 45.62$ $S = 5.694$ $df = 13 - 1 = 12$

95% Confidence Interval, $\alpha/2 = .025$

$t_{.025,12} = 2.179$

$$\overline{X} \pm t\frac{S}{\sqrt{n}} = 45.62 \pm 2.179\frac{5.694}{\sqrt{13}} = 45.62 \pm 3.44 = \mathbf{42.18 \le \mu \le 49.06}$$

8.17 $n = 27$ $\overline{X} = 128.4$ $S = 20.64$ $df = 27 - 1 = 26$

98% Confidence Interval
$\alpha/2 = .01$

$t_{.01,26} = 2.479$

$$\overline{X} \pm t \frac{S}{\sqrt{n}} = 128.4 \pm 2.479 \frac{20.6}{\sqrt{27}} = 128.4 \pm 9.83 = \mathbf{118.57 \le \mu \le 138.23}$$

$\overline{X} = \mathbf{128.4}$ **Point Estimate**

8.19 $n = 25$ $\overline{X} = 16.088$ $S = .817$ $df = 25 - 1 = 24$

99% Confidence Interval

$\alpha/2 = .005$

$t_{.005,24} = 2.797$

$$\overline{X} \pm t \frac{S}{\sqrt{n}} = 16.088 \pm 2.797 \frac{.817}{\sqrt{25}} = 16.088 \pm .457 = \mathbf{15.631 \le \mu \le 16.545}$$

$\overline{X} = \mathbf{16.088}$ **Point Estimate**

8.21 $n = 20$ $df = 19$ **95% CI** $t_{.025,19} = 2.093$

$\overline{X} = 2.36116$ $S = 0.19721$

$$2.36116 \pm 2.093 \frac{0.1972}{\sqrt{20}} = 2.36116 \pm 0.0923 = \mathbf{2.26886 \le \mu \le 2.45346}$$

Point Estimate = **2.36116**

Error = **0.0923**

8.23 n=10 $\overline{X} = 49.8$ S = 18.22   df = 10 − 1 = 9

   95% Confidence   α/2=.025 $t_{.025,9} = 2.262$

$$\overline{X} \pm t \frac{S}{\sqrt{n}} = 49.8 \pm 2.262 \frac{18.22}{\sqrt{10}} = 49.8 \pm 13.03 = \mathbf{36.77 \leq \mu \leq 62.83}$$

8.25 a) n = 44 $\hat{p} = .51$ 99% C.I. $Z_{.005} = 2.575$

$$\hat{p} \pm Z \sqrt{\frac{\hat{p} \cdot \hat{q}}{n}} = .51 \pm 2.575 \sqrt{\frac{(.51)(.49)}{44}} = .51 \pm .194 = \mathbf{.316 \leq P \leq .704}$$

b) n = 300 $\hat{p} = .82$ 95% C.I. $Z_{.025} = 1.96$

$$\hat{p} \pm Z \sqrt{\frac{\hat{p} \cdot \hat{q}}{n}} = .82 \pm 1.96 \sqrt{\frac{(.82)(.18)}{300}} = .82 \pm .043 = \mathbf{.777 \leq P \leq .863}$$

c) n=1150 $\hat{p} = .48$ 90% C.I. $Z_{.05} = 1.645$

$$\hat{p} \pm Z \sqrt{\frac{\hat{p} \cdot \hat{q}}{n}} = .48 \pm 1.645 \sqrt{\frac{(.48)(.52)}{1150}} = .48 \pm .024 = \mathbf{.456 \leq P \leq .504}$$

d) n=95 $\hat{p} = .32$ 88% C.I. $Z_{.06} = 1.555$

$$\hat{p} \pm Z \sqrt{\frac{\hat{p} \cdot \hat{q}}{n}} = .32 \pm 1.555 \sqrt{\frac{(.32)(.68)}{95}} = .32 \pm .074 = \mathbf{.246 \leq P \leq .394}$$

8.27   n=85   X=40   90% C.I. $Z_{.05} = 1.645$

$$\hat{p} = \frac{x}{n} = \frac{40}{85} = .47$$

$$\hat{p} \pm Z\sqrt{\frac{\hat{p} \cdot \hat{q}}{n}} = .47 \pm 1.645\sqrt{\frac{(.47)(.53)}{85}} = .47 \pm .09 = \mathbf{.38 \leq P \leq .56}$$

95% C.I. $Z_{.025} = 1.96$

$$\hat{p} \pm Z\sqrt{\frac{\hat{p} \cdot \hat{q}}{n}} = .47 \pm 1.96\sqrt{\frac{(.47)(.53)}{85}} = .47 \pm .106 = \mathbf{.364 \leq P \leq .576}$$

99% C.I. $Z_{.005} = 2.575$

$$\hat{p} \pm Z\sqrt{\frac{\hat{p} \cdot \hat{q}}{n}} = .47 \pm 2.575\sqrt{\frac{(.47)(.53)}{85}} = .47 \pm .14 = \mathbf{.33 \leq P \leq .61}$$

All things being constant, as the confidence increased, the width of the interval increased.

8.29   n = 560 $\hat{p} = .47$ 95% CI $Z_{.025} = 1.96$

$$\hat{p} \pm Z\sqrt{\frac{\hat{p} \cdot \hat{q}}{n}} = .47 \pm 1.96\sqrt{\frac{(.47)(.53)}{560}} = .47 \pm .0413 = \mathbf{.4287 \leq P \leq .5113}$$

n = 560 $\hat{p} = .28$ 90% CI $Z_{.05} = 1.645$

$$\hat{p} \pm Z\sqrt{\frac{\hat{p} \cdot \hat{q}}{n}} = .28 \pm 1.645\sqrt{\frac{(.28)(.72)}{560}} = .28 \pm .0312 = \mathbf{.2488 \leq P \leq .3112}$$

8.31   n = 3481   X=927

$$\hat{p} = \frac{x}{n} = \frac{927}{3481} = .266$$

a) $\hat{p} = .266$ **Point Estimate**

b) 99% C.I. $Z_{.005} = 2.575$

$$\hat{p} \pm Z\sqrt{\frac{\hat{p} \cdot \hat{q}}{n}} = .266 \pm 2.575\sqrt{\frac{(.266)(.734)}{3481}} = .266 \pm .02 =$$

.246 ≤ P ≤ .286

8.33 $\hat{p} = .63$ n = 672 95% Confidence $Z = \pm 1.96$

$$\hat{p} \pm Z\sqrt{\frac{\hat{p} \cdot \hat{q}}{n}} = .63 \pm 1.96\sqrt{\frac{(.63)(.37)}{672}} = .63 \pm .0365 = \mathbf{.5935 \leq P \leq .6665}$$

8.35   n = 16 $S^2 = 37.18333$

For 98% C.I., $\alpha = .02$ and $\alpha/2 = .01$ df = 16 – 1 = 15

$\chi^2_{.99,15} = 5.22935$ $\chi^2_{.01,15} = 30.5779$

$$\frac{(16-1)(37.18333)}{30.5779} \leq \sigma^2 \leq \frac{(16-1)(37.18333)}{5.22935}$$

18.24 ≤ σ² ≤ 106.66

Point Estimate = $S^2 = 37.18333$

8.37 $n = 152 \; S^2 = 3.067$ 99% C.I. $df = 15 - 1 = 14$

$\chi^2_{.995,14} = 4.07468$ $\chi^2_{.005,14} = 31.3193$

$$\frac{(15-1)(3.067)}{31.3193} \le \sigma^2 \le \frac{(15-1)(3.067)}{24.07468}$$

$1.37 \le \sigma^2 \le 10.54$

8.39 a) $\sigma = 36$ $E = 5$ 95% Confidence $Z_{.025} = 1.96$

$$n = \frac{Z^2\sigma^2}{E^2} = \frac{(1.96)^2(36)^2}{5^2} = 199.15$$

Sample 200

b) $\sigma = 4.13$ $E = 1$ 99% Confidence $Z_{.005} = 2.575$

$$n = \frac{Z^2\sigma^2}{E^2} = \frac{(2.575)^2(4.13)^2}{1^2} = 113.1$$

Sample 114

c) $W = 4$ $\sigma = 17$ 90% confidence $Z_{.05} = 1.645$

$$n = \frac{4Z^2\sigma^2}{W^2} = \frac{4(1.645)^2(17)^2}{4^2} = 195.5$$

Sample 196

d) $E = 10$ Range $= 500 - 80 = 420$

1/4 Range $= (.25)(420) = 105$

90% Confidence $Z_{.05} = 1.645$

$$n = \frac{Z^2\sigma^2}{E^2} = \frac{(1.645)^2(105)^2}{10^2} = 298.3$$

Sample 299

e) E=3   Range = 108 - 50 = 58

1/4 Range = (.25)(58) = 14.5

88% Confidence $Z_{.06} = 1.555$

$$n = \frac{Z^2\sigma^2}{E^2} = \frac{(1.555)^2(14.5)^2}{3^2} = 56.5$$

Sample 57

f) W = 5   Range = 52 - 10 = 42

$\sigma = 1/4$ range = (.25)(42) = 10.5

98% confidence, $Z_{01} = 2.33$

$$n = \frac{4Z^2\sigma^2}{W^2} = \frac{4(2.33)^2(10.5)^2}{5^2} = 95.8$$

Sample 96

8.41   E = \$200 $\sigma = \$1,000$ 99% Confidence $Z_{.005} = 2.575$

$$n = \frac{Z^2\sigma^2}{E^2} = \frac{(2.575)^2(1000)^2}{200^2} = 165.77$$

Sample 166

8.43   W=\$200   Range = \$2,500 - \$600 = \$1,900

$\sigma \approx 1/4$ Range = (.25)(\$1,900) = \$475

90% Confidence $Z_{.05} = 1.645$

$$n = \frac{4Z^2\sigma^2}{W^2} = \frac{4(1.645)^2(475)^2}{200^2} = 61.05$$

Sample 62

8.45   P=.50   Q=.50   W=.10

95% Confidence, $Z_{.025} = 1.96$

$$n = \frac{4Z^2 P \cdot Q}{W^2} = \frac{4(1.96)^2(.50)(.50)}{(.10)^2} = 384.16$$

Sample 385

8.47 $\overline{X} = 45.6$ S = 7.7467   n = 35

80% confidence $Z_{.10} = 1.28$

$$\overline{X} \pm Z \frac{S}{\sqrt{n}} = 45.6 \pm 1.28 \frac{7.7467}{\sqrt{35}} = 45.6 \pm 1.676$$

43.924 $\leq \mu \leq$ 47.276

94% confidence $Z_{.03} = 1.88$

$$\overline{X} \pm Z \frac{S}{\sqrt{n}} = 45.6 \pm 1.88 \frac{7.7467}{\sqrt{35}} = 45.6 \pm 2.462$$

43.138 $\leq \mu \leq$ 48.062

98% confidence $Z_{.01} = 2.33$

$$\overline{X} \pm Z \frac{S}{\sqrt{n}} = 45.6 \pm 2.33 \frac{7.7467}{\sqrt{35}} = 45.6 \pm 3.051$$

42.549 $\leq \mu \leq$ 48.651

8.49 a) n = 715   X = 329

$$\hat{p} = \frac{329}{715} = .46$$

95% confidence $Z_{.025} = 1.96$

$$\hat{p} \pm Z\sqrt{\frac{\hat{p} \cdot \hat{q}}{n}} = .46 \pm 1.96\sqrt{\frac{(.46)(.54)}{715}} = .46 \pm .0365$$

.4235 $\leq$ P $\leq$ .4965

b) n = 284 $\hat{p} = .71$ 90% confidence $Z_{.05} = 1.645$

$$\hat{p} \pm Z\sqrt{\frac{\hat{p} \cdot \hat{q}}{n}} = .71 \pm 1.645\sqrt{\frac{(.71)(.29)}{284}} = .71 \pm .0443$$

.6657 $\leq$ P $\leq$ .7543

c) n = 1250 $\hat{p} = .48$ 95% confidence $Z_{.025} = 1.96$

$$\hat{p} \pm Z\sqrt{\frac{\hat{p} \cdot \hat{q}}{n}} = .48 \pm 1.96\sqrt{\frac{(.48)(.52)}{1250}} = .48 \pm .0277$$

.4523 $\leq$ P $\leq$ .5077

d) n = 457   X = 270   98% confidence $Z_{.01} = 2.33$

$$\hat{p} = \frac{270}{457} = .591$$

$$\hat{p} \pm Z\sqrt{\frac{\hat{p} \cdot \hat{q}}{n}} = .591 \pm 2.33\sqrt{\frac{(.591)(.409)}{457}} = .591 \pm .0536$$

.5374 $\leq$ P $\leq$ .6446

8.51 a) $\sigma = 44$ $E = 3$ 95% confidence $Z_{.025} = 1.96$

$$n = \frac{Z^2 \sigma^2}{E^2} = \frac{(1.96)^2 (44)^2}{3^2} = 826.4$$

Sample 827

b) $W = 4$ Range $= 88 - 20 = 68$

use $= 1/4(\text{range}) = (.25)(68) = 17$

90% confidence $Z_{.05} = 1.645$

$$\frac{4Z^2 \sigma^2}{W^2} = \frac{4(1.645)^2 (17)^2}{4^2} = 195.5$$

Sample 196

c) $E = .04$ $P = .50$ $Q = .50$

98% confidence $Z_{.01} = 2.33$

$$\frac{Z^2 P \cdot Q}{E^2} = \frac{(2.33)^2 (.50)(.50)}{(.04)^2} = 848.3$$

Sample 849

d) $W = .06$ $P = .70$ $Q = .30$

95% confidence $Z_{.025} = 1.96$

$$\frac{4Z^2 P \cdot Q}{W^2} = \frac{4(1.96)^2 (.70)(.30)}{(.06)^2} = 896.4$$

Sample 897

8.53   P=.40   W=.06   90% Confidence $Z_{.05} = 1.645$

$$n = \frac{4Z^2 P \cdot Q}{W^2} = \frac{4(1.645)^2 (.40)(.60)}{(.06)^2} = 721.61$$

Sample 722

8.55   n = 45 $\overline{X} = 213$ S = 48

98% Confidence $Z_{.01} = 2.33$

$$\overline{X} \pm Z \frac{S}{\sqrt{n}} = 213 \pm 2.33 \frac{48}{\sqrt{45}} = 213 \pm 16.67$$

196.33 $\leq \mu \leq$ 229.67

8.57 $\sigma = 6$ E=1   98% Confidence $Z_{.98} = 2.33$

$$n = \frac{Z^2 \sigma^2}{E^2} = \frac{(2.33)^2 (6)^2}{1^2} = 195.44$$

Sample 196

8.59   n = 25   S = 21 $\overline{X} = 128$ 98% C.I.   df = 25 − 1 = 24

$t_{.01,24} = 2.492$

Point Estimate = \$128

$$\overline{X} \pm t \frac{S}{\sqrt{n}} = 128 \pm 2.492 \frac{21}{\sqrt{25}} = 128 \pm 10.466$$

117.534 $\leq \mu \leq$ 138.466

Interval Width = 138.466 − 117.534 = 20.932

8.61 $E = \$20$ Range = $\$600 - \$30 = \$570$

1/4 Range = $(.25)(\$570) = \$142.50$

95% Confidence $Z_{.025} = 1.96$

$$n = \frac{Z^2\sigma^2}{E^2} = \frac{(1.96)^2(142.50)^2}{20^2} = 195.02$$

Sample 196

8.63 $n = 90$ $X = 30$ 95% Confidence $Z_{.025} = 1.96$

$$\hat{p} = \frac{x}{n} = \frac{30}{90} = .33$$

$$\hat{p} \pm Z\sqrt{\frac{\hat{p} \cdot \hat{q}}{n}} = .33 \pm 1.96\sqrt{\frac{(.33)(.67)}{90}} = .33 \pm .097$$

.233 $\leq$ P $\leq$ .427

8.65 $n = 27$ $\overline{X} = 4.82$ $S = 0.37$ $df = 26$

95% CI: $t_{.025,26} = 2.056$

$$\overline{X} \pm t\frac{S}{\sqrt{n}} = 4.82 \pm 2.056\frac{0.37}{\sqrt{27}} = 4.82 \pm .1464$$

4.6736 $\leq \mu \leq$ 4.9664

We are 95% confident that μ does not equal 4.50.

8.67 $n = 560$ $\hat{p} = .33$

99% Confidence $Z_{.005} = 2.575$

$$\hat{p} \pm Z \sqrt{\frac{\hat{p} \cdot \hat{q}}{n}} = .33 \pm 2.575 \sqrt{\frac{(.33)(.67)}{560}} = .33 \pm (2.575) = .33 \pm .05$$

.28 $\leq$ P $\leq$ .38

8.69 $n = 27$ $\overline{X} = 2.10$ $S = 0.86$ $df = 27 - 1 = 26$

98% confidence $\alpha/2 = .01$ $t_{.01,26} = 2.479$

$$\overline{X} \pm t \frac{S}{\sqrt{n}} = 2.10 \pm 2.479 \frac{0.86}{\sqrt{27}} = 2.10 \pm (2.479) = 2.10 \pm 0.41$$

1.69 $\leq$ μ $\leq$ 2.51

8.71 $n = 39$ $\overline{X} = 1.294$ $S = 0.205$ 99% Confidence $Z_{.005} = 2.575$

$$\overline{X} \pm Z \frac{S}{\sqrt{n}} = 1.294 \pm 2.575 \frac{0.205}{\sqrt{39}} = 1.294 \pm (2.575) = 1.294 \pm .085$$

1.209 $\leq$ μ $\leq$ 1.379

8.73   The point estimate for the average length of burn of the new bulb is 2208.415 hours. Eighty-four bulbs were included in this study. A 90% confidence interval can be constructed from the information given. The error of the confidence interval is $\pm$ 24.682. Combining this with the point estimate yields the 90% confidence interval of 2208.415 $\pm$ 24.682 = 2183.733 $\leq \mu \leq$ 2233.097.

8.75   A poll of 781 American workers was taken. Of these, 506 drive their cars to work. Thus, the point estimate for the population proportion is 506/781 = .648. A 95% confidence interval to estimate the population proportion shows that we are 95% confident that the actual value lies between .613 and .681. The error of this interval is $\pm$ .034.

Chapter 9
Statistical Inference:
Hypothesis Testing for Single Populations

LEARNING OBJECTIVES

The main objective of Chapter 9 is to help you to learn how to test hypotheses on single populations, thereby enabling you to:

1. Understand the logic of hypothesis testing and know how to establish null and alternate hypotheses.

2. Understand Type I and Type II errors and know how to solve for Type II errors.

3. Use large samples to test hypotheses about a single population mean and a single population proportion.

4. Test hypotheses about a single population mean using small samples when σ is unknown and the population is normally distributed.

5. Test hypotheses about a single population variance.

CHAPTER OUTLINE

KEY WORDS

Alpha(α)

Alternative Hypothesis

Beta(β)

Critical Value

Critical Value Method

Hypothesis Testing

Level of Significance

Nonrejection Region

Null Hypothesis

Observed Significance Level

One-tailed Test

Operating-Characteristic Curve (OC)

p-Value Method

Power

Power Curve

Rejection Region

Two-tailed Test

Type I Error

Type II Error

STUDY QUESTIONS

1. The first step in testing a hypothesis is to establish a(n) _____ hypothesis and a(n) _____ hypothesis.

2. In testing hypotheses, the researcher initially assumes that the _____ hypothesis is true.

3. The region of the distribution in hypothesis testing in which the null hypothesis is rejected is called the _____ region.

4. The rejection and acceptance regions are divided by a point called the _____ value.

5. The portion of the distribution which is not in the rejection region is called the _____ region.

6. The probability of committing a Type I error is called _____.

7. Another name for alpha is _____ _____ _____.

8. When a true null hypothesis is rejected, the researcher has committed a _____ error.

9. When a researcher fails to reject a false null hypothesis, a _____ error has been committed.

10. The probability of committing a Type II error is represented by _____.

11. Power is equal to _____.

12. Whenever hypotheses are established such that the alternative hypothesis is directional, then the researcher is conducting a _____-tailed test.

13. A _____-tailed test is nondirectional.

14. If in testing hypotheses, the researcher uses a method in which the probability of the calculated statistic is compared to alpha to reach a decision, the researcher is using the _____ method.

15. Suppose H_o: $\mu = 95$ and H_a: $\mu \neq 95$. If the sample size is 50 and $\alpha = .05$, the critical value of Z is _____.

16. Suppose H_o: $\mu = 2.36$ and H_a: $\mu < 2.36$. If the sample size is 64 and $\alpha = .01$, the critical value of Z is _____.

17.   Suppose H_o: $\mu = 24.8$ and H_a: $\mu \neq 24.8$. If the sample size is 49 and   = .10, the critical value of Z is _____.

18.   Suppose a researcher is testing a null hypothesis that $\mu = 61$. A random sample of n = 38 is taken resulting in $\overline{X} = 63$ and S = 8.76. The calculated Z value is _____.

19.   Suppose a researcher is testing a null hypothesis that $\mu = 413$. A random sample of n = 70 is taken resulting in $\overline{X} = 405$. The population standard deviation is 34. The calculated Z value is _____.

20.   A researcher is testing a hypothesis of a single mean. The critical Z value for $\alpha = .05$ and a one-tailed test is 1.645. The calculated Z value from sample data is 1.13. The decision made by the researcher based on this information is to _____ the null hypothesis.

21.   A researcher is testing a hypothesis of a single mean. The critical Z value for $\alpha = .05$ and a two-tailed test is ± 1.96. The calculated Z value from sample data is -1.85. The decision made by the researcher based on this information is to _____ the null hypothesis.

22.   A researcher is testing a hypothesis of a single mean. The critical Z value for $\alpha = .01$ and a one-tailed test is -2.33. The calculated Z value from sample data is -2.45. The decision made by the researcher based on this information is to _____ the null hypothesis.

23.   A researcher has a theory that the average age of managers in a particular industry is over 35-years-old. The null hypothesis to conduct a statistical test on this theory would be

_____.

24.   A company produces, among other things, a metal plate that is supposed to have a six inch hole punched in the center. A quality control inspector is concerned that the machine which punches the hole is "out-of-control". In an effort to test this, the inspector is going to gather a sample of metal plates punched by the machine and measure the diameter of the hole. The alternative hypothesis used to statistical test to determine if the machine is out-of-control is _____.

25.   The following hypotheses are being tested:

H_o: $\mu = 4.6$
H_a: $\mu \neq 4.6$

The value of alpha is .05. To test these hypotheses, a random sample of 22 items is selected resulting in a sample mean of 4.1 with a sample standard deviation of 1.8. It can be assumed that this measurement is normally distributed in the population. The degrees of freedom associated with the t test used in this problem are _____.

26.   The critical t value for the problem presented in question 25 is _____.

27.   The problem presented in question 25 contains hypotheses which lead to a _____-tailed test.

28.   The calculated value of t for the problem presented in question 25 is _____.

29.   Based on the results of the calculated t value and the critical table t value, the researcher should _____ the null hypothesis in the problem presented in question 25.

30.   It is believed that the average time to assemble a given product is less than 2 hours. To test this, a sample of 18 assemblies is taken resulting in a sample mean of 1.91 hours with a sample standard deviation of 0.73 hours. Suppose $\alpha = .01$. If a hypothesis test is done on this problem, the table value is _____. The calculated value is _____. The decision is _____.

31.   A political scientist want to statistically test the null hypothesis that her candidate for governor is currently carrying at least 57% of the vote in the state. She has her assistants randomly sample 550 eligible voters in the state by telephone and only 300 declare that they support her candidate. The calculated Z value for this problem is _____.

32.   Problem 31 is a _____-tailed test.

33.   Suppose that the value of alpha for problem 31 is .05. After comparing the calculated value to the critical value, the political scientist decided to _____ the null hypothesis.

34.   A company believes that it controls .27 of the total market share in the South for one of its products. To test this belief, a random sample of 1150 purchases of this product in the South are contracted. 385 of the 1150 purchased this company's brand of the product. If a researcher wants to conduct a statistical test for this problem, the alternative hypothesis would be _____.

35.   The calculated value of Z for problem 34 is _____.

36.   Problem 34 would result in a _____-tailed test.

37.   Suppose that a .01 value of alpha were used in problem 34. The critical value of Z for the problem is _____.

38.   Upon comparing the calculated value of Z to the critical value of Z, it is determined to _____ the null hypothesis in problem 34.

39.   A production process produces parts with a normal variance of 27.3. Engineers are concerned that the process may now be producing parts with greater variance than that. To test this concern, a sample of 9 newly produced parts is taken. The sample standard deviation is 5.93. Let $\alpha = .01$. The null hypothesis for this problem is _____.

40.   The critical table value of σ^2 for problem 39 is _____.

41.   The calculated value of chi-square in problem 39 is _____.

42.   The decision reached for problem 39 is _____.

43.   The null hypothesis for a test is H_0: $\mu = 30$. After taking a sample of 49 items and
       computing a mean and standard deviation, it is decided to fail to reject the null hypothesis.
       Let $\alpha = .05$. Suppose the sample standard deviation is .63. If the null hypothesis is not true
       and if the true alternative hypothesis is 29.6, the value of beta is

       _____.

44.   Suppose the alternative mean in problem 43 is really 29.9, the value of beta is

       _____.

45.   Plotting the power values against the various values of the alternative hypotheses produces
       a _____ curve.

46.   Plotting the values of   against various values of the alternative hypothesis produces a
       _____ curve.

ANSWERS TO STUDY QUESTIONS

1. Null, Alternative

2. Null

3. Rejection

4. Critical

5. Nonrejection Region

6. Alpha

7. Level of Significance

8. Type I

9. Type II

10. Beta

11. $1 - \beta$

12. One

13. Two

14. p-value

15. 1.96

16. -2.33

17. ± 1.645

18. 1.41

19. -1.97

20. Fail to Reject

21. Fail to Reject

22. Reject

23. $\mu = 35$

24. $\mu \neq 6"$

25. 32

26. ± 2.08

27. Two

28. -1.30

29. Fail to Reject

30. $-2.567, -0.52$, Fail to Reject

31. -1.16

32. One

33. Fail to Reject

34. $P \neq .27$

35. 4.95

36. Two

37. ± 2.575

38. Reject

39. H_0: $\sigma^2 = 27.3$

40. 20.0902

41. 10.3047

42. Fail to Reject the Null Hypothesis

43. .0026

44. .7019

45. Power

46. Operating Characteristic

SOLUTIONS TO ODD-NUMBERED PROBLEMS IN CHAPTER 9

9.1 a) H_o: $\mu = 25$
H_a: $\mu \neq 25$

$\overline{X} = 28.1$ $n = 57$ $S = 8.46$ $\alpha = .01$

For two-tail, $\alpha/2 = .005 Z_c = 2.575$

$$Z = \frac{\overline{X} - \mu}{\dfrac{S}{\sqrt{n}}} = \frac{28.1 - 25}{\dfrac{8.46}{\sqrt{57}}} = \mathbf{2.77}$$

calculated $Z = 2.77 > Z_c = 2.575$

Reject the null hypothesis

b) critical mean values:

$$Z_c = \frac{\overline{X}_c - \mu}{\dfrac{S}{\sqrt{n}}}$$

$$\pm 2.575 = \frac{\overline{X}_c - 25}{\dfrac{8.46}{\sqrt{57}}}$$

$\overline{X}_c = 25 \pm 2.885$

$\overline{X}_c = \mathbf{27.885}$ **(upper value)**

$\overline{X}_c = \mathbf{22.115}$ **(lower value)**

9.3 a) H_o: $\mu = 1{,}200$
   H_a: $\mu > 1{,}200$

$\overline{X} = 1{,}215$ \qquad $n = 113$ \qquad $S = 100$ \qquad $\alpha = .10$

For one-tail, $\alpha = .10$ \qquad $Z_c = 1.28$

$$Z = \frac{\overline{X} - \mu}{\dfrac{S}{\sqrt{n}}} = \frac{1{,}215 - 1{,}200}{\dfrac{100}{\sqrt{113}}} = \mathbf{1.59}$$

observed $Z = 1.59 > Z_c = 1.28$

Reject the null hypothesis

b) Probability $\geq$ calculated $Z = 1.59$ is **.0559** which is less than $\alpha = .10$.
   Reject the null hypothesis.

c) Critical mean value:

$$Z_c = \frac{\overline{X}_c - \mu}{\dfrac{S}{\sqrt{n}}}$$

$$1.28 = \frac{\overline{X}_c - 1{,}200}{\dfrac{100}{\sqrt{113}}}$$

$$\overline{X}_c = 1{,}200 + 12.04$$

Since calculated $\overline{X} = 1{,}215$ which is greater than the critical $\overline{X} = 1212.04$, reject the null hypothesis.

9.5 H_0: $\mu = \$424.20$
      H_a: $\mu \neq \$424.20$

$\overline{X} = \$432.69$ $n = 54$ $S = \$33.90$ $\alpha = .05$

2-tailed test, $\alpha/2 = .025$ $Z_{.025} = \pm 1.96$

$$ Z = \frac{\overline{X} - \mu}{\frac{S}{\sqrt{n}}} = \frac{432.69 - 424.20}{\frac{33.90}{\sqrt{54}}} = \mathbf{1.84} $$

Since the observed $Z = 1.85 < Z_{.025} = 1.96$, the decision is to **fail** to reject the null hypothesis.

9.7 H_0: $\mu = 5$
      H_a: $\mu \neq 5$

$\overline{X} = 5.0611$ $n = 42$ $S = 0.2803$ $\alpha = .10$

2-tailed test, $\alpha/2 = .05$ $Z_{.05} = \pm 1.645$

$$ Z = \frac{\overline{X} - \mu}{\frac{S}{\sqrt{n}}} = \frac{5.0611 - 5}{\frac{0.2803}{\sqrt{42}}} = \mathbf{1.41} $$

Since the observed $Z = 1.41 < Z_{.05} = 1.645$, the decision is to **fail to reject** the null hypothesis.

9.9 H_o: $\mu = \$4{,}292$
      H_a: $\mu < \$4{,}292$

$\overline{X} = \$4{,}008$ $n = 55$ $S = \$386$ $\alpha = .01$

For one-tailed test, $\alpha = .01$, $Z_{.01} = -2.33$

$$Z = \frac{\overline{X} - \mu}{\dfrac{S}{\sqrt{n}}} = \frac{\$4{,}008 - \$4{,}292}{\dfrac{\$386}{\sqrt{55}}} = \textbf{-5.46}$$

Since the observed Z = -5.46 < $Z_{.01}$ = -2.33, the decision is to
Reject the null hypothesis

9.11 $n = 20$ $\overline{X} = 16.45$ $S = 3.59$ $df = 20 - 1 = 19$ $\alpha = .05$

H_o: $\mu = 16$
H_a: $\mu \neq 16$

For two-tail test, $\alpha/2 = .025$,   critical $t_{.025,19} = \pm 2.093$

$$t = \frac{\overline{X} - \mu}{\dfrac{S}{\sqrt{n}}} = \frac{16.45 - 16}{\dfrac{3.59}{\sqrt{20}}} = \textbf{0.56}$$

Observed t = 0.56 < $t_{.025,19}$ = 2.093

The decision is to **Fail to reject the null hypothesis**

9.13 $n = 11$ $\overline{X} = 1{,}235.36$ $S = 103.81$ $df = 11 - 1 = 10$ $\alpha = .05$

H_o: $\mu = 1{,}160$
H_a: $\mu > 1{,}160$

For one-tail test, $\alpha = .05$ critical $t_{.05,10} = 1.812$

$$t = \frac{\overline{X} - \mu}{\dfrac{S}{\sqrt{n}}} = \frac{1{,}236.36 - 1{,}160}{\dfrac{103.81}{\sqrt{11}}} = \textbf{2.44}$$

Observed $t = 2.44 > t_{.05,10} = 1.812$

The decision is to **Reject the null hypothesis**

9.15 $n = 12$ $\overline{X} = 1.85083$ $S = .02353$ $df = 12 - 1 = 11$ $\alpha = .10$

H_0: $\mu = 1.84$
H_a: $\mu \neq 1.84$

For a two-tailed test, $\alpha/2 = .05$ critical $t_{.05,11} = 1.796$

$$t = \frac{\overline{X} - \mu}{\dfrac{S}{\sqrt{n}}} = \frac{1.85083 - 1.84}{\dfrac{.02353}{\sqrt{12}}} = \textbf{1.59}$$

Since $t = 1.59 < t_{11,.05} = 1.796$,

The decision is to **fail to reject the null hypothesis**.

9.17 $n = 19$ $\overline{X} = \$31.67$ $S = \$1.29$ $df = 19 - 1 = 18$ $\alpha = .05$

H_0: $\mu = \$32.28$
H_a: $\mu \neq \$32.28$

Two-tailed test, $\alpha/2 = .025$ $t_{.025,18} = \pm 2.101$

$$t = \frac{\overline{X} - \mu}{\frac{S}{\sqrt{n}}} = \frac{31.67 - 32.28}{\frac{1.29}{\sqrt{19}}} = \mathbf{-2.06}$$

The observed $t = -2.06 > t_{.025,18} = -2.101$,

The decision is to **fail to reject the null hypothesis**

9.19 H_0: $P = .45$
        H_a: $P > .45$

$n = 310$ $\hat{p} = .465$ $\alpha = .05$

For one-tail, $\alpha = .05$ $Z_{.05} = 1.645$

$$Z = \frac{\hat{p} - P}{\sqrt{\frac{P \cdot Q}{n}}} = \frac{.465 - .45}{\sqrt{\frac{(.45)(.55)}{310}}} = \mathbf{0.53}$$

observed $Z = 0.53 < Z_{.05} = 1.645$

The decision is to **Fail to reject the null hypothesis**

9.21 H_o: $P = .29$
        H_a: $P \neq .29$

$n = 740 \; X = 207$ $\hat{p} = \dfrac{x}{n} = \dfrac{207}{740} = .28$ $\alpha = .05$

For two-tail, $\alpha/2 = .025$ $Z_{.025} = \pm 1.96$

$$Z = \frac{\hat{p} - P}{\sqrt{\dfrac{P \cdot Q}{n}}} = \frac{.28 - .29}{\sqrt{\dfrac{(.29)(.71)}{740}}} = \mathbf{-0.60}$$

observed $Z = -0.60 > Z_c = -1.96$

The decision is to **Fail to reject the null hypothesis**

Solving for critical values:

$$Z = \frac{\hat{p}_c - P}{\sqrt{\dfrac{P \cdot Q}{n}}}$$

$$\pm 1.96 = \frac{\hat{p}_c - .29}{\sqrt{\dfrac{(.29)(.71)}{740}}}$$

$$\hat{p}_c = .29 \pm .033$$

.257 and .323

Sample $p = \hat{p} = .28$ not outside critical values in tails

Again, the decision is to **Fail to reject the null hypothesis**

_P_-Value Method:

Z = -0.60

from Table A.5, area = .2257

Area in tail = .5000 - .2257 = **.2743**

.2743 > .025

Again, the decision is to **Fail to reject the null hypothesis**

9.23 H_o: P = .79
H_a: P < .79

n = 415   X = 303 α = .01 $Z_{.01}$ = -2.33

$$\hat{p} = \frac{x}{n} = \frac{303}{415} = .7301$$

$$Z = \frac{\hat{p} - P}{\sqrt{\dfrac{P \cdot Q}{n}}} = \frac{7301 - .79}{\sqrt{\dfrac{(.79)(.21)}{415}}} = \mathbf{-3.00}$$

Since the observed Z = -3.00 is less than $Z_{.01}$= -2.33, The decision is to **reject the null hypothesis**.

9.25 H_o: $P = .18$
H_a: $P > .18$

$n = 376$ $\hat{p} = .22$ $\alpha = .01$

one-tailed test, $Z_{.01} = 2.33$

$$Z = \frac{\hat{p} - P}{\sqrt{\dfrac{P \cdot Q}{n}}} = \frac{.22 - .18}{\sqrt{\dfrac{(.18)(.82)}{376}}} = \textbf{2.02}$$

Since the observed $Z = 2.02$ is less than $Z_{.01} = 2.33$, The decision is to **fail to reject the null hypothesis**. There is not enough evidence to declare that the proportion is greater than .18.

9.27 H_o: $P = .47$
H_a: $P \neq .47$

$n = 67$ $X = 40$ $\alpha = .05$ $\alpha/2 = .025$

For a two-tailed test, $Z_{.025} = \pm 1.96$

$$\hat{p} = \frac{x}{n} = \frac{40}{67} = .597$$

$$Z = \frac{\hat{p} - P}{\sqrt{\dfrac{P \cdot Q}{n}}} = \frac{.597 - .47}{\sqrt{\dfrac{(.47)(.53)}{67}}} = \textbf{2.08}$$

Since the observed $Z = 2.08$ is greater than $Z_{.025} = 1.96$, The decision is to **reject the null hypothesis**.

9.29 H_0: $\sigma^2 = 14$ $\alpha = .05$ $\alpha/2 = .025$ $n = 12$ $df = 12 - 1 = 11$ $S^2 = 30.0833$
      H_a: $\sigma^2 \neq 14$

$\chi^2_{.025,11} = 21.92$ $\chi^2_{.975,11} = 3.81575$

$$\chi^2 = \frac{(12-1)(30.0833)}{14} = \mathbf{23.64}$$

Since $\chi^2 = 23.64 < \chi^2_{.025,11} = 21.92$, the decision is to **reject the null hypothesis**.

9.31 H_0: $\sigma^2 = 199{,}996{,}164$ $\alpha = .10$ $\alpha/2 = .05$ $n = 13$ $df = 13 - 1 = 12$
      H_a: $\sigma^2 \neq 199{,}996{,}164$ $S^2 = 832{,}089{,}743.7$

$\chi^2_{.05,12} = 21.0261$ $\chi^2_{.95,12} = 5.22603$

$$\chi^2 = \frac{(13-1)(832{,}089{,}743.7)}{199{,}996{,}164} = \mathbf{49.93}$$

Since $\chi^2 = 49.93 > \chi^2_{.05,12} = 21.0261$, the decision is to **reject the null hypothesis**. The variance has changed.

9.33 H_o: $\mu = 100$
H_a: $\mu < 100$
$n = 48$ $\mu = 99$ $S = 14$

a) $\alpha = .10$ $Z_{.10} = -1.28$

$$Z_c = \frac{\overline{X}_c - \mu}{\frac{S}{\sqrt{n}}}$$

$$-1.28 = \frac{\overline{X}_c - 100}{\frac{14}{\sqrt{48}}}$$

$$\overline{X}_c = 97.4$$

$$Z = \frac{\overline{X}_c - \mu}{\frac{S}{\sqrt{n}}} = \frac{97.4 - 99}{\frac{14}{\sqrt{48}}} = -0.79$$

from Table A.5, area for $Z = -0.79$ is .2852

$\beta = .2852 + .5000 = $ **.7852**

b) $\alpha = .05$ $Z_{.05} = -1.645$

$$Z_c = \frac{\overline{X}_c - \mu}{\frac{S}{\sqrt{n}}}$$

$$-1.645 = \frac{\overline{X}_c - 100}{\frac{14}{\sqrt{48}}}$$

$$\overline{X}_c = 96.68$$

$$Z = \frac{\overline{X}_c - \mu}{\dfrac{S}{\sqrt{n}}} = \frac{96.68 - 99}{\dfrac{14}{\sqrt{48}}} = -1.15$$

from Table A.5, area for $Z = -1.15$ is $.3749$

$\beta = .3749 + .5000 = $ **.8749**

c) $\alpha = .01$ $Z_{.01} = -2.33$

$$Z_c = \frac{\overline{X}_c - \mu}{\dfrac{S}{\sqrt{n}}}$$

$$-2.33 = \frac{\overline{X}_c - 100}{\dfrac{14}{\sqrt{48}}}$$

$\overline{X}_c = 95.29$

$$Z = \frac{\overline{X}_c - \mu}{\dfrac{S}{\sqrt{n}}} = \frac{95.29 - 99}{\dfrac{14}{\sqrt{48}}} = -1.84$$

from Table A.5, area for $Z = -1.84$ is $.4671$

$\beta = .4671 + .5000 = $ **.9671**

d)   As gets smaller (other variables remaining constant), beta gets larger. Decreasing the probability of committing a Type I error increases the probability of committing a Type II error if other variables are held constant.

9.35 H_o: $\mu = 50$
        H_a: $\mu \neq 50$

$\mu_a = 53$ $n = 35$ $S = 7$ $\alpha = .01$

Since this is two-tailed, $\alpha/2 = .005$ $Z_{.005} = \pm 2.575$

$$Z_c = \frac{\overline{X}_c - \mu}{\frac{S}{\sqrt{n}}}$$

$$\pm 2.575 = \frac{\overline{X}_c - 50}{\frac{7}{\sqrt{35}}}$$

$$\overline{X}_c = 50 \pm 3.05$$

46.95 and 53.05

$$Z = \frac{\overline{X}_c - \mu}{\frac{S}{\sqrt{n}}} = \frac{53.05 - 53}{\frac{7}{\sqrt{35}}} = 0.04$$

from Table A.5 for Z = 0.04, area = .0160

Other end:

$$Z = \frac{\overline{X}_c - \mu}{\frac{S}{\sqrt{n}}} = \frac{46.9 - 53}{\frac{7}{\sqrt{35}}} = -5.11$$

Area associated with Z = -5.11 is .5000

$\beta = .5000 + .0160 = \mathbf{.5160}$

9.37 $n = 58$ $\overline{X} = 45.1$ $S = 8.7$ $\alpha = .05$ $\alpha/2 = .025$

H_0: $\mu = 44$
H_a: $\mu \neq 44$ $Z_{.025} = \pm 1.96$

$$Z = \frac{45.1 - 44}{\frac{8.7}{\sqrt{58}}} = 0.96$$

Since $Z = 0.96 < Z_c = 1.96$, the decision is to fail to reject the null hypothesis.

$$\pm 1.96 = \frac{\overline{X}_c - 44}{\frac{8.7}{\sqrt{58}}}$$

$$\pm 2.239 = \overline{X}_c - 44$$

$$\overline{X}_c = 46.239 \text{ and } 41.761$$

For 45 years:

$$Z = \frac{46.29 - 45}{\frac{8.7}{\sqrt{58}}} = 1.08$$

from Table A.5, the area for $Z = 1.08$ is .3599

$\beta = .5000 + .3599 = \mathbf{.8599}$

Power $= 1 - \beta = 1 - .8599 = .1401$

For 46 years:

$$Z = \frac{46.239 - 46}{\frac{8.7}{\sqrt{58}}} = 0.21$$

From Table A.5, the area for $Z = 0.21$ is .0832

$\beta = .5000 + .0832 = \mathbf{.5832}$

Power = 1 - β = 1 - .5832 = .4168

For 47 years:

$$Z = \frac{46.9 - 47}{\frac{8.7}{\sqrt{58}}} = -0.67$$

From Table A.5, the area for Z = -0.67 is .2486

β = .5000 - .2486 = **.2514**

Power = 1 - β = 1 - .2514 = .7486

For 48 years:

$$Z = \frac{46.248 - 48}{\frac{8.7}{\sqrt{58}}} = 1.54$$

From Table A.5, the area for Z = 1.54 is .4382

β = .5000 - .4382 = **.0618**

Power = 1 - β = 1 - .0618 = .9382

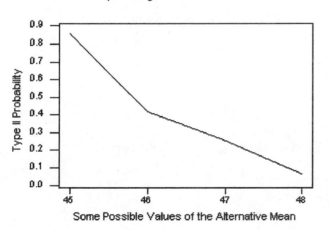

Operating Characteristic Curve

Some Possible Values of the Alternative Mean

Power Curve

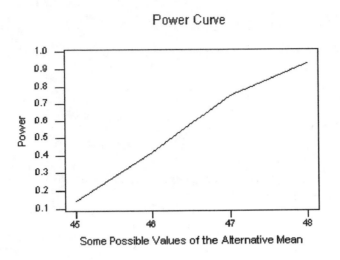

Some Possible Values of the Alternative Mean

9.39

1) H_o: $\mu = 36$
   H_a: $\mu \neq 36$

2) $Z = \dfrac{\overline{X} - \mu}{\dfrac{S}{\sqrt{n}}}$

3) $\alpha = .01$

4) two-tailed test, $\alpha/2 = .005$, $Z_{.005} = \pm 2.575$
   If the observed value of Z is greater than 2.575 or less than -2.575, the decision will be to reject the null hypothesis.

5) $n = 63$, $\overline{X} = 38.4$, $S = 5.93$

6) $Z = \dfrac{\overline{X} - \mu}{\dfrac{S}{\sqrt{n}}} = \dfrac{38.4 - 36}{\dfrac{5.93}{\sqrt{63}}} = \mathbf{3.21}$

7) Since the observed value of $Z = 3.21$ is greater than $Z_{.005} = 2.575$, the decision is to **reject the null hypothesis.**

8) The mean is likely to be greater than 36.

9.41   a.   1) H_o: P = .28
H_a: P > .28

2) $Z = \dfrac{\hat{p} - P}{\sqrt{\dfrac{P \cdot Q}{n}}}$

3) α = .10

4) This is a one-tailed test, $Z_{.10}$ = 1.28. If the observed value of Z is greater than 1.28, the decision will be to reject the null hypothesis.

5) n = 783   X = 230

$\hat{p} = \dfrac{230}{783} = .2937$

6) $Z = \dfrac{.2937 - .28}{\sqrt{\dfrac{(.28)(.72)}{783}}} = \mathbf{0.85}$

7) Since **Z = 0.85** is less than $Z_{.10}$ = 1.28, the decision is to **fail to reject the null hypothesis**.

8) There is not enough evidence to declare that P is not .28.

b.   1) H_o: P = .61
H_a: P ≠ .61

2) $Z = \dfrac{\hat{p} - P}{\sqrt{\dfrac{P \cdot Q}{n}}}$

3) α = .05

4) This is a two-tailed test, $Z_{.025}$ = ± 1.96. If the observed value of Z is greater than 1.96 or less than -1.96, then the decision will be to reject the null hypothesis.

5) n = 401 $\hat{p}$ = .56

6) $Z = \dfrac{.56 - .61}{\sqrt{\dfrac{(.61)(.39)}{401}}} = \mathbf{-2.05}$

7) Since Z = -2.05 is less than $Z_{.025}$ = -1.96, the decision is to **reject the null hypothesis.**

8) The population proportion is not likely to be .61.

9.43 a) H_0: $\mu = 130$
H_a: $\mu > 130$

n = 75 $\sigma = 12$ $\alpha = .01$ $Z_{.01} = 2.33$ $\mu_a = 135$

Solving for $\overline{X}_c$:

$$Z_c = \dfrac{\overline{X}_c - \mu}{\dfrac{\sigma}{\sqrt{n}}}$$

$$2.33 = \dfrac{\overline{X}_c - 130}{\dfrac{12}{\sqrt{75}}}$$

$$\overline{X}_c = 133.23$$

$$Z = \dfrac{133.23 - 135}{\dfrac{12}{\sqrt{75}}} = -1.28$$

from table A.5, area for Z = -1.28 is .3997

$\beta = .5000 - .3997 = \mathbf{.1003}$

b) H_0: $P = .44$
    H_a: $P < .44$

   $n = 1095$ $\alpha = .05$ $P_a = .42$ $Z_{.05} = -1.645$

$$Z_c = \frac{\hat{p}_c - P}{\sqrt{\dfrac{P \cdot Q}{n}}}$$

$$-1.645 = \frac{\hat{p}_c - .44}{\sqrt{\dfrac{(.44)(.56)}{1095}}}$$

$$\hat{p}_c = .4153$$

$$Z = \frac{.4153 - .42}{\sqrt{\dfrac{(.42)(.58)}{1095}}} = \mathbf{-0.32}$$

from table A.5, area for Z = -0.32 is .1255

$\beta = .5000 + .1255 = \mathbf{.6255}$

9.45 $\overline{X} = 3.45$ $n = 64$ $\sigma^2 = 1.31$ $\alpha = .05$

   H_o: $\mu = 3.3$
   H_a: $\mu \neq 3.3$

   For two-tail, $\alpha/2 = .025$ $Z_c = \pm 1.96$

$$Z = \frac{\overline{X} - \mu}{\dfrac{\sigma}{\sqrt{n}}} = \frac{3.45 - 3.3}{\dfrac{\sqrt{1.31}}{\sqrt{64}}} = \mathbf{1.05}$$

Since the observed Z = 1.05 < Z_c = 1.96, the decision is to **Fail to reject the null hypothesis**.

9.47 H_0: $\sigma^2 = 16$ $n = 12$ $\sigma = .05$ $df = 12 - 1 = 11$
       H_a: $\sigma^2 > 16$

   $S = 0.4987864$ ft. $= 5.98544$ in.

   $\chi^2_{.05,11} = 19.6751$

   $$\chi^2 = \frac{(12-1)(5.98544)^2}{16} = \mathbf{24.63}$$

   Since $\chi^2 = 24.63 > \chi^2_{.05,11} = 19.6751$, the decision is to **reject the null**   **hypothesis.**

9.49 $\overline{X} = \$26,650$ $n = 100$ $S = \$12,000$

   a) H_0: $\mu = \$25,000$
       H_a: $\mu > \$25,000$ $\alpha = .05$

   For one-tail, $\alpha = .05$ $Z_{.05} = 1.645$

   $$Z = \frac{\overline{X} - \mu}{\frac{S}{\sqrt{n}}} = \frac{26,650 - 25,000}{\frac{12,000}{\sqrt{100}}} = \mathbf{1.38}$$

   Since the observed $Z = 1.38 < Z_{.05} = 1.645$, the decision is to **fail to reject the null hypothesis**.

   b) $\mu_a = \$30,000$ $Z_c = 1.645$

   Solving for $\overline{X}_c$:

   $$Z_c = \frac{\overline{X}_c - \mu}{\frac{S}{\sqrt{n}}}$$

$$1.645 = \frac{(\overline{X}_c - 25,000}{\frac{12,000}{\sqrt{100}}}$$

$$\overline{X}_c = 25,000 + 1,974 = 26,974$$

$$Z = \frac{26,974 - 30,000}{\frac{12,000}{\sqrt{100}}} = \textbf{-2.52}$$

from Table A.5, the area for Z = -2.52 is .4941

β = .5000 - .4941 = **.0059**

9.51 H_0: P = .46
H_a: P > .46

n = 125 X = 66 α = .05 $\hat{p} = \frac{X}{n} = \frac{66}{125} = .528$

Using a one-tailed test, $Z_{.05}$ = 1.645

$$Z = \frac{\hat{p} - P}{\sqrt{\frac{P \cdot Q}{n}}} = \frac{.528 - .46}{\sqrt{\frac{(.46)(.54)}{125}}} = \textbf{1.53}$$

Since the observed value of Z = 1.53 < $Z_{.05}$ = 1.645, the decision is to **fail to reject the null hypothesis**.

Solving for $\hat{p}_c$:

$$Z_c = \frac{\hat{p}_c - P}{\sqrt{\dfrac{P \cdot Q}{n}}}$$

$$1.645 = \frac{\hat{p}_c - .46}{\sqrt{\dfrac{(.46)(.54)}{125}}}$$

$$\hat{p}_c = .533$$

$$Z = \frac{\hat{p}_c - P_a}{\sqrt{\dfrac{P_a \cdot Q_a}{n}}} = \frac{.533 - .50}{\sqrt{\dfrac{(.50)(.50)}{125}}} = \mathbf{0.74}$$

from Table A.5, the area for $Z = 0.74$ is .2704

$$\beta = .5000 + .2704 = \mathbf{.7704}$$

9.53 H_0: $P = .16$
       H_a: $P > .16$

$n = 428$ $X = 84$ $\alpha = .01$ $\hat{p} = \dfrac{X}{n} = \dfrac{84}{428} = .1963$

For a one-tailed test, $Z_{.01} = 2.33$

$$Z = \frac{\hat{p} - P}{\sqrt{\dfrac{P \cdot Q}{n}}} = \frac{.1963 - .16}{\sqrt{\dfrac{(.16)(.84)}{428}}} = \mathbf{2.05}$$

Since the observed $Z = 2.05 < Z_{.01} = 2.33$, the decision is to **fail to reject the null hypothesis**.

The probability of committing a Type I error is **.01**.

Solving for $\hat{p}_c$:

$$Z_c = \frac{\hat{p}_c - P}{\sqrt{\dfrac{P \cdot Q}{n}}}$$

$$2.33 = \frac{\hat{p}_c - .16}{\sqrt{\dfrac{(.16)(.84)}{428}}}$$

$$\hat{p}_c = .2013$$

$$Z = \frac{\hat{p}_c - P_a}{\sqrt{\dfrac{P_a \cdot Q_a}{n}}} = \frac{.2013 - .21}{\sqrt{\dfrac{(.21)(.79)}{428}}} = \textbf{-0.44}$$

from Table A.5, the area for $Z = -0.44$ is .1700

$\beta = .5000 - .1700 = \textbf{.3300}$

9.55 H_0: $\sigma^2 = 16$ $n = 22$ $df = 22 - 1 = 21$ $S = 6$ $\alpha = .05$

   H_a: $\sigma^2 > 16$

$\chi^2_{.05,21} = 32.6705$

$$\chi^2 = \frac{(22-1)(6)^2}{16} = \textbf{47.25}$$

Since the observed $\chi^2 = 47.25 > \chi^2_{.05,21} = 32.6705$, the decision is to **reject the null hypothesis**.

9.57 a) H_o: $\mu = 23.58$
H_a: $\mu \neq 23.58$

$n = 95$ $\overline{X} = 22.83$ $S = 5.11$ $\alpha = .05$

Since this is a two-tailed test and using $\alpha/2 = .025$: $Z_{.025} = \pm 1.96$

$$Z = \frac{\overline{X} - \mu}{\frac{S}{\sqrt{n}}} = \frac{22.83 - 23.58}{\frac{5.11}{\sqrt{95}}} = \textbf{-1.43}$$

Since the observed $Z = -1.43 > Z_{.025} = -1.96$, the decision is to **fail to reject the null hypothesis**.

b) $$Z_c = \frac{\overline{X}_c - \mu}{\frac{S}{\sqrt{n}}}$$

$$\pm 1.96 = \frac{\overline{X}_c - 23.58}{\frac{5.11}{\sqrt{95}}}$$

$\overline{X}_c = 23.58 \pm 1.03$

$\overline{X}_c = 22.55, \ 24.61$

for H_a: $\mu = 22.30$

$$Z = \frac{\overline{X}_c - \mu_a}{\frac{S}{\sqrt{n}}} = \frac{22.55 - 22.30}{\frac{5.11}{\sqrt{95}}} = \textbf{0.48}$$

$$Z = \frac{\overline{X}_c - \mu_a}{\frac{S}{\sqrt{n}}} = \frac{24.61 - 22.30}{\frac{5.11}{\sqrt{95}}} = \textbf{4.41}$$

from Table A.5, the areas for $Z = 0.48$ and $Z = 4.41$ are   .1844 and .5000

$\beta = .5000 - .1844 = \textbf{.3156}$

The upper tail has no effect on β.

9.59   The sample size is 22. $\overline{X}$ is 4.03   S = 0.92   df = 21

The test statistic is:

$$t = \frac{\overline{X} - \mu}{\dfrac{S}{\sqrt{n}}}$$

The observed t = -1.89. The p-value is .037.

The results are statistical significant at   = .05.

The decision is to reject the null hypothesis.

9.61 H_0: μ = 2.51
H_a: μ > 2.51

This is a one-tailed test. The sample mean is 2.528138 which is more than the hypothesized value. The observed t value is 0.418896 with an associated p-value of .339366 for a one-tailed test. Because the p-value is greater than α = .05 or even α = .10, the decision is to fail to reject the null hypothesis. There is not enough evidence to conclude that beef prices are higher.

Chapter 10
Statistical Inferences About Two Populations

LEARNING OBJECTIVES

The general focus of Chapter 10 is on testing hypotheses and constructing confidence intervals about parameters from two populations, thereby enabling you to

1. Test hypotheses and construct confidence intervals about the difference in two population means using data from large samples.

2. Test hypotheses and establish confidence intervals about the difference in two population means using data from small samples when the population variances are unknown and the populations are normally distributed.

3. Test hypotheses and construct confidence intervals about the difference in two related populations when the differences are normally distributed.

4. Test hypotheses and construct confidence intervals about the difference in two population proportions.

5. Test hypotheses and construct confidence intervals about two population variances when the two populations are normally distributed.

CHAPTER OUTLINE

10.1   Hypothesis Testing and Confidence Intervals about the Difference in Two Means: Large
       Samples or Variances Known, Independent Samples

      Hypothesis Testing

      Confidence Intervals

      Using the Computer to Test Hypotheses and Construct Confidence
      Intervals about the Difference in Two Population Means Using the Z Test

10.2   Hypothesis Testing and Confidence Intervals about the Difference in Two Means: Small
       Independent Samples and Population Variances Unknown

      Hypothesis Testing

      Using the Computer to Test Hypotheses and Construct Confidence
      Intervals about the Difference in Two Population Means Using the t Test

      Confidence Intervals

10.3   Statistical Inferences For Two Related Populations

      Hypothesis Testing

      Using the Computer to Make Statistical Inferences about Two Related
      Populations

      Confidence Intervals

10.4   Statistical Inferences About Two Population Proportions

      Hypothesis Testing

      Confidence Intervals

      Using the Computer to Analyze the Difference in Two Proportions

10.5   Testing Hypotheses About Two Population Variances

      Using the Computer to Test Hypotheses about Two Population Variances

KEY WORDS

Dependent Samples
F Distribution
F Value
Independent Samples

Matched-Pairs Data
Matched-Pairs Test
Paired Data
Related Measures

STUDY QUESTIONS

1. A researcher wants to estimate the difference in the means of two populations. A random sample of 40 items from the first population results in a sample mean of 433 with a sample standard deviation of 112. A random sample of 50 items from the second population results in a sample mean of 467 with a sample standard deviation of 120. From this information, a point estimate of the difference of population means can be computed as

    _____ .

2. Using the information from question 1, the researcher can compute a 95% confidence interval to estimate the difference in population means. The resulting confidence interval is

    _____ .

3. A random sample of 32 items is taken from a population which has a population variance of 93. The resulting sample mean is 45.6. A random sample of 37 items is taken from a population which has a population variance of 88. The resulting sample mean is 49.4. Using this information, a 98% confidence interval can be computed to estimate the difference in means of these two populations. The resulting interval is

    _____ .

4. A researcher desires to estimate the difference in means of two populations. To accomplish this, he/she takes a random sample of 85 items from the first population. The sample yields a mean of 168 with a variance of 783. A random sample of 70 items is taken from the second population yielding a mean of 161 with a variance of 780. A 94% confidence interval is computed to estimate the difference in population means. The resulting confidence interval is _____ .

5. Is there a difference in the average number years of experience of assembly line employees between company A and company B? A researcher wants to conduct a statistical test to answer this question. He is likely to be conducting a _____ -tailed test.

6.   The researcher who is conducting the test to determine if there is a difference in the average number of years of experience of assembly line workers between companies A and B is using an alpha of .10. The critical value of Z for this problem is _____.

7.   Suppose the researcher conducting an experiment to compare the ages of workers at two companies. The researcher randomly samples forty-five assembly-line workers from company A and discovers that the sample average is 7.1 years with a sample standard deviation of 2.3. Fifty-two assembly-line workers from company B are randomly selected resulting in a sample average of 6.2 years and a sample standard deviation of 2.7. The calculated Z value for this problem is _____.

8.   Using an alpha of .10 and the critical values determined in questions 6 and 7, the decision is to _____ the null hypothesis.

9.   A researcher has a theory that the mean for population A is less than the mean for population B. To test this, she randomly samples thirty-eight items from population A and determines that the sample average is 38.4 with a variance of 50.5 She randomly samples thirty-two items from population B and determines that the sample average is 44.3 with a variance of 48.6 Alpha is .05. She is going to conduct a _____-tailed test.

10.   Using the information from question 9, the critical Z value is _____.

11.   Using the information from question 9, the calculated value of Z is _____.

12.   Using the results determined in question 10 and 11, the decision is to _____ the null hypothesis.

13.   A researcher is interested in testing to determine if the mean of population one is greater than the mean of population two. He uses the following hypotheses to test this theory:

$$H_o: \mu_1 - \mu_2 = 0$$
$$H_a: \mu_1 - \mu_2 > 0$$

He randomly selects a sample of 8 items from population one resulting in a mean of 14.7 and a standard deviation of 3.4. He randomly selects a sample of 12 items from population two resulting in a mean of 11.5 and a standard deviation 2.9. He is using an alpha value of .10 to conduct this test. The degrees of freedom for this problem are _____. It is assumed that these values are normally distributed in both populations.

14.   The critical table t value used to conduct the hypothesis test in question 13 is

_____.

15.   The t value calculated from the sample data is _____.

16.   Based on the calculated t value obtained in question 15 and the critical table t value in question 14, the researcher should _____ the null hypothesis.

17.   What is the difference in the means of two populations? A researcher wishes to determine this by taking random samples of size 14 from each population and computing a 90% confidence interval. The sample from the first population produces a mean of 780 with a standard deviation of 245. The sample from the second population produces a mean of 890 with a standard deviation of 256. The point estimate for the difference in the means of these two populations is _____. Assume that the values are normally distributed in each population.

18.   The table t value used to construct the confidence interval for the problem in question 17 is

    _____.

19.   The confidence interval constructed for the problem in question 17 is _____.

20.   The matched-pairs t test deals with _____ samples.

21.   A researcher wants to conduct a before/after study on 13 subjects to determine if a treatment results in higher scores. The hypotheses are:

$$H_o: \ D = 0$$
$$H_a: \ D < 0$$

Scores are obtained on the subjects both before and after the treatment. After subtracting the after scores from the before scores, the resulting value of $\overline{d}$ is -2.85 with a S_d of 1.01. The degrees of freedom for this test are _____. Assume that the data are normally distributed in the population.

22.   The critical table t value for the problem in question 21 is _____ if $\alpha = .01$.

23.   The calculated t value for the problem in question 21 is _____.

24.   For the problem in question 21 based on the critical table t value obtained in question 22 and the calculated t value obtained in question 23, the decision should be to _____ the null hypothesis.

25.   A researcher is conducting a matched-pairs study. She gathers data on each pair in the study resulting in:

Pair	Group 1	Group 2
1	10	12
2	13	14
3	11	15
4	14	14
5	12	11
6	12	15
7	10	16
8	8	10

Assuming that the data are normally distributed in the population, the computed value of $\bar{d}$ is _____.

26.   The value of S_d for the problem in question 25 is _____.

27.   The degrees of freedom for the problem in question 25 is _____.

28.   The calculated value of t for the problem in question 25 is _____.

29.   A researcher desires to estimate the difference between two related populations. He gathers pairs of data from the populations. The data are below:

Pair	Group 1	Group 2
1	360	280
2	345	290
3	355	300
4	325	270
5	340	300
6	365	310

It is assumed that the data are normally distributed in the population. Using this data, the value of $\bar{d}$ is _____.

30.   For the problem in 29, the value of S_d is _____.

31.   The point estimate for the population difference for the problem in question 29 is _____.

32.   The researcher conducting the study for the problem in question 29 wants to use a 95% level of confidence. The table t value for this confidence interval is _____.

33.   The confidence interval computed for the problem in question 29 is _____.

34.   A researcher is interested in estimating the difference in two populations proportions. A sample of 1000 from each population results in sample proportions of .61 and .64. The point estimate of the difference in the population proportions is _____.

35.   Using the data from question 34, the researcher computes a 90% confidence interval to estimate the difference in population proportions. The resulting confidence interval is

       _____.

36.   A random sample of 400 items from a population shows that 110 of the sample items possess a given characteristic. A random sample of 550 items from a second population resulted in 154 of the sample items possessing the characteristic. Using this data, a 99% confidence interval is constructed to estimate the difference in population proportions which possess the given characteristic. The resulting confidence interval is

       _____.

37.   A researcher desires to estimate the difference in proportions of two populations. To accomplish this, he/she samples 338 and 332 items respectively from each population. The resulting sample proportions are .71 and .68 respectively. Using this data, a 90% confidence interval can be computed to estimate the difference in population proportions. The resulting confidence interval is _____.

38.   A statistician is being asked to test a new theory that the proportion of population A possessing a given characteristic is greater than the proportion of population B possessing the characteristic. A random sample of 625 from population A has been taken and it is determined that 463 possess the characteristic. A random sample of 704 taken from population B results in 428 possessing the characteristic. The alternative hypothesis for this problem is _____.

39.   The calculated value of Z for question 38 is _____.

40.   Suppose alpha is .10. The critical value of Z for question 38 is _____.

41.   Based on the results of question 39 and 40, the decision for the problem in question 38 is to _____ the null hypothesis.

42.   In testing hypotheses about two population variances, use the _____ distribution.

43.   Suppose we want to test the following hypothesis:

       $H_0: \sigma_1^2 = \sigma_2^2$ and $H_a: \sigma_1^2 > \sigma_2^2$

       A sample of 9 items from population one yielded a sample standard deviation of 8.6.
       A sample of 8 items from population two yielded a sample standard deviation of 6.9.
       If alpha is .05, the critical F value is _____.

44.   The calculated F value for question 45 is _____. The resulting decision is _____.

ANSWERS TO STUDY QUESTIONS

1. -34

2. $-82.07 \leq \mu_1 - \mu_2 \leq 14.07$

3. $-9.16 \leq \mu_1 - \mu_2 \leq 1.56$

4. $-1.48 \leq \mu_1 - \mu_2 \leq 15.48$

5. Two

6. ± 1.645

7. 1.77

8. Reject

9. One

10. -1.645

11. -3.50

12. Reject

13. 18

14. 1.33

15. 2.26

16. Reject

17. -110

18. 1.706

19. $-271.56 \leq \mu_1 - \mu_2 \leq 51.56$

20. Related

21. 12

22. -2.681

23. -10.17

24. Reject

25. -2.125

26. 2.232

27. 7

28. -2.69

29. 56.67

30. 12.91

31. 56.67

32. 2.571

33. $43.12 \leq D \leq 70.22$

34. $-.03$

35. $-.066 \leq P_1 - P_2 \leq .006$

36. $-.081 \leq P_1 - P_2 \leq .071$

37. $-.0285 \leq P_1 - P_2 \leq .0885$

38. $P_A - P_B > 0$

39. 5.14

40. 1.28

41. Reject

42. F

43. 3.73

44. 1.55, Fail to Reject the Null Hypothesis

SOLUTIONS TO ODD-NUMBERED PROBLEMS IN CHAPTER 10

10.1
	Sample 1	Sample 2

$\overline{X}_1 = 51.3$ $\overline{X}_2 = 53.2$

$S^2_1 = 52$ $S^2_2 = 60$

$n_1 = 32$ $n_2 = 32$

a) H_o: $\mu_1 - \mu_2 = 0$

   H_a: $\mu_1 - \mu_2 < 0$

For one-tail test, $\alpha = .10$ $Z_{.10} = -1.28$

$$Z = \frac{(\overline{X}_1 - \overline{X}_2) - (\mu_1 - \mu_2)}{\sqrt{\dfrac{S_1^2}{n_1} + \dfrac{S_2^2}{n_2}}} = \frac{(51.3 - 53.2) - (0)}{\sqrt{\dfrac{52}{32} + \dfrac{60}{32}}} = -1.02$$

Since the observed $Z = -1.02 > Z_c = -1.645$, the decision is to **fail to reject the null hypothesis**.

b) Critical value method:

$$Z_c = \frac{(\overline{X}_1 - \overline{X}_2)_c - (\mu_1 - \mu_2)}{\sqrt{\dfrac{S_1^2}{n_1} + \dfrac{S_2^2}{n_2}}}$$

$$-1.645 = \frac{(\overline{X}_1 - \overline{X}_2)_c - (0)}{\sqrt{\dfrac{52}{32} + \dfrac{60}{32}}}$$

$$(\overline{X}_1 - \overline{X}_2)_c = -3.08$$

c) The area for $Z = -1.02$ using Table A.5 is .3461.

   The *p*-value is $.5000 - .3461 = $ **.1539**

10.3   a) Sample 1   Sample 2

$\overline{X}_1 = 88.23$ $\overline{X}_2 = 81.2$
$S_1^2 = 22.74$ $S_2^2 = 26.65$
$n_1 = 30$ $n_2 = 30$

H_o: $\mu_1 - \mu_2 = 0$
H_a: $\mu_1 - \mu_2 \neq 0$

For two-tail test, use $\alpha/2 = .01$ $Z_{.01} = \pm 2.33$

$$Z = \frac{(\overline{X}_1 - \overline{X}_2) - (\mu_1 - \mu_2)}{\sqrt{\dfrac{S_1^2}{n_1} + \dfrac{S_2^2}{n_2}}} = \frac{(88.23 - 81.2) - (0)}{\sqrt{\dfrac{22.74}{30} + \dfrac{26.65}{30}}} = 5.48$$

Since the observed $Z = 5.48 > Z_{.01} = 2.33$, the decision is to **reject the null hypothesis**.

b) $(\overline{X}_1 - \overline{X}_2) \pm Z \sqrt{\dfrac{S_1^2}{n_1} + \dfrac{S_2^2}{n_2}}$

$(88.23 - 81.2) \pm 2.33 \sqrt{\dfrac{22.74}{30} + \dfrac{26.65}{30}}$

7.03 ± 2.99

$4.04 \leq \mu \leq 10.02$

This supports the decision made in a) to reject the null hypothesis because zero is not in the interval.

10.5
	$\underline{A}$	$\underline{B}$

$$n_1 = 40 \qquad n_2 = 37$$
$$\overline{X}_1 = 5.3 \qquad \overline{X}_2 = 6.5$$
$$S_1^2 = 1.99 \qquad S_2^2 = 2.36$$

For a 95% C.I., $Z_{.025} = 1.96$

$$(\overline{X}_1 - \overline{X}_2) \pm Z \sqrt{\frac{S_1^2}{n_1} + \frac{S_2^2}{n_2}}$$

$$(5.3 - 6.5) \pm 1.96 \sqrt{\frac{1.99}{40} + \frac{2.36}{37}}$$

-1.2 ± .66   **-1.86 ≤ μ ≤ -.54**

The results indicate that we are 95% confident that, on average, Plumber B does between 0.54 and 1.86 more jobs per day than Plumber A. Since zero does not lie in this interval, we are confident that there <u>is</u> a difference between Plumber A and Plumber B.

10.7
	$\underline{1992}$	$\underline{1999}$

$$\overline{X}_1 = 190 \qquad \overline{X}_2 = 198$$
$$S_1 = 18.50 \qquad S_2 = 15.60$$
$$n_1 = 51 \qquad n_2 = 47 \qquad \alpha = .01$$

H_0: $\mu_1 - \mu_2 = 0$
H_a: $\mu_1 - \mu_2 < 0$
For a one-tailed test, $Z_{.01} = -2.33$

$$Z = \frac{(\overline{X}_1 - \overline{X}_2) - (\mu_1 - \mu_2)}{\sqrt{\dfrac{S_1^2}{n_1} + \dfrac{S_2^2}{n_2}}} = \frac{(190 - 198) - (0)}{\sqrt{\dfrac{(18.50)^2}{51} + \dfrac{(15.60)^2}{47}}} = \textbf{-2.32}$$

Since the observed $Z = -2.32 > Z_{.01} = -2.33$, the decision is to **fail to reject the null hypothesis**.

10.9   Canon   Pioneer

$\overline{X}_1 = 5.8$ $\overline{X}_2 = 5.0$
$S_1 = 1.7$ $S_2 = 1.4$
$n_1 = 36$ $n_2 = 45$

$H_o:$ $\mu_1 - \mu_2 = 0$
$H_a:$ $\mu_1 - \mu_2 \neq 0$

For two-tail test, $\alpha/2 = .025$ $Z_{.025} = \pm 1.96$

$$Z = \frac{(\overline{X}_1 - \overline{X}_2) - (\mu_1 - \mu_2)}{\sqrt{\dfrac{S_1^2}{n_1} + \dfrac{S_2^2}{n_2}}} = \frac{(5.8 - 5.0) - (0)}{\sqrt{\dfrac{(1.7)^2}{36} + \dfrac{(1.4)}{45}}} = \mathbf{2.27}$$

Since the observed Z = 2.27 > Z_c = 1.96, the decision is to **reject the null hypothesis**.

10.11 $H_o: \mu_1 - \mu_2 = 0$ $\alpha = .01$
        $H_a: \mu_1 - \mu_2 < 0$ df = 8 + 11 - 2 = 17

        Sample 1   Sample 2

        $n_1 = 8$ $n_2 = 11$
        $\overline{X}_1 = 24.56$ $\overline{X}_2 = 26.42$
        $S_1^2 = 12.4$ $S_2^2 = 15.8$

        For one-tail test, $\alpha = .01$ Critical $t_{.01,19} = -2.567$

$$t = \frac{(\overline{X}_1 - \overline{X}_2) - (\mu_1 - \mu_2)}{\sqrt{\dfrac{S_1^2(n_1 - 1) + S_2^2(n_2 - 1)}{n_1 + n_2 - 2}} \sqrt{\dfrac{1}{n_1} + \dfrac{1}{n_2}}} = \frac{(24.56 - 26.42) - (0)}{\sqrt{\dfrac{12.4(7) + 15.8(10)}{8 + 11 - 2}} \sqrt{\dfrac{1}{8} + \dfrac{1}{11}}} = \mathbf{-1.05}$$

Since the observed t = -1.05 > $t_{.01,19}$ = -2.567, the decision is to **fail to reject the null hypothesis**.

10.13 H_o: $\mu_1 - \mu_2 = 0$ $\alpha = .05$

         H_a: $\mu_1 - \mu_2 > 0$ $df = n_1 + n_2 - 2 = 10 + 10 - 2 = 18$

Sample 1   **Sample 2**

$n_1 = 10$ $n_2 = 10$

$\overline{X}_1 = 45.38$ $\overline{X}_2 = 40.49$

$S_1 = 2.357$ $S_2 = 2.355$

For one-tail test, $\alpha = .05$ Critical $t_{.05,18} = 1.734$

$$t = \frac{(\overline{X}_1 - \overline{X}_2) - (\mu_1 - \mu_2)}{\sqrt{\dfrac{S_1^2(n_1 - 1) + S_2^2(n_2 - 1)}{n_1 + n_2 - 2}}\sqrt{\dfrac{1}{n_1} + \dfrac{1}{n_2}}} =$$

$$t = \frac{(45.38 - 40.49) - (0)}{\sqrt{\dfrac{(2.357)^2(9) + (2.355)^2(9)}{10 + 10 - 2}}\sqrt{\dfrac{1}{10} + \dfrac{1}{10}}} = \mathbf{4.64}$$

Since the observed t = 4.64 > $t_{.05,18}$ = 1.734, the decision is to **reject the null hypothesis**.

10.15   <u>Peoria</u>   <u>Evansville</u>

$n_1 = 21$ $n_2 = 26$

$\overline{X} = 86,900$ $\overline{X} = 84,000$

$S_1 = 2,300$ $S_2 = 1,750$ $df = 21 + 26 - 2$

90% level of confidence, $\alpha/2 = .05$ $t_{.05,45} = 1.684$ (used df = 40)

$$(\overline{X}_1 - \overline{X}_2) \pm t\sqrt{\frac{S_1^2(n_1 - 1) + S_2^2(n_2 - 1)}{n_1 + n_2 - 2}}\sqrt{\frac{1}{n_1} + \frac{1}{n_2}} =$$

$$(86,900 - 84,000) \pm 1.684\sqrt{\frac{(2300)^2(20) + (1750)^2(25)}{21 + 26 - 2}}\sqrt{\frac{1}{21} + \frac{1}{26}} =$$

$2,900 \pm 994.62$

$\mathbf{1905.38 \leq \mu_1 - \mu_2 \leq 3894.62}$

10.17 Let Boston be group 1

1) H_o: $\mu_1 - \mu_2 = 0$
    H_a: $\mu_1 - \mu_2 > 0$

2) $t = \dfrac{(\overline{X_1} - \overline{X_2}) - (\mu_1 - \mu_2)}{\sqrt{\dfrac{S_1^2(n_1 - 1) + S_2^2(n_2 - 1)}{n_1 + n_2 - 2}}\sqrt{\dfrac{1}{n_1} + \dfrac{1}{n_2}}}$

3) $\alpha = .01$

4) For a one-tailed test and df = 8 + 9 - 2 = 15, $t_{.01,15} = 2.602$. If the observed value of t is greater than 2.602, the decision is to reject the null hypothesis.

5) <u>Boston</u>   <u>Dallas</u>

   $n_1 = 8$ $n_2 = 9$
   $\overline{X}_1 = 47$ $\overline{X}_2 = 44$
   $S_1 = 3$ $S_2 = 3$

6) $t = \dfrac{(47 - 44) - (0)}{\sqrt{\dfrac{7(3)^2 + 8(3)^2}{15}}\sqrt{\dfrac{1}{8} + \dfrac{1}{9}}} = \mathbf{2.06}$

7) Since $t = 2.06 < t_{.01,15} = 2.602$, the decision is to fail to reject the null hypothesis.

8) There is no significant difference in rental rates between Boston and Dallas.

10.19 H_o: $\mu_1 - \mu_2 = 0$
         H_a: $\mu_1 - \mu_2 \neq 0$

df $= n_1 + n_2 - 2 = 11 + 11 - 2 = 20$

Toronto   Mexico City

$n_1 = 11$ $n_2 = 11$
$\overline{X}_1 = \$67,381.82$ $\overline{X}_2 = \$63,481.82$
$S_1 = \$2,067.28$ $S_2 = \$1,594.25$

For a two-tail test, $\alpha/2 = .005$ Critical $t_{.005,20} = \pm 2.845$

$$t = \frac{(\overline{X}_1 - \overline{X}_2) - (\mu_1 - \mu_2)}{\sqrt{\dfrac{S_1^2(n_1 - 1) + S_2^2(n_2 - 1)}{n_1 + n_2 - 2}}\sqrt{\dfrac{1}{n_1} + \dfrac{1}{n_2}}} =$$

$$t = \frac{(67,381.82 - 63,481.82) - (0)}{\sqrt{\dfrac{(2,067.28)^2(10) + (1,594.25)^2(10)}{11 + 11 - 2}}\sqrt{\dfrac{1}{11} + \dfrac{1}{11}}} = \mathbf{4.95}$$

Since the observed t = 4.95 > $t_{.005,20}$ = 2.845, the decision is to **Reject the null hypothesis**.

10.21 H_o: $D = 0$
H_a: $D > 0$

Sample 1	Sample 2	d
38	22	16
27	28	-1
30	21	9
41	38	3
36	38	-2
38	26	12
33	19	14
35	31	4
44	35	9

n=9 $\bar{d}$ =7.11 S_d=6.45 α = .01

df = n - 1 = 9 - 1 = 8

For one-tail test and α = .01,   the critical $t_{.01,8}$ = ±2.896

$$t = \frac{\bar{d} - D}{\frac{S_d}{\sqrt{n}}} = \frac{7.11 - 0}{\frac{6.45}{\sqrt{9}}} = \mathbf{3.31}$$

Since the observed t = 3.31 > $t_{.01,8}$ = 2.896, the decision is to **reject the null hypothesis**.

10.23   n = 22 $\bar{d}$ = 40.56 S_d = 26.58

For a 98% Level of Confidence, α/2 = .01, and df = n - 1 = 22 - 1 = 21

$t_{.01,21}$ = 2.518

$$\bar{d} \pm t \frac{S_d}{\sqrt{n}}$$

$$40.56 \pm (2.518)\frac{26.58}{\sqrt{22}}$$

$$40.56 \pm 14.27$$

$$\mathbf{26.29 \leq D \leq 54.83}$$

10.25

City	Cost	Resale	d
Atlanta	20427	25163	-4736
Boston	27255	24625	2630
Des Moines	22115	12600	9515
Kansas City	23256	24588	-1332
Louisville	21887	19267	2620
Portland	24255	20150	4105
Raleigh-Durham	19852	22500	-2648
Reno	23624	16667	6957
Ridgewood	25885	26875	- 990
San Francisco	28999	35333	-6334
Tulsa	20836	16292	4544

$\bar{d} = 1302.82$ $S_d = 4938.22$ $n = 11$, $df = 10$

$\alpha = .01$ $\alpha/2 = .005$ $t_{.005,10} = 3.169$

$$\bar{d} \pm t \frac{S_d}{\sqrt{n}} = 1302.82 \pm 3.169 \frac{4938.22}{\sqrt{11}} = 1302.82 \pm 4718.42$$

-3415.6 $\leq$ D $\leq$ 6021.2

10.27

Before	After	d
255	197	58
230	225	5
290	215	75
242	215	27
300	240	60
250	235	15
215	190	25
230	240	-10
225	200	25
219	203	16
236	223	13

$n = 11$ $\overline{d} = 28.09$ $S_d = 25.813$ $df = n - 1 = 11 - 1 = 10$

For a 98% level of confidence and $\alpha/2 = .01$, $t_{.01,10} = 2.764$

$$\overline{d} \pm t \frac{S_d}{\sqrt{n}}$$

$$28.09 \pm (2.764) \frac{25.813}{\sqrt{11}} = 28.09 \pm 21.51$$

6.58 $\leq$ D $\leq$ 49.60

10.29 $n = 21$ $\overline{d} = 75$ $S_d = 30$ $df = 21 - 1 = 20$

For a 90% confidence level, $\alpha/2 = .05$ and $t_{.05,20} = 1.725$

$$\overline{d} \pm t \frac{S_d}{\sqrt{n}}$$

$$75 \pm 1.725 \frac{30}{\sqrt{21}} = 75 \pm 11.29$$

63.71 $\leq$ D $\leq$ 86.29

10.31 a)

Sample 1	Sample 2
$n_1 = 368$	$n_2 = 405$
$x_1 = 175$	$x_2 = 182$

$$\hat{p}_1 = \frac{X_1}{n_1} = \frac{175}{368} = .476 \quad \hat{p}_2 = \frac{X_2}{n_2} = \frac{182}{405} = .449$$

$$\overline{P} = \frac{X_1 + X_2}{n_1 + n_2} = \frac{175 + 182}{368 + 405} = \frac{357}{773} = .462$$

H_o: $P_1 - P_2 = 0$
H_a: $P_1 - P_2 \neq 0$

For two-tail, $\alpha/2 = .025$ and $Z_{.025} = \pm 1.96$

$$Z = \frac{(\hat{p}_1 - \hat{p}_2) - (P_1 - P_2)}{\sqrt{\overline{P} \cdot \overline{Q} \left(\frac{1}{n_1} + \frac{1}{n} \right)}} = \frac{(.476 - .449) - (0)}{\sqrt{(.462)(.538) \left(\frac{1}{368} + \frac{1}{405} \right)}} = \mathbf{0.75}$$

Since the observed $Z = 0.75 < Z_c = 1.96$, the decision is to **fail to reject the null hypothesis**.

b)

Sample 1	Sample 2
$\hat{p}_1 = .38$	$\hat{p}_2 = .25$
$n_1 = 649$	$n_2 = 558$

$$\overline{P} = \frac{n_1 \hat{p}_1 + n_2 \hat{p}_2}{n_1 + n_2} = \frac{649(.38) + 558(.25)}{649 + 558} = .32$$

H_o: $P_1 - P_2 = 0$
H_a: $P_1 - P_2 > 0$

For a one-tail test and $\alpha = .10$, $Z_{.10} = 1.28$

$$Z = \frac{(\hat{p}_1 - \hat{p}_2) - (P_1 - P_2)}{\sqrt{\overline{P} \cdot \overline{Q} \left(\frac{1}{n_1} + \frac{1}{n} \right)}} = \frac{(.38 - .25) - (0)}{\sqrt{(.32)(.68) \left(\frac{1}{649} + \frac{1}{558} \right)}} = \mathbf{4.83}$$

Since the observed $Z = 4.83 > Z_c = 1.28$, the decision is to **reject the null hypothesis**.

10.33 H_0: $P_m - P_w = 0$
        H_a: $P_m - P_w < 0$ $n_m = 374$ $n_w = 481$ $\hat{p}_m = .59$ $\hat{p}_w = .70$

For a one-tailed test and $\alpha = .05$, $Z_{.05} = -1.645$

$$\overline{P} = \frac{n_m \hat{p}_m + n_w \hat{p}_w}{n_m + n_w} = \frac{374(.59) + 481(.70)}{374 + 481} = .652$$

$$Z = Z = \frac{(\hat{p}_1 - \hat{p}_2) - (P_1 - P_2)}{\sqrt{\overline{P} \cdot \overline{Q}\left(\dfrac{1}{n_1} + \dfrac{1}{n}\right)}} = \frac{(.59 - .70) - (0)}{\sqrt{(.652)(.348)\left(\dfrac{1}{374} + \dfrac{1}{481}\right)}} = -3.35$$

Since the observed $Z = -3.35 < Z_{.05} = -1.645$, the decision is to **reject the null hypothesis**.

10.35   <u>Computer Firms</u>   <u>Banks</u>

$\hat{p}_1 = .48$ $\hat{p}_2 = .56$
$n_1 = 56$ $n_2 = 89$

$$\overline{P} = \frac{n_1 \hat{p}_1 + n_2 \hat{p}_2}{n_1 + n_2} = \frac{56(.48) + 89(.56)}{56 + 89} = .529$$

H_o: $P_1 - P_2 = 0$
H_a: $P_1 - P_2 \neq 0$

For two-tail test, $\alpha/2 = .10$ and $Z_c = \pm 1.28$

$$Z = Z = \frac{(\hat{p}_1 - \hat{p}_2) - (P_1 - P_2)}{\sqrt{\overline{P} \cdot \overline{Q}\left(\dfrac{1}{n_1} + \dfrac{1}{n}\right)}} = \frac{(.48 - .56) - (0)}{\sqrt{(.529)(.471)\left(\dfrac{1}{56} + \dfrac{1}{89}\right)}} = -0.94$$

Since the observed $Z = -0.94 > Z_c = -1.28$, the decision is to **fail to reject the null hypothesis**.

10.37 H_0: $P_1 - P_2 = 0$
H_a: $P_1 - P_2 \neq 0$

$\alpha = .10$ $\hat{p}_1 = .09$ $\hat{p}_2 = .06$ $n_1 = 780$ $n_2 = 915$

For a two-tailed test, $\alpha/2 = .05$ and $Z_{.05} = \pm 1.645$

$$\overline{P} = \frac{n_1 \hat{p}_1 + n_2 \hat{p}_2}{n_1 + n_2} = \frac{780(.09) + 915(.06)}{780 + 915} = .0738$$

$$Z = \frac{(\hat{p}_1 - \hat{p}_2) - (P_1 - P_2)}{\sqrt{\overline{P} \cdot \overline{Q}\left(\frac{1}{n_1} + \frac{1}{n}\right)}} = \frac{(.09 - .06) - (0)}{\sqrt{(.0738)(.9262)\left(\frac{1}{780} + \frac{1}{915}\right)}} = \mathbf{2.35}$$

Since the observed Z = 2.35 > $Z_{.05}$ = 1.645, the decision is to **reject the null hypothesis**.

10.39 H_0: $\sigma_1^2 = \sigma_2^2$ $\alpha = .01$ $n_1 = 10$ $S_1^2 = 562$
H_a: $\sigma_1^2 < \sigma_2^2$ $n_2 = 12$ $S_2^2 = 1013$

$df_{num} = 12 - 1 = 11$ $df_{denom} = 10 - 1 = 9$

Table $F_{.01,10,9} = 5.26$

$$F = \frac{S_2^2}{S_1^2} = \frac{1013}{562} = \mathbf{1.80}$$

Since the observed F = 1.80 < $F_{.01,10,9}$ = 5.26, the decision is to **fail to reject the null hypothesis**.

10.41   <u>City 1</u>   <u>City 2</u>

    1.18   1.08
    1.15   1.17
    1.14   1.14
    1.07   1.05
    1.14   1.21
    1.13   1.14
    1.09   1.11
    1.13   1.19
    1.13   1.12
    1.03   1.13

$n_1 = 10$ $df_1 = 9$ $n_2 = 10$ $df_2 = 9$

$S_1^2 = .0018989$ $S_2^2 = .0023378$

H_0: $\sigma_1^2 = \sigma_2^2$ $\alpha = .10$ $\alpha/2 = .05$
H_a: $\sigma_1^2 \neq \sigma_2^2$

Upper tail critical F value $= F_{.05,9,9} = 3.18$

Lower tail critical F value $= F_{.95,9,9} = 0.314$

$$F = \frac{S_1^2}{S_2^2} = \frac{.0018989}{.0023378} = \mathbf{0.81}$$

Since the observed $F = 0.81$ is greater than the lower tail critical value of 0.314 and less than the upper tail critical value of 3.18, the decision is to **fail to reject the null hypothesis**

10.43 H_0: $\sigma_1^2 = \sigma_2^2$ $\alpha = .05$ $n_1 = 12$ $S_1 = 7.52$
         H_a: $\sigma_1^2 > \sigma_2^2$ $n_2 = 15$ $S_2 = 6.08$
         $df_{num} = 12 - 1 = 11$ $df_{denom} = 15 - 1 = 14$

The critical table F value is $F_{.05,10,14} = 5.26$

$$F = \frac{S_1^2}{S_2^2} = \frac{(7.52)^2}{(6.08)^2} = \mathbf{1.53}$$

Since the observed $F = 1.53 < F_{.05,10,14} = 2.60$, the decision is to **fail to reject the null hypothesis**.

10.45 H_o: $\mu_1 - \mu_2 = 0$
         H_a: $\mu_1 - \mu_2 \neq 0$

For $\alpha = .10$ and a two-tailed test, $\alpha/2 = .05$ and $Z_{.05} = \pm 1.645$

Sample 1	Sample 2
$\overline{X_1} = 138.4$	$\overline{X_2} = 142.5$
$S_1 = 6.71$	$S_2 = 8.92$
$n_1 = 48$	$n_2 = 39$

$$Z = \frac{(\overline{X_1} - \overline{X_2}) - (\mu_1 - \mu_2)}{\sqrt{\dfrac{S_1^2}{n_1} + \dfrac{S_2^2}{n_2}}} = \frac{(138.4 - 142.5) - (0)}{\sqrt{\dfrac{(6.71)^2}{48} + \dfrac{(8.92)}{39}}} = \mathbf{-2.38}$$

Since the observed value of $Z = -2.38$ is less than the critical value of $Z = -1.645$, the decision is to **reject the null hypothesis**. There is a significant difference in the means of the two populations.

10.47 H_o: $\mu_1 - \mu_2 = 0$
        H_a: $\mu_1 - \mu_2 > 0$

Sample 1	Sample 2
$\overline{X_1} = 2.06$	$\overline{X_2} = 1.93$
$S_1^2 = .176$	$S_2^2 = .143$
$n_1 = 12$	$n_2 = 15$

This is a one-tailed test with df $= 12 + 15 - 2 = 25$.   The critical value is
$t_{.05,25} = 1.708$. If the observed value is greater than 1.708, the decision will be to reject
the null hypothesis.

$$t = \frac{(\overline{X_1} - \overline{X_2}) - (\mu_1 - \mu_2)}{\sqrt{\dfrac{S_1^2(n_1 - 1) + S_2^2(n_2 - 1)}{n_1 + n_2 - 2}} \sqrt{\dfrac{1}{n_1} + \dfrac{1}{n_2}}}$$

$$t = \frac{(2.06 - 1.93) - (0)}{\sqrt{\dfrac{(.176)(11) + (.143)(14)}{25}} \sqrt{\dfrac{1}{12} + \dfrac{1}{15}}} = \mathbf{0.85}$$

Since the observed value of $t = 0.85$ is less than the critical value of $t = 1.708$, the
decision is to **fail to reject the null hypothesis**. The mean for population one is not
significantly greater than the mean for population two.

10.49 H_o: $D = 0$ $\alpha = .01$
        H_a: $D < 0$

        $n = 21$ df $= 20$ $\overline{d} = -1.16$ $S_d = 1.01$

The critical $t_{.01,20} = -2.528$. If the observed t is less than -2.528, then the decision will be
to reject the null hypothesis.

$$t = \frac{\overline{d} - D}{\dfrac{S_d}{\sqrt{n}}} = \frac{-1.16 - 0}{\dfrac{1.01}{\sqrt{21}}} = \mathbf{-5.26}$$

Since the observed value of $t = -5.26$ is less than the critical t value of -2.528, the
decision is to **reject the null hypothesis**. The population difference is less
than zero.

10.51 H_o: $P_1 - P_2 = 0$ $\alpha = .05$ $\alpha/2 = .025$

H_a: $P_1 - P_2 \neq 0$ $Z_{.025} = \pm 1.96$

If the observed value of Z is greater than 1.96 or less than -1.96, then the decision will be to reject the null hypothesis.

<u>Sample 1</u>   <u>Sample 2</u>

$X_1 = 345$ $X_2 = 421$
$n_1 = 783$ $n_2 = 896$

$$\overline{P} = \frac{X_1 + X_2}{n_1 + n_2} = \frac{345 + 421}{783 + 896} = .4562$$

$$\hat{p}_1 = \frac{X_1}{n_1} = \frac{345}{783} = .4406 \qquad\qquad \hat{p}_2 = \frac{X_2}{n_2} = \frac{421}{896} = .4699$$

$$Z = \frac{(\hat{p}_1 - \hat{p}_2) - (P_1 - P_2)}{\sqrt{\overline{P} \cdot \overline{Q}\left(\frac{1}{n_1} + \frac{1}{n}\right)}} = \frac{(.4406 - .4699) - (0)}{\sqrt{(.4562)(.5438)\left(\frac{1}{783} + \frac{1}{896}\right)}} = \mathbf{-1.20}$$

Since the observed value of Z = -1.20 is greater than -1.96,   the decision is to **fail to reject the null hypothesis**.   There is no significant difference in the population proportions.

10.53 H_0: $\sigma_1^2 = \sigma_2^2$ $\alpha = .05$ $n_1 = 8$ $S_1^2 = 46$

H_a: $\sigma_1^2 \neq \sigma_2^2$ $n_2 = 10$ $S_2^2 = 37$

$df_{num} = 8 - 1 = 7$ $df_{denom} = 10 - 1 = 9$
The critical F values are: $F_{.025,7,9} = 4.20$ $F_{.975,9,7} = .238$

If the observed value of F is greater than 4.20 or less than .238, then the decision will be to reject the null hypothesis.

$$F = \frac{S_1^2}{S_2^2} = \frac{46}{37} = \mathbf{1.24}$$

Since the observed $F = 1.24$ is less than $F_{.025,7,9} = 4.20$ and greater than $F_{.975,9,7} = .238$, the decision is to **fail to reject the null hypothesis**. There is no significant difference in the variances of the two populations.

10.55

Morning	Afternoon	d
43	41	2
51	49	2
37	44	-7
24	32	-8
47	46	1
44	42	2
50	47	3
55	51	4
46	49	-3

$n = 9$ $\overline{d} = -0.444$ $S_d = 4.447$ $df = 9 - 1 = 8$

For a 90% Confidence Level: $\alpha/2 = .05$ and $t_{.05,8} = 1.86$

$$\overline{d} \pm t \frac{S_d}{\sqrt{n}}$$

$-0.444 \pm (1.86) \dfrac{4.447}{\sqrt{9}}$ $=$ -0.444 ± 2.757

-3.201 $\leq$ D $\leq$ 2.313

10.57

Accounting	Data Entry
$n_1 = 16$	$n_2 = 14$
$\overline{X}_1 = 26,400$	$\overline{X}_2 = 25,800$
$S_1 = 1,200$	$S_2 = 1,050$

H_0: $\sigma_1^2 = \sigma_2^2$
H_a: $\sigma_1^2 \neq \sigma_2^2$

$df_{num} = 16 - 1 = 15$ $df_{denom} = 14 - 1 = 13$

The critical F values are: $F_{.025,15,13} = 3.05$ $F_{.975,15,13} = 0.33$

$$F = \frac{S_1^2}{S_2^2} = \frac{1,440,000}{1,102,500} = \mathbf{1.31}$$

Since the observed F = 1.31 is less than $F_{.025,15,13} = 3.05$ and greater than $F_{.975,15,13} = 0.33$, the decision is to **fail to reject the null hypothesis**.

10.59   Men   Women

$n_1 = 60$ $n_2 = 41$

$\overline{X}_1 = 631$ $\overline{X}_2 = 848$

$S_1 = 100$ $S_2 = 100$

For a 95% Confidence Level, $\alpha/2 = .025$ and $Z_{.025} = 1.96$

$$(\overline{X}_1 - \overline{X}_2) \pm Z\sqrt{\frac{S_1^{\,2}}{n_1} + \frac{S_2^{\,2}}{n_2}}$$

$$(631 - 848) \pm 1.96\sqrt{\frac{100^2}{60} + \frac{100^2}{41}} \;\; = \;\; -217 \pm 39.7$$

$-256.7 \leq \mu_1 - \mu_2 \leq -177.3$

10.61   With Fertilizer   Without Fertilizer

$\overline{X}_1 = 38.4$ $\overline{X}_2 = 23.1$

$S_1 = 9.8$ $S_2 = 7.4$

$n_1 = 35$ $n_2 = 35$

H_o: $\mu_1 - \mu_2 = 0$

H_a: $\mu_1 - \mu_2 > 0$

For one-tail test, $\alpha = .01$ and $Z_{.01} = 2.33$

$$Z = \frac{(\overline{X}_1 - \overline{X}_2) - (\mu_1 - \mu_2)}{\sqrt{\dfrac{S_1^{\,2}}{n_1} + \dfrac{S_2^{\,2}}{n_2}}} = \frac{(38.4 - 23.1) - (0)}{\sqrt{\dfrac{(9.8)^2}{35} + \dfrac{(7.4)}{35}}} = 7.37$$

Since the observed $Z = 7.37 > Z_{.01} = 2.33$, the decision is to **reject the null hypothesis**.

10.63 H_0: $\sigma_1^2 = \sigma_2^2$ $\alpha = .05$ $n_1 = 27$ $S_1 = 22{,}000$
H_a: $\sigma_1^2 \neq \sigma_2^2$ $n_2 = 29$ $S_2 = 15{,}500$

$df_{num} = 27 - 1 = 26$ $df_{denom} = 29 - 1 = 28$

The critical F values are: $F_{.025,24,28} = 2.17$ $F_{.975,28,24} = .46$

$$F = \frac{S_1^2}{S_2^2} = \frac{22{,}000^2}{15{,}500^2} = \mathbf{2.01}$$

Since the observed F = 2.01 < $F_{.025,24,28}$ = 2.17 and > than $F_{.975,28,24}$ = .46, the decision is to **fail to reject the null hypothesis**.

10.65 H_o: $\mu_1 - \mu_2 = 0$ $\alpha = .01$
H_a: $\mu_1 - \mu_2 < 0$ df = 23 + 19 - 2 = 40

	Wisconsin		Tennessee

Wisconsin

$n_1 = 23$

$\overline{X}_1 = 69.652$

$S_1^2 = 9.9644$

Tennessee

$n_2 = 19$

$\overline{X}_2 = 71.7368$

$S_2^2 = 4.6491$

For one-tail test, $\alpha = .01$ and the critical $t_{.01,40} = -2.423$

$$t = \frac{(\overline{X}_1 - \overline{X}_2) - (\mu_1 - \mu_2)}{\sqrt{\dfrac{S_1^2(n_1 - 1) + S_2^2(n_2 - 1)}{n_1 + n_2 - 2}} \sqrt{\dfrac{1}{n_1} + \dfrac{1}{n_2}}}$$

$$t = \frac{(69.652 - 71.7368) - (0)}{\sqrt{\dfrac{(9.9644)(22) + (4.6491)(18)}{40}} \sqrt{\dfrac{1}{23} + \dfrac{1}{19}}} = \mathbf{-2.44}$$

Since the observed t = -2.44 < $t_{.01,40}$ = -2.423, the decision is to **reject the null hypothesis**.

10.67 H_o: $P_1 - P_2 = 0$ $\alpha = .05$
H_a: $P_1 - P_2 \neq 0$

Machine 1	Machine 2
$X_1 = 38$	$X_2 = 21$
$n_1 = 191$	$n_2 = 202$

$$\hat{p}_1 = \frac{X_1}{n_1} = \frac{38}{191} = .199 \qquad\qquad \hat{p}_2 = \frac{X_2}{n_2} = \frac{21}{202} = .104$$

$$\overline{P} = \frac{n_1\hat{p}_1 + n_2\hat{p}_2}{n_1 + n_2} = \frac{(.199)(191) + (.104)(202)}{191 + 202} = .15$$

For two-tail, $\alpha/2 = .025$ and the critical Z values are: $Z_{.025} = \pm 1.96$

$$Z = \frac{(\hat{p}_1 - \hat{p}_2) - (P_1 - P_2)}{\sqrt{\overline{P} \cdot \overline{Q}\left(\frac{1}{n_1} + \frac{1}{n}\right)}} = \frac{(.199 - .104) - (0)}{\sqrt{(.15)(.85)\left(\frac{1}{191} + \frac{1}{202}\right)}} = \textbf{2.64}$$

Since the observed Z = 2.64 > Z_c = 1.96, the decision is to **reject the null hypothesis**.

10.69 | Aerospace | Automobile |
|----------------------|----------------------|
| $n_1 = 33$ | $n_2 = 35$ |
| $\overline{X}_1 = 12.4$ | $\overline{X}_2 = 4.6$ |
| $S_1 = 2.9$ | $S_2 = 1.8$ |

For a 99% Confidence Level, $\alpha/2 = .005$ and $Z_{.005} = 2.575$

$$(\overline{X}_1 - \overline{X}_2) \pm Z\sqrt{\frac{S_1^{\,2}}{n_1} + \frac{S_2^{\,2}}{n_2}}$$

$$(12.4 - 4.6) \pm 2.575\sqrt{\frac{(2.9)^2}{33} + \frac{(1.8)^2}{35}} = 7.8 \pm 1.52$$

$6.28 \leq \mu_1 - \mu_2 \leq 9.32$

10.71

Before	After	d
12	8	4
7	3	4
10	8	2
16	9	7
8	5	3

$n = 5$ $\quad$ $\overline{d} = 4.0$ $\quad$ $S_d = 1.8708$ $\quad$ $df = 5 - 1 = 4$

H_o: $D = 0$ $\qquad$ $\alpha = .01$
H_a: $D > 0$

For one-tail test, $\alpha = .01$ and the critical $t_{.01,4} = 3.747$

$$t = \frac{\overline{d} - D}{\dfrac{S_d}{\sqrt{n}}} = \frac{4.0 - 0}{\dfrac{1.8708}{\sqrt{5}}} = \textbf{4.78}$$

Since the observed $t = 4.78 > t_{.01,4} = 3.747$, the decision is to **reject the null hypothesis**.

10.73   A t test was used to test to determine if Hong Kong has significantly higher rates than Bombay. Let group 1 be Hong Kong.

H_o: $\qquad$ $\mu_1 - \mu_2 = 0$
H_a: $\qquad$ $\mu_1 - \mu_2 > 0$

$n_1 = 19$ $\quad$ $n_2 = 23$ $\quad$ $\overline{X}_1 = 131.5$ $\quad$ $\overline{X}_2 = 123.1$

$S_1 = 11.8$ $\quad$ $S_2 = 14.3$ $\quad$ $\alpha = .01$

$t = 2.06$ with a p-value of .023 which is not significant at of .01.

10.75   The point estimates from the sample data indicate that in the northern city the market share is .3108 and in the southern city the market share is .2701. The point estimate for the difference in the two proportions of market share are .0407. Since the 99% confidence interval ranges from -.0394 to +.1207 and zero <u>is</u> in the interval, any hypothesis testing decision based on this interval would result in failure to reject the null hypothesis. Alpha is .01 with a two-tailed test. This is underscored by a calculated Z value of 1.31 which has an associated *p*-value of .191 which, of course, is not significant for any of the usual values of α.

Chapter 11
Analysis of Variance and
Design of Experiments

LEARNING OBJECTIVES

The focus of this chapter is learning about the design of experiments and the analysis of variance thereby enabling you to:

1. Understand the differences between various experiment designs and when to use them.

2. Compute and interpret the results of a one-way ANOVA.

3. Compute and interpret the results of a random block design.

4. Compute and interpret the results of a two-way ANOVA.

5. Understand and interpret interaction.

6. Know when and how to use multiple comparison techniques.

CHAPTER OUTLINE

KEY WORDS

a posteriori
a priori
Analysis of Variance (ANOVA)
Blocking Variable
Classification Variables
Classifications
Completely Randomized Design
Concomitant Variables
Confounding Variables
Dependent Variable
Experimental Design
F Distribution
F Value
Factorial Design

Factors
Independent Variable
Interaction
Levels
Multiple Comparisons
One-way Analysis of Variance
Post-hoc
Randomized Block Design
Repeated Measures Design
Treatment Variable
Tukey-Kramer Procedure
Tukey's HSD Test
Two-way Analysis of Variance

STUDY QUESTIONS

1. A plan for testing hypotheses in which the researcher either controls or manipulates one or more variables is called a(n) _____.

2. A variable that is either controlled or manipulated is called a(n) _____ variable.

3. An independent variable is sometimes referred to as a _____ variable, a _____ variable, or a _____.

4. Each independent variable contains two or more _____ or _____.

5. The response to the different levels of the independent variables is called the _____ variable.

6. The experimental design that contains only one independent variable with two or more treatment levels is called a _____.

7. In chapter 11, the experimental designs are analyzed statistically using _____ _____.

8. Suppose we want to analyze the data shown below using analysis of variance.

1	2	3	4
3	5	4	1
2	6	2	2
4	7	2	2
3	6	2	1
2	7	3	1
3			2

The degrees of freedom numerator for this analysis are _____.
The degrees of freedom denominator for this analysis are _____.

9. Assuming that = .05, for the problem presented in question 8, the critical F value is _____.

10. For the problem presented in question 8, the sum of squares between is _____ and the sum of squares error is _____. The mean square between is _____ and the mean square error is _____. The calculated value of F for this problem is _____. The decision is to _____.

11.   A set of techniques used to make comparisons between groups after an overall significant F value has been obtained is called _____.

12.   The two types of multiple comparison techniques presented in chapter 11 are
_____ and _____.

13.   In conducting multiple comparisons with unequal sample sizes with techniques presented in chapter 11 of the text, you would use which procedure? _____

14.   Suppose the following data are taken as samples from three populations and that an ANOVA results in an overall significant F value of 404.80. The mean square error for this ANOVA is 1.58.

1	2	3
11	24	27
9	25	30
10	25	29
12	26	28
11	24	31
8		29
10		

The Tukey-Kramer significant difference for groups 1 and 2 is _____.
For groups 1 and 3, it is _____. For groups 2 and 3, it is
_____. The following groups are significantly different
_____ using $\alpha = .01$.

15.   Suppose the following data represent four samples of size five which are taken from four populations. An ANOVA revealed a significant overall F value.

1	2	3	4
5	11	12	21
8	9	11	18
7	9	13	20
8	10	14	21
6	11	14	23

The mean square error for this problem is 1.92. The number of populations (C) for this problem is _____. The degrees of freedom error are _____. The value of q is _____. The value of HSD for this problem is _____. The following pairs of means are significantly different according to Tukey's HSD _____. Let $\alpha = .05$

16.   A research design that is similar to the completely randomized design except that it includes a second variable referred to as a blocking variable is called a(n)
_____.

17.   In the randomized block design, the variable that the researcher desires to control but is not the treatment variable of interest is called the _____ variable.

18.   Consider the following randomized block design.

Treatment Level

	1	2	3
Block			
1	2	4	8
2	3	4	9
3	2	5	7
4	4	6	6
5	3	5	9

The degrees of freedom treatment are _____. The degrees of freedom blocking are _____. The degrees of freedom error are _____.

19.   For the problem in question 18, the sum of squares treatment is _____. The sum of squares blocking are _____. The sum of squares error are

_____.

20.   For the problem in question 18, the mean square treatment is _____. The mean square blocking is _____. The mean square error is _____. The calculated F value for treatment is _____. The calculated F value for blocking is _____. Using = .01, the following effects are significant based on these F values _____.

21.   One advantage of a two-way design over the completely randomized design and the randomized block design is that the researcher can test for _____ if multiple measures are taken under every combination of treatment levels of the two treatments.

22.   The ANOVA table shown below is compiled from the analysis of a two-way factorial design with three rows and four columns. There were a total of 48 values in this design.

Effect	SS	df	MS	F
Row	29.3			
Column	17.1			
Interaction	14.7			
Error	55.8			
Total				

The sum of squares total is _____. The degrees of freedom for rows are _____. The degrees of freedom for columns are _____. The degrees of freedom for interaction are _____. The degrees of freedom for error are _____. The total degrees of freedom are _____. The mean square for rows is _____. The mean square for columns is _____. The mean squares for interaction is _____. The mean squares for error is _____. The calculated F value for rows is _____. The calculated F value for columns is _____. The calculated F value for interaction is _____. The following effects are statistically significant using = .05 _____.

23.   Perform a two-way ANOVA on the data given below.

Column Effects

		1	2	3
		2	5	5
	1	3	2	6
Row		2	4	5
Effects				
		4	8	7
	2	6	4	6
		6	7	7

The sum of squares rows is _____. The sum of squares columns is _____. The sum of squares interaction is _____. The sum of squares error is _____. The degrees of freedom for rows are _____. The degrees of freedom for columns are _____. The degrees of freedom for interaction are _____. The degrees of freedom for error are _____. The mean square for rows is _____. The mean square for columns is _____. The mean squares for interaction is _____. The mean squares for error is _____. The calculated F value for rows is _____. The calculated F value for columns is _____. The calculated F value for interaction is _____. The following effects are statistically significant using = .05 _____.

ANSWERS TO STUDY QUESTIONS

1. Experimental Design

2. Independent

3. Classification, Treatment, Factor

4. Levels, Classifications

5. Dependent

6. Completely Randomized Design

7. Analysis of Variance (ANOVA)

8. 3, 18

9. 3.16

10. 64.939, 10.333, 21.646, 0.574, 37.71, Reject the Null Hypothesis

11. Multiple Comparisons

12. Tukey's Honestly Significant Difference Test (HSD) and Tukey-Kramer Procedure

13. Tukey-Kramer Procedure

14. 2.514, 2.388, 2.60. All are significantly different

15. 4, 16, 4.05, 2.51. All are significantly different

16. Randomized Block Design

17. Blocking

18. 2, 4, 8

19. 63.33, 2.40, 10.00

20. 31.67, 0.60, 1.25, 25.34, 0.48, Treatment

21. Interaction

22. 116.9, 2, 3, 6, 36, 47, 14.65, 5.70, 2.45, 1.55, 9.45, 3.68, 1.58, Rows and Columns

23. 24.50, 14.11, 2.33, 18.00, 1, 2, 2, 12, 24.50, 7.06, 1.17, 1.50, 16.33, 4.71, 0.78, Rows and Columns

SOLUTIONS TO ODD-NUMBERED PROBLEMS IN CHAPTER 11

11.1 a) Time Period, Market Condition, Day of the Week, Season of the Year

b) Time Period - 4 P.M. to 5 P.M. and 5 P.M. to 6 P.M.
   Market Condition - Bull Market and Bear Market
   Day of the Week - Monday, Tuesday, Wednesday, Thursday, Friday
   Season of the Year - Summer, Winter, Fall, Spring

c) Volume, Value of the Dow Jones Average, Earnings of Investment Houses

11.3 a) Type of Card, Age of User, Economic Class of Cardholder, Geographic Region

b) Type of Card - Mastercard, Visa, Discover, American Express
   Age of User - 21-25 y, 26-32 y, 33-40 y, 41-50 y, over 50
   Economic Class - Lower, Middle, Upper
   Geographic Region - NE, South, MW, West

c) Average number of card usages per person per month,
   Average balance due on the card, Average per expenditure per person,
   Number of cards possessed per person

11.5

Source	Df	SS	MS	F
Treatment	2	22.20	11.10	11.07
Error	14	14.03	1.00	
Total	16	36.24		

$\alpha = .05$ Critical $F_{.05,2,14} = 3.74$

Since the observed $F = 11.07 > F_{.05,2,14} = 3.74$, the decision is to **reject the null hypothesis**.

11.7

Source	Df	SS	MS	F
Treatment	3	544.2	181.4	13.00
Error	12	167.5	14.0	
Total	15	711.8		

$\alpha = .01$ Critical $F_{.01,3,12} = 5.95$

Since the observed $F = 13.00 > F_{.01,3,12} = 5.95$, the decision is to **reject the null hypothesis**.

11.9

Source	DF	SS	MS	F
Treatment	**4**	583.39	**145.8475**	**7.50**
Error	**50**	972.18	**19.4436**	
Total	**54**	1,555.57		

11.11

Source	Df	SS	MS	F
Treatment	3	.007076	.002359	10.10
Error	15	.003503	.000234	
Total	18	.010579		

$\alpha = .01$ Critical $F_{.01,3,15} = 5.42$

Since the observed $F = 10.10 > F_{.01,3,15} = 5.42$, the decision is to **reject the null hypothesis**.

11.13

Source	Df	SS	MS	F
Treatment	2	29.61	14.80	11.76
Error	15	18.89	1.26	
Total	17	48.50		

$\alpha = .05$ Critical $F_{.05,2,15} = 3.68$

Since the observed $F = 11.76 > F_{.05,2,15} = 3.68$, the decison is to **reject the null hypothesis**.

11.15 There are **4 treatment levels**. The sample sizes are **18, 15, 21, and 11.** The F value is **2.95** with a p-value of **.04.** There is an overall significant difference at alpha of .05. The means are **226.73, 238.79, 232.58, and 239.82.**

11.17 There were 5 treatment levels in the study. The sample sizes were 7, 5, 8, 12, 11 respectively. Since the p value is .213, there is no significant difference between the means at a = .05 because the smallest value of alpha for which the null hypothesis can be rejected is .213 and this is greater than .05. The means for groups 1 through 5 are 53.042, 48.481, 56.257, 53.138, and 57.977 respectively. The confidence intervals contain considerable overlap and underscore the notion that there is no significant overall difference in treatment means.

11.19 $C = 4$ $n = 6$ $N = 24$ $df_{error} = N - C = 24 - 4 = 20$

$MSE = 2.389$ $q_{.05,4,20} = 3.96$

$$HSD = q\sqrt{\frac{MSE}{n}} = (3.96)\sqrt{\frac{2.389}{6}} = \mathbf{2.50}$$

11.21   From problem 11.6,   MSE $= 1.48$ $C = 5$ $N = 23$

$n_2 = 5$ $n_4 = 5$ $\alpha = .01$ $q_{.01,5,23} = 5.29$

$$HSD = 5.29\sqrt{\frac{1.48}{2}\left(\frac{1}{5}+\frac{1}{5}\right)} = 2.88$$

$\overline{X}_2 = 10$ $\overline{X}_4 = 16$

$\left|\overline{X}_3 - \overline{X}_6\right| = |10 - 16| = 6$

Since $6 > 2.88$, **there is a significant difference in the means of groups 2 and 4**.

11.23 $n = 7$ $C = 2$ MSE $= 3.62$ $N = 14$ $N - C = 14 - 2 = 12$

$\alpha = .05$ $q_{.05,2,12} = 3.08$

$$HSD = q\sqrt{\frac{MSE}{n}} = 3.08\sqrt{\frac{3.62}{7}} = 2.215$$

$\overline{X}_1 = 29$ and $\overline{X}_2 = 24.71$

Since $\overline{X}_1 - \overline{X}_2 = 4.29 > HSD = 2.215$, the decision is to **reject the null hypothesis**.

11.25 $\alpha = .01$ $k = 3$ $n = 5$ $N = 15$ $N - k = 12$ $MSE = 975,000$

$$HSD = q \sqrt{\frac{MSE}{n}} = 5.04 \sqrt{\frac{975,000}{5}} = 2,225.6$$

$\overline{X}_1 = 28,400$ $\overline{X}_2 = 36,900$ $\overline{X}_3 = 32,800$

$\left| \overline{X}_1 - \overline{X}_2 \right|$ = **8,500**

$\left| \overline{X}_1 - \overline{X}_3 \right|$ = **4,400**

$\left| \overline{X}_2 - \overline{X}_3 \right|$ = **4,100**

Using Tukey's HSD, **all three pairwise comparisons are significantly different**.

11.27 $\alpha = .05$ $n = 5$ $C = 4$ $N = 20$ $N - C = 16$ $MSE = 13,798$

$\overline{X}_1 = 591$ $\overline{X}_2 = 350$ $\overline{X}_3 = 776$ $\overline{X}_4 = 563$

$$HSD = q \sqrt{\frac{MSE}{n}} = 4.05 \sqrt{\frac{13,798}{5}} = \mathbf{212.75}$$

$\left| \overline{X}_1 - \overline{X}_2 \right|$ = 241 $\left| \overline{X}_1 - \overline{X}_3 \right|$ = 185 $\left| \overline{X}_1 - \overline{X}_4 \right|$ = 28

$\left| \overline{X}_2 - \overline{X}_3 \right|$ = 426 $\left| \overline{X}_2 - \overline{X}_4 \right|$ = 213 $\left| \overline{X}_3 - \overline{X}_4 \right|$ = 213

Using Tukey's HSD = 212.75, only means 1 and 2 and means 2 and 3 are significantly different.

11.29 H_0: $\mu_1 = \mu_2 = \mu_3 = \mu_4$
H_a: At least one treatment mean is different from the others

Source	Df	SS	MS	F
Treatment	3	62.95	20.98	5.56
Blocks	4	257.50	64.38	17.07
Error	12	45.30	3.77	
Total	19	365.75		

$\alpha = .05$ Critical $F_{.05,3,12} = 3.49$ for treatments

For treatments, the observed $F = 5.56 > F_{.05,3,12} = 3.49$, the decision is to **reject the null hypothesis**.

11.31

Source	Df	SS	MS	F
Treatment	5	2477.53	495.506	1.91
Blocks	9	3180.48	353.387	1.36
Error	45	11661.38	259.142	
Total	59	17319.39		

$\alpha = .05$ Critical $F_{.05,5,45} = 2.45$ for treatments

For treatments, the observed $F = 1.91 < F_{.05,5,45} = 2.45$ and decision is to **fail to reject the null hypothesis**.

11.33

Source	Df	SS	MS	F
Treatment	3	2302.5	767.5	15.66
Blocks	9	5402.5	600.3	12.25
Error	27	1322.5	49.0	
Total	39	9027.5		

$\alpha = .05$ Critical $F_{.05,3,27} = 2.96$ for treatments

For treatments, the observed $F = 15.66 > F_{.05,3,27} = 2.96$ and the decision is to **reject the null hypothesis**.

11.35   This a randomized block design with 3 treatments (machines) and 5 block levels (operators). The F for treatments is 6.72 with a p-value of .019. There is a significant difference in machines at $= .05$. The F for blocking effects is 0.22 with a p-value of .807. There are no significant blocking effects. The blocking effects reduced the power of the treatment effects since the blocking effects were not significant.

11.37   This is a two-way factorial design with two independent variables and one dependent variable. It is 2x4 in that there are two row treatment levels and four column treatment levels. Since there are three measurements per cell, interaction can be analyzed.

$Df_{row\ treatment} = 1$ $Df_{column\ treatment} = 3$ $Df_{interaction} = 3,$

$Df_{error} = 16$ $Df_{total} = 23$

11.39

Source	Df	SS	MS	F
Row	3	126.98	42.327	3.46
Column	4	37.49	9.373	0.77
Interaction	12	380.82	31.735	2.60
Error	60	733.65	12.228	
Total	79	1278.94		

$\alpha = .05$ Critical $F_{.05,3,60} = 2.76$ for rows

For rows, the observed $F = 3.46 > F_{.05,3,60} = 2.76$ and the decision is to **reject the null hypothesis**.

Critical $F_{.05,4,60} = 2.53$ for columns

For columns, the observed $F = 0.77 < F_{.05,4,60} = 2.53$ and the decision is to **fail to reject the null hypothesis**.

Critical $F_{.05,12,60} = 1.92$ for interaction

For interaction, the observed $F = 2.60 > F_{.05,12,60} = 1.92$ and the decision is to **reject the null hypothesis**.

Since there is significant interaction, the researcher should exercise extreme caution in analyzing the "significant" row effects.

11.41

Source	Df	SS	MS	F
Row	1	60.750	60.750	38.37
Column	2	14.000	7.000	4.42
Interaction	2	2.000	1.000	0.63
Error	6	9.500	1.583	
Total	11	86.250		

$\alpha = .01$ Critical $F_{.01,1,6} = 13.75$ for rows

For rows, the observed $F = 38.37 > F_{.01,1,6} = 13.75$ and the decision is to **reject the null hypothesis**.

Critical $F_{.01,2,6} = 10.92$ for columns

For columns, the observed $F = 4.42 < F_{.01,2,6} = 10.92$ and the decision is to **fail to reject the null hypothesis**.

Critical $F_{.01,2,6} = 10.92$ for interaction

For interaction, the observed $F = 0.63 < F_{.01,2,6} = 10.92$ and the decision is to **fail to reject the null hypothesis**.

11.43

Source	Df	SS	MS	F
Row	3	42.4583	14.1528	14.77
Column	2	49.0833	24.5417	25.61
Interaction	6	4.9167	0.8194	0.86
Error	12	11.5000	0.9583	
Total	23	107.9583		

$\alpha = .05$ Critical $F_{.05,3,12} = 3.49$ for rows

For rows, the observed $F = 14.77 > F_{.05,3,12} = 3.49$ and the decision is to **reject the null hypothesis**.

Critical $F_{.05,2,12} = 3.89$ for columns

For columns, the observed $F = 25.61 > F_{.05,2,12} = 3.89$ and the decision is to **reject the null hypothesis**.

Critical $F_{.05,6,12} = 3.00$ for interaction

For interaction, the observed $F = 0.86 < F_{.05,6,12} = 3.00$ and **fail to reject the null hypothesis**.

11.45   This two-way design has 3 row treatments and 5 column treatments. There are 45 total observations with 3 in each cell.

$$F_R = \frac{MS_R}{MS_E} = \frac{46.16}{3.49} = 13.23$$

p-value = .000 and the decision is to **reject the null hypothesis for rows**.

$$F_C = \frac{MS_C}{MS_E} = \frac{249.70}{3.49} = 71.57$$

p-value = .000 and the decision is to **reject the null hypothesis for columns**.

$$F_I = \frac{MS_I}{MS_E} = \frac{55.27}{3.49} = 15.84$$

p-value = .000 and the decision is to reject the null hypothesis for interaction.

Because there is significant interaction, **the analysis of main effects is confounded**. The graph of means displays the crossing patterns of the line segments indicating the presence of interaction.

11.47   This two-way design has 3 row treatments and 3 column treatments. There are 3
        observations per cell.

$$F_R = \frac{MS_R}{MS_E} = \frac{19.11}{2.70} = 7.08$$

$F_{.05,2,18} = 3.55$ **The decision is to reject the null hypothesis for rows.**

$$F_C = \frac{MS_C}{MS_E} = \frac{196.33}{2.70} = 72.71$$

$F_{.05,2,18} = 3.55$ **The decision is to reject the null hypothesis for columns.**

$$F_I = \frac{MS_I}{MS_E} = \frac{3.11}{2.70} = 1.15$$

$F_{.05,4,18} = 2.93$ **The decision is to fail to reject the null hypothesis for interaction.**

The graph shows almost parallel lines supporting the interaction decision.

11.49

Source	Df	SS	MS	F
Treatment	6	68.19	11.365	0.87
Error	19	249.61	13.137	
Total	25	317.80		

11.51

Source	Df	SS	MS	F
Treatment	2	150.91	75.46	16.19
Error	22	102.53	4.66	
Total	24	253.44		

$\alpha = .01$ Critical $F_{.01,2,22} = 5.72$

Since the observed $F = 16.19 > F_{.01,2,22} = 5.72$, the decision is to **reject the null hypothesis**.

$$\overline{X}_1 = 9.200 \qquad \overline{X}_2 = 14.250 \qquad \overline{X}_3 = 8.714$$

$n_1 = 10$ $n_2 = 8$ $n_3 = 7$

$MSE = 4.66$ $C = 3$ $N = 25$ $N - C = 22$

$\alpha = .01$ $q_{.01,3,22} = 4.64$

$$HSD_{1,2} = 4.64 \sqrt{\frac{4.66}{2}\left(\frac{1}{10} + \frac{1}{8}\right)} = 3.36$$

$$HSD_{1,3} = 4.64 \sqrt{\frac{4.66}{2}\left(\frac{1}{10} + \frac{1}{7}\right)} = 3.49$$

$$HSD_{2,3} = 4.64 \sqrt{\frac{4.66}{2}\left(\frac{1}{8} + \frac{1}{7}\right)} = 3.14$$

$\left|\overline{X}_1 - \overline{X}_2\right| =$ **5.05** and $\left|\overline{X}_2 - \overline{X}_3\right| =$ **5.54** are **significantly different** at $\alpha = .01$

11.53

Source	Df	SS	MS	F
Treatment	3	20,994	6998.00	5.58
Blocks	9	16,453	1828.11	1.46
Error	27	33,891	1255.22	
Total	39	71,338		

$\alpha = .05$ Critical $F_{.05,3,27} = 2.96$ for treatments

Since the calculated $F = 5.58 > F_{.05,3,27} = 2.96$ for treatments, the decision is to **reject the null hypothesis**.

11.55

Source	Df	SS	MS	F
Treatment 1	4	29.13	7.2825	1.98
Treatment 2	1	12.67	12.6700	3.45
Interaction	4	73.49	18.3725	5.00
Error	30	110.30	3.6767	
Total	39	225.59		

$\alpha = .05$ Critical $F_{.05,4,30} = 2.69$ for treatment 1

For treatment 1, the observed $F = 1.98 < F_{.05,4,30} = 2.69$ and the decision is to **fail to reject the null hypothesis**.

Critical $F_{.05,1,30} = 4.17$ for treatment 2

For treatment 2 observed $F = 3.45 < F_{.05,1,30} = 4.17$ and the decision is to **fail to reject the null hypothesis**.

Critical $F_{.05,4,30} = 2.69$ for interaction

For interaction, the observed $F = 5.00 > F_{.05,4,30} = 2.69$ and the decision is to **reject the null hypothesis**.

Since there are significant interaction effects, examination of the main effects should not be done in the usual manner. However, in this case, there are no significant treatment effects anyway.

11.57

Source	Df	SS	MS	F
Row	2	49.3889	24.6944	38.65
Column	3	1.2222	0.4074	0.64
Interaction	6	1.2778	0.2130	0.33
Error	24	15.3333	0.6389	
Total	35	67.2222		

$\alpha = .05$ Critical $F_{.05,2,24} = 3.40$ for rows

For the row effects, the observed $F = 38.65 > F_{.05,2,24} = 3.40$ and the decision is to **reject the null hypothesis**.

Critical $F_{.05,3,24} = 3.01$ for columns

For the column effects, the observed $F = 0.64 < F_{.05,3,24} = 3.01$ and the decision is to **fail to reject the null hypothesis**.

Critical $F_{.05,6,24} = 2.51$ for interaction

For interaction effects, the observed $F = 0.33 < F_{.05,6,24} = 2.51$ and the decision is to **fail to reject the null hypothesis**.

There are no significant interaction effects. Only the row effects are significant.

Computing Tukey's HSD for rows:

$$\overline{X}_1 = 2.667 \qquad \overline{X}_2 = 4.917 \qquad \overline{X}_3 = 2.250$$

$$n = 12 \quad k = 3 \quad N = 36 \quad N - k = 33$$

MSE is recomputed by folding together the interaction and column sum of squares and degrees of freedom with previous error terms:

$$MSE = (1.2222 + 1.2778 + 15.3333)/(3 + 6 + 24) = 0.5404$$

$$q_{.05,3,33} = 3.49$$

$$HSD = q \sqrt{\frac{MSE}{n}} = (3.49) \sqrt{\frac{.5404}{12}} = 0.7406$$

Using HSD, there are significant pairwise differences between means 1 and 2 and between means 2 and 3.

Shown below is a graph of the interaction using the cell means by row.

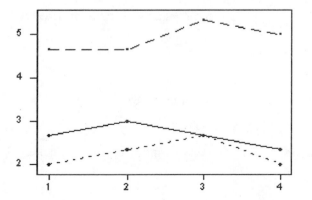

11.59

Source	Df	SS	MS	F
Treatment	2	460,353	230,176	103.70
Blocks	5	33,524	6,705	3.02
Error	10	22,197	2,220	
Total	17	516,074		

$\alpha = .01$ Critical $F_{.05,2,10} = 4.10$ for treatments

Since the treatment observed $F = 103.70 > F_{.05,2,10} = 4.10$, the decision is to **reject the null hypothesis**.

11.61

Source	Df	SS	MS	F
Row	2	4.875	2.437	5.16
Column	3	17.083	5.694	12.06
Interaction	6	2.292	0.382	0.81
Error	36	17.000	0.472	
Total	47	41.250		

$\alpha = .05$ Critical $F_{.05,2,36} = 3.32$ for rows

For rows, the observed $F = 5.16 > F_{.05,2,36} = 3.32$ and the decision is to **reject the null hypothesis**.

Critical $F_{.05,3,36} = 2.92$ for columns

For columns, the observed $F = 12.06 > F_{.05,3,36} = 2.92$ and the decision is to **reject the null hypothesis**.

Critical $F_{.05,6,36} = 2.42$ for interaction

For interaction, the observed $F = 0.81 < F_{.05,6,36} = 2.42$ and the decision is to **fail to reject the null hypothesis**.

There are no significant interaction effects. There are significant row and column effects at $\alpha = .05$.

11.63   This is a one-way ANOVA with four treatment levels. There are 36 observations in the study. An examination of the mean analysis shows that the sample sizes are different with sizes of 8, 7, 11, and 10 respectively. The p value of .04 indicates that there is a significant overall difference in the means at a = .05. No multiple comparison technique was used here to conduct pairwise comparisons. However, a study of sample means shows that the two most extreme means are from levels one and four. These two means would be the most likely candidates for multiple comparison tests.

11.65   This is a two-way ANOVA factorial design with interaction.   There are 5 levels of the row treatment, 2 levels of the column treatment, and 20 total observations with two observations per cell. The critical value for interaction effects is $F_{.05,4,10} = 3.48$. The observed F for interaction effects is $MS_I / MS_E = 160.9 / 28.0 = 5.75$. Since this observed value is greater than the critical value, there are significant interaction effects which confound the study.   Examining the observed F values and reaching conclusions about the row and/or column effects would be fruitless since there are significant interaction effects. The graph of cell means shown in the problem indicates the presence of interaction by the crossing of line segments.

11.67   This was a random block design with 5 treatment levels and 5 blocking levels. For both treatment and blocking effects, the critical value is $F_{.05,4,16} = 3.01$. The observed F value for treatment effects is $MS_C / MS_E = 35.98 / 7.36 = 4.89$ which is greater than the critical value. The null hypothesis for treatments is rejected, and we conclude that there is a significant different in treatment means. No multiple comparisons have been computed in the output.   However, a visual examination of sample means and there confidence intervals indicates that the mean for sample 1 appears to be quite higher than the other means.   The observed F value for blocking effects is $MS_R / MS_E = 10.36 /7.36 = 1.41$ which is less than the critical value. There are no significant blocking effects. Using random block design on this experiment might have cost a loss of power.

Chapter 12
Simple Regression and Correlation Analysis

LEARNING OBJECTIVES

The overall objective of this chapter is to give you an understanding of bivariate regression and correlation analysis, thereby enabling you to:

1. Be able to determine the equation of a simple regression line from a sample of data and interpret the slope and intercept of the equation.

2. Be able to understand the usefulness of residual analysis in testing the assumptions underlying regression analysis and in examining the fit of the regression line to the data.

3. Compute a standard error of the estimate and interpret its meaning.

4. Compute a coefficient of determination and interpret it.

5. Test hypotheses about the slope of the regression model and interpret the results.

6. Estimate values of Y using the regression model.

7. Compute a coefficient of correlation and interpret it.

CHAPTER OUTLINE

KEY WORDS

Coefficient of Determination (r^2)

Correlation

Covariance

Dependent Variable

Deterministic Model

Heteroscedasticity

Homoscedasticity

Independent Variable

Least Squares Analysis

Outliers

Pearson Product-Moment

Correlation Coefficient (r)

Probabilistic Model

Regression

Residual

Residual Plot

Scatter Plot

Simple Regression

Standard Error of the Estimate (S_e)

Sum of Squares of Error (SSE)

STUDY QUESTIONS

1. _____ is a measure of the degree of relatedness of two variables.

2. The process of constructing a mathematical model or function that can be used to predict or determine one variable by another variable is _____ .

3. Bivariate linear regression is often termed _____ regression.

4. In regression, the variable being predicted is usually referred to as the _____ variable.

5. In regression, the predictor is called the _____ variable.

6. The first step in simple regression analysis often is to graph or construct a _____ .

7. In regression analysis, β_1 represents the population _____ .

8. In regression analysis, b_o represents the sample _____ .

9. A researcher wants to develop a regression model to predict the price of gold by the prime interest rate. The dependent variable is _____ .

10. In an effort to develop a regression model, the following data were gathered:

    X: 2, 9, 11, 19, 21, 25
    Y: 26, 17, 18, 15, 15, 8

    The slope of the regression line determined from these data is _____ . The Y intercept is _____ .

11. A researcher wants to develop a regression line from the data given below:

    X: 12, 11, 5, 6, 9
    Y: 31, 25, 14, 12, 16

    The equation of the regression line is _____ .

12. In regression, the value of $Y - \hat{Y}$ is called the _____ .

13. Data points that lie apart from the rest of the points are called _____ .

14. The regression assumption of constant error variance is called _____ .

    If the error variances are not constant, it is called _____ .

15.   Suppose the graph of residuals looks like:

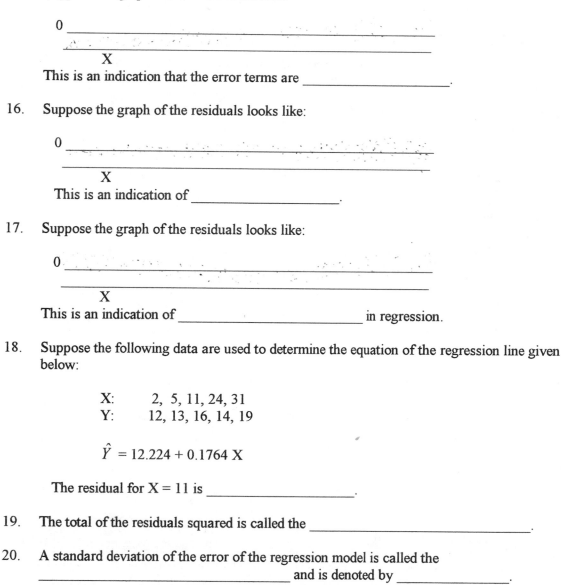

       This is an indication that the error terms are _____.

16.   Suppose the graph of the residuals looks like:

       This is an indication of _____.

17.   Suppose the graph of the residuals looks like:

       This is an indication of _____ in regression.

18.   Suppose the following data are used to determine the equation of the regression line given
       below:

              X: 2, 5, 11, 24, 31
              Y: 12, 13, 16, 14, 19

              $\hat{Y} = 12.224 + 0.1764\ X$

       The residual for X = 11 is _____.

19.   The total of the residuals squared is called the _____.

20.   A standard deviation of the error of the regression model is called the
       _____ and is denoted by _____.

21.   Suppose a regression model is developed for ten pairs of data resulting in S.S.E. = 1,203.
       The standard error of the estimate is _____.

22.   A regression analysis results in the following data:

       X = 276 $X^2 = 12{,}014$ XY = 2,438
       Y = 77 $Y^2 = 1{,}183$ n = 7

       The value of S.S.E. is _____.

23.   The value of S_e is computed from the data of question 22 is _____.

24.   Suppose a regression model results in a value of $S_e = 27.9$. 95% of the residuals should fall within _____ .

25.   Coefficient of determination is denoted by _____ .

26.   _____ is the proportion of variability of the dependent variable accounted for or explained by the independent variable.

27.   The value of r^2 always falls between _____ and _____ inclusive.

28.   Suppose a regression analysis results in the following:

$$b_1 = .19364 \qquad Y = 1,019$$
$$b_0 = 59.4798 \qquad Y^2 = 134,451$$
$$n = 8 \qquad XY = 378,932$$

The value of r^2 for this regression model is _____ .

29.   Suppose the data below are used to determine the equation of a regression line:

X: 18, 14, 9, 6, 2
Y: 14, 25, 22, 23, 27

The value of r^2 associated with this model is _____ .

30.   A researcher has developed a regression model from sixteen pairs of data points. He wants to test to determine if the slope is significantly different from zero. He uses a two-tailed test and $\alpha = .01$. The critical table t value is _____ .

31.   The following data are used to develop a simple regression model:

X: 22, 20, 15, 15, 14, 9
Y: 31, 20, 12, 9, 10, 6

The calculated t value used to test the slope of this regression model is _____ .

32.   If = .05 and a two-tailed test is being conducted, the critical table t value to test the slope of the model developed in question 31 is _____ .

33.   The decision reached about the slope of the model computed in question 31 is to _____ the null hypothesis.

34.   The Pearson product-moment correlation coefficient is denoted by _____ .

35.   The value of r varies from _____ .

36.   Perfect positive correlation results in an r value of _____ .

37.   Squaring the value of the coefficient of correlation results in the value of _____ .

38.   The variance of X and Y together is called _____.

39.   The value of the coefficient of correlation from the following data is _____.

> X: 19, 20, 26, 31, 34, 45, 45, 51
> Y: 78, 100, 125, 120, 119, 130, 145, 143

40.   The value of r from the following data is _____.

> X: -10, -6,   1,   4, 15
> Y: -26, -44, -36, -39, -43

ANSWERS TO STUDY QUESTIONS

1. Correlation

2. Regression

3. Simple

4. Dependent

5. Independent

6. Scatter Plot

7. Slope

8. Y Intercept

9. Price of Gold

10. -0.626, 25.575

11. -1.253 + 2.425 X

12. Residual

13. Outliers

14. Homoscedasticity, Heteroscadasticity

15. Nonindependent

16. Nonconstant Error Variance

17. Nonlinearity

18. 1.8356

19. Sum of Squares of Error

20. Standard Error of the Estimate, S_e

21. 12.263

22. 20.015

23. 2.00

24. 0 ± 55.8

25. r^2

26. Coefficient of Determination

27. 0, 1

28. .900

29. .578

30. 2.977

31. 4.72

32. ± 2.776

33. Reject

34. r

35. -1 to 0 to $+1$

36. $+1$

37. r^2

38. Covariance

39. .876

40. -.581

SOLUTIONS TO ODD-NUMBERED PROBLEMS IN CHAPTER 12

12.1

X	Y
6	5
11	2
9	3
14	1
5	7
3	11

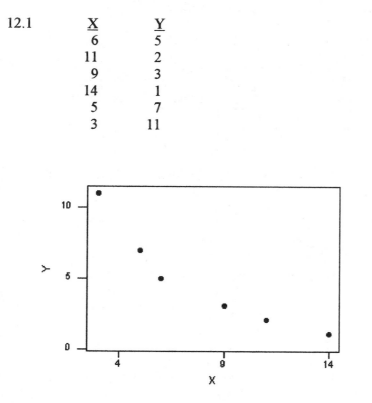

12.3 $b_1 = \dfrac{SS_{XY}}{SS_X} = \dfrac{\sum XY - \dfrac{\sum X \sum Y}{n}}{\sum X^2 - \dfrac{(\sum X)^2}{n}} = \dfrac{6{,}596 - \dfrac{(261)(148)}{9}}{11{,}219 - \dfrac{(261)^2}{9}} = \dfrac{2{,}304}{3{,}650} = \mathbf{0.631}$

$b_0 = \dfrac{\sum Y}{n} - b_1 \dfrac{\sum X}{n} = \dfrac{148}{9} - 0.631 \dfrac{261}{9} = \mathbf{-1.855}$

$\hat{Y} = \mathbf{-1.855 + 0.631\ X}$

12.5

X	Y
12	17
21	15
28	22
8	19
20	24

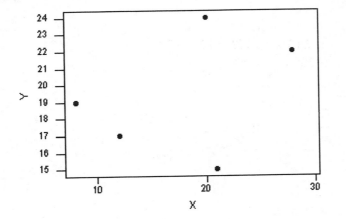

$\Sigma X = 89$ $\Sigma Y = 97$ $\Sigma XY = 1{,}767$

$\Sigma X^2 = 1{,}833$ $\Sigma Y^2 = 1{,}935$ $n = 5$

$$b_1 = \frac{SS_{XY}}{SS_X} = \frac{\sum XY - \dfrac{\sum X \sum Y}{n}}{\sum X^2 - \dfrac{(\sum X)^2}{n}} = \frac{1{,}767 - \dfrac{(89)(97)}{5}}{1{,}833 - \dfrac{(89)^2}{5}} = \mathbf{0.162}$$

$$b_0 = \frac{\sum Y}{n} - b_1 \frac{\sum X}{n} = \frac{97}{5} - 0.162 \frac{89}{5} = \mathbf{16.5}$$

$$\hat{Y} = \mathbf{16.5 + 0.162\ X}$$

12.7

(Advertising) X	(Sales) Y
12.5	148
3.7	55
21.6	338
60.0	994
37.6	541
6.1	89
16.8	126
41.2	379

$\Sigma X = 199.5$ $\Sigma Y = 2{,}670$ $\Sigma XY = 107{,}610.4$

$\Sigma X^2 = 7{,}667.15$ $\Sigma Y^2 = 1{,}587{,}328$ $n = 8$

$$b_1 = \frac{SS_{XY}}{SS_X} = \frac{\sum XY - \frac{\sum X \sum Y}{n}}{\sum X^2 - \frac{(\sum X)^2}{n}} = \frac{107{,}610.4 - \frac{(199.5)(2{,}670)}{8}}{7{,}667.15 - \frac{(199.5)^2}{8}} = 15.24$$

$$b_0 = \frac{\sum Y}{n} - b_1 \frac{\sum X}{n} = \frac{2{,}670}{8} - 15.24\frac{199.5}{8} = -46.29$$

$$\hat{Y} = -46.29 + 15.24\ X$$

12.9

Starts	Failures
233,710	57,097
199,091	50,361
181,645	60,747
158,930	88,140
155,672	97,069
164,086	86,133
166,154	71,558
188,387	71,128
168,158	71,931
170,475	83,384

$\Sigma X = 1{,}786{,}308$ $\Sigma Y = 737{,}548$ $\Sigma X^2 = 324{,}104{,}880{,}400$

$\Sigma Y^2 = 56{,}403{,}139{,}750$ $\Sigma XY = 129{,}257{,}084{,}500$ $n = 10$

$$b_1 = \frac{SS_{XY}}{SS_X} = \frac{\sum XY - \dfrac{\sum X \sum Y}{n}}{\sum X^2 - \dfrac{(\sum X)^2}{n}} = \frac{129{,}257{,}084{,}500 - \dfrac{(1{,}786{,}308)(737{,}548)}{10}}{324{,}104{,}880{,}400 - \dfrac{(1{,}786{,}308)^2}{10}} =$$

$$b_1 = -0.496825$$

$$b_0 = \frac{\sum Y}{n} - b_1 \frac{\sum X}{n} = \frac{737{,}548}{10} - (-0.496825)\frac{1{,}786{,}308}{10} = 162{,}503.1$$

$$\hat{Y} = 162{,}503.1 - 0.496825\,X$$

12.11

Steel	New Orders
99.9	2.74
97.9	2.87
98.9	2.93
87.9	2.87
92.9	2.98
97.9	3.09
100.6	3.36
104.9	3.61
105.3	3.75
108.6	3.95

$\sum X = 994.8$ $\sum Y = 32.15$ $\sum X^2 = 99{,}293.28$

$\sum Y^2 = 104.9815$ $\sum XY = 3{,}216.652$ $n = 10$

$$b_1 = \frac{SS_{XY}}{SS_X} = \frac{\sum XY - \dfrac{\sum X \sum Y}{n}}{\sum X^2 - \dfrac{(\sum X)^2}{n}} = \frac{3{,}216.652 - \dfrac{(994.8)(32.15)}{10}}{99{,}293.28 - \dfrac{(994.8)^2}{10}} = 0.05557$$

$$b_0 = \frac{\sum Y}{n} - b_1 \frac{\sum X}{n} = \frac{32.15}{10} - (0.05557)\frac{994.8}{10} = -2.31307$$

$$\hat{Y} = -2.31307 + 0.05557\,X$$

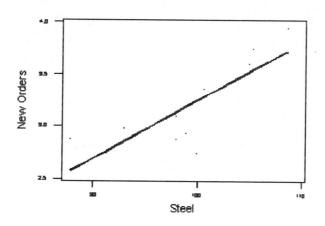

12.13

X	Y	Predicted ($\hat{Y}$)	Residuals (Y-$\hat{Y}$)
12	17	18.4582	-1.4582
21	15	19.9196	-4.9196
28	22	21.0563	0.9437
8	19	17.8087	1.1913
20	24	19.7572	4.2428

$$\hat{Y} = 16.5 + 0.162 \, X$$

12.15

X	Y	Predicted ($\hat{Y}$)	Residuals (Y-$\hat{Y}$)
12.5	148	144.2053	3.7947
3.7	55	10.0953	44.9047
21.6	338	282.8873	55.1127
60.0	994	868.0945	125.9055
37.6	541	526.7236	14.2764
6.1	89	46.6708	42.3292
16.8	126	209.7364	-83.7364
41.2	379	581.5868	-202.5868

$$\hat{Y} = -46.29 + 15.24 \, X$$

12.17

X	Y	Predicted ($\hat{Y}$)	Residuals (Y-$\hat{Y}$)
5	47	42.2756	4.7244
7	38	38.9836	-0.9836
11	32	32.3996	-0.3996
12	24	30.7537	-6.7537
19	22	19.2317	2.7683
25	10	9.3558	0.6442

$$\hat{Y} = 50.5056 - 1.6460 \, X$$

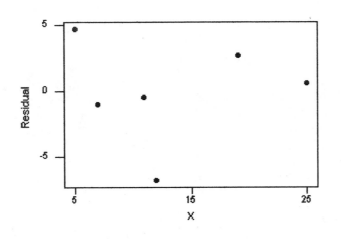

No apparent violation of assumptions

12.19

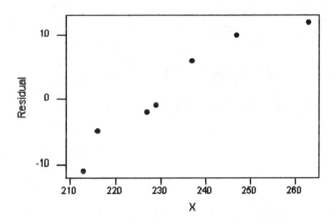

Error terms appear to be non independent

12.21

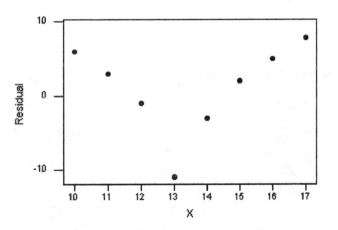

There appears to be nonlinear regression

12.23 $SSE = \Sigma Y^2 - b_0 \Sigma Y - b_1 \Sigma XY = 1,935 - (16.51)(97) - 0.1624(1767) = 46.5692$

$$S_e = \sqrt{\frac{SSE}{n-2}} = \sqrt{\frac{46.5692}{3}} = \textbf{3.94}$$

Approximately 68% of the residuals should fall within ±1Se.

3 out of 5 or 60% of the actually residuals in 11.13 fell within ± 1Se.

12.25 $SSE = \Sigma Y^2 - b_0 \Sigma Y - b_1 \Sigma XY = 1,587,328 - (-46.29)(2,670) - 15.24(107,610.4) =$

SSE = 70,940

$$S_e = \sqrt{\frac{SSE}{n-2}} = \sqrt{\frac{70,940}{6}} = \textbf{108.7}$$

Six out of eight (75%) of the sales estimates are within $108.7 million.

12.27

$(Y-\hat{Y})$	$(Y-\hat{Y})^2$
4.7244	22.3200
-0.9836	.9675
-0.3996	.1597
-6.7537	45.6125
2.7683	7.6635
0.6442	.4150

$$\Sigma(Y-\hat{Y})^2 = 77.1382$$

$$SSE = \sum(Y-\hat{Y})^2 = 77.1382$$

$$S_e = \sqrt{\frac{SSE}{n-2}} = \sqrt{\frac{77.1382}{4}} = \textbf{4.391}$$

12.29

Volume (X)	Sales (Y)
728.6	10.5
497.9	48.1
439.1	64.8
377.9	20.1
375.5	11.4
363.8	123.8
276.3	89.0

$n=7$ $\Sigma X = 3059.1$ $\Sigma Y = 367.7$

$\Sigma X^2 = 1,464,071.97$ $\Sigma Y^2 = 30,404.31$ $\Sigma XY = 141,558.6$

$b_1 = -.1504$ $b_0 = 118.257$

$\hat{Y} = 118.257 - .1504$

$SSE = \Sigma Y^2 - b_0 \Sigma Y - b_1 \Sigma XY$

$= 30,404.31 - (118.257)(367.7) - (-0.1504)(141,558.6) = 8211.6245$

$S_e = \sqrt{\dfrac{SSE}{n-2}} = \sqrt{\dfrac{8211.6245}{5}} = \mathbf{40.5256}$

This is a relatively large standard error of the estimate given the sales values (ranging from 10.5 to 123.8).

12.31 $r^2 = 1 - \dfrac{SSE}{\sum Y^2 - \dfrac{(\sum Y)^2}{n}} = 1 - \dfrac{272.12}{45,154 - \dfrac{(498)^2}{7}} = .972$

This is a high value of r^2

12.33 $r^2 = 1 - \dfrac{SSE}{\sum Y^2 - \dfrac{(\sum Y)^2}{n}} = 1 - \dfrac{19.8885}{524 - \dfrac{(48)^2}{5}} = .685$

This value of r^2 is a modest value.
68.5% of the variation of Y is accounted for by X but 31.5% is unaccounted for.

12.35

CCI	Median Income
116.8	37.415
91.5	36.770
68.5	35.501
61.6	35.047
65.9	34.700
90.6	34.942
100.0	35.887
104.6	36.306
125.4	37.005

$\Sigma X = 323.573$ $\Sigma Y = 824.9$ $\Sigma X^2 = 11,640.93413$

$\Sigma Y^2 = 79,718.79$ $\Sigma XY = 29,804.4505$ $n = 9$

$$b_1 = \frac{SS_{XY}}{SS_X} = \frac{\sum XY - \dfrac{\sum X \sum Y}{n}}{\sum X^2 - \dfrac{(\sum X)^2}{n}} = \frac{29,804.4505 - \dfrac{(323.573)(824.9)}{9}}{11,640.93413 - \dfrac{(323.573)^2}{9}} =$$

$b_1 = \textbf{19.2204}$

$$b_0 = \frac{\sum Y}{n} - b_1 \frac{\sum X}{n} = \frac{824.9}{9} - (19.2204)\frac{323.573}{9} = \textbf{-599.3674}$$

$\hat{Y} = \textbf{-599.3674} + \textbf{19.2204 X}$

$SSE = \Sigma Y^2 - b_0 \Sigma Y - b_1 \Sigma XY =$

$79,718.79 - (-599.3674)(824.9) - 19.2204(29,804.4505) = 1283.13435$

$$S_e = \sqrt{\frac{SSE}{n-2}} = \sqrt{\frac{1283.13435}{7}} = \textbf{13.539}$$

$$r^2 = 1 - \frac{SSE}{\sum Y^2 - \dfrac{(\sum Y)^2}{n}} = 1 - \frac{1283.13435}{79,718.79 - \dfrac{(824.9)^2}{9}} = \textbf{.688}$$

12.37 $S_b = \dfrac{S_e}{\sqrt{\sum X^2 - \dfrac{(\sum X)^2}{n}}} = \dfrac{7.376}{\sqrt{58,293 - \dfrac{(571)^2}{7}}} = .068145$

$b_1 = -0.898$

$H_o:\ \beta = 0$ $\alpha = .01$
$H_a:\ \beta \neq 0$

Two-tail test, $\alpha/2 = .005$ $df = n - 2 = 7 - 2 = 5$

$t_{.005,5} = \pm 4.032$

$t = \dfrac{b_1 - \beta_1}{S_b} = \dfrac{-0.898 - 0}{.068145} = \mathbf{-13.18}$

Since the observed t = -13.18 < $t_{.005,5}$ = -4.032, the decision is to **reject the null hypothesis**.

12.39 $S_b = \dfrac{S_e}{\sqrt{\sum X^2 - \dfrac{(\sum X)^2}{n}}} = \dfrac{2.575}{\sqrt{421 - \dfrac{(41)^2}{5}}} = .27963$

$b_1 = -0.715$

$H_o:\ \beta = 0$ $\alpha = .05$
$H_a:\ \beta \neq 0$

For a two-tail test, $\alpha/2 = .025$ $df = n - 2 = 5 - 2 = 3$

$t_{.025,3} = \pm 3.182$

$t = \dfrac{b_1 - \beta_1}{S_b} = \dfrac{-0.715 - 0}{.27963} = \mathbf{-2.56}$

Since the observed t = -2.56 > $t_{.025,3}$ = -3.182, the decision is to **fail to reject the null hypothesis**.

12.41 $F = 8.26$ with a p-value of .021. The overall model is significant at $\alpha = .05$ but not at $\alpha = .01$. For simple regression,

$$t = \sqrt{F} = 2.8674$$

$t_{.05,5} = 2.015$ but $t_{.01,5} = 3.365$. The slope is significant at $\alpha = .05$ but not at $\alpha = .01$.

12.43 $X_0 = 100$ For 90% confidence, $\alpha/2 = .05$
        $df = n - 2 = 7 - 2 = 5$ $t_{.05,5} = \pm 2.015$

$$\overline{X} = \frac{\sum X}{n} = \frac{571}{7} = 81.57143$$

$\sum X = 571$ $\sum X^2 = 58{,}293$ $S_e = 7.377$

$$\hat{Y} = 144.414 - .0898(100) = 54.614$$

$$\hat{Y} \pm t_{/2,n\text{-}2}\, S_e \sqrt{1 + \frac{1}{n} + \frac{(X_0 - \overline{X})^2}{\sum X^2 - \dfrac{(\sum X)^2}{n}}} =$$

$$54.614 \pm 2.015(7.377) \sqrt{1 + \frac{1}{7} + \frac{(100 - 81.57143)^2}{58{,}293 - \dfrac{(571)^2}{7}}} =$$

$$54.614 \pm 2.015(7.377)(1.08252) = 54.614 \pm 16.091$$

$38.523 \le Y \le 70.705$

For $X_0 = 130,$ $\hat{Y} = 144.414 - .0898(130) = 27.674$

$$Y \pm t_{/2,n\text{-}2}\, S_e \sqrt{1 + \frac{1}{n} + \frac{(X_0 - \overline{X})^2}{\sum X^2 - \dfrac{(\sum X)^2}{n}}} =$$

$$27.674 \pm 2.015(7.377)\sqrt{1+\frac{1}{7}+\frac{(130-81.57143)^2}{58{,}293-\frac{(571)^2}{7}}} =$$

$$27.674 \pm 2.015(7.377)(1.1589) = \qquad 27.674 \pm 17.227$$

$10.447 \le Y \le 44.901$

The width of this confidence interval of Y for $X_0 = 130$ is <u>wider</u> that the confidence interval of Y for $X_0 = 100$ because $X_0 = 100$ is nearer to the value of $X = 81.57$ than is $X_0 = 130$.

12.45   **$X_0 = 10$**   For 99% confidence $\alpha/2 = .005$
       df = n - 2 = 5 - 2 = 3 $t_{.005,3} = 5.841$

$$\overline{X} = \frac{\sum X}{n} = \frac{41}{5} = 8.20$$

$\sum X = 41$ $\sum X^2 = 421$ $S_e = 2.575$

$$\hat{Y} = 15.46 - 0.715(10) = 8.31$$

$$\hat{Y} \pm t_{/2,n-2}\, S_e \sqrt{\frac{1}{n}+\frac{(X_0-\overline{X})^2}{\sum X^2-\frac{(\sum X)^2}{n}}}$$

$$8.31 \pm 5.841(2.575)\sqrt{\frac{1}{5}+\frac{(10-8.2)^2}{421-\frac{(41)^2}{5}}} =$$

$$8.31 \pm 5.841(2.575)(.488065) = 8.31 \pm 7.34$$

$0.97 \le E(Y_{10}) \le 15.65$

If the prime interest rate is 10%, we are 99% confident that the average bond rate is between 0.97% and 15.65%.

12.47 $\Sigma X = 93$ $\Sigma X^2 = 1,619$ $\Sigma Y = 103$
         $\Sigma Y^2 = 1,811$ $\Sigma XY = 1,691$ $n = 7$

$$r = \frac{\sum XY - \dfrac{\sum X \sum Y}{n}}{\sqrt{\left[\sum X^2 - \dfrac{(\sum X)^2}{n}\right]\left[\sum Y^2 - \dfrac{(\sum Y)^2}{n}\right]}} =$$

$$r = \frac{1,691 - \dfrac{(93)(103)}{7}}{\sqrt{\left[1,619 - \dfrac{(93)^2}{7}\right]\left[1,811 - \dfrac{(103)^2}{7}\right]}} =$$

$$r = \frac{322.5714}{\sqrt{(383.4286)(295.4286)}} = \frac{322.5714}{336.5647} = \mathbf{0.958}$$

12.49

Delta (X)	SW (Y)
47.6	15.1
46.3	15.4
50.6	15.9
52.6	15.6
52.4	16.4
52.7	18.1

$\Sigma X = 302.2$ $\Sigma Y = 96.5$ $\Sigma XY = 4,870.11$
$\Sigma X^2 = 15,259.62$ $\Sigma Y^2 = 1,557.91$

$$r = \frac{\sum XY - \dfrac{\sum X \sum Y}{n}}{\sqrt{\left[\sum X^2 - \dfrac{(\sum X)^2}{n}\right]\left[\sum Y^2 - \dfrac{(\sum Y)^2}{n}\right]}} =$$

$$r = \frac{4,870.11 - \dfrac{(302.2)(96.5)}{6}}{\sqrt{\left[15,259.62 - \dfrac{(302.2)^2}{6}\right]\left[1,557.91 - \dfrac{(96.5)^2}{6}\right]}} = \mathbf{.6445}$$

12.51 $\Sigma X = 6,087$ $\Sigma X^2 = 6,796,149$

$\Sigma Y = 1,050$ $\Sigma Y^2 = 194,526$

$\Sigma XY = 1,130,483$ $n = 9$

$$r = \frac{\sum XY - \dfrac{\sum X \sum Y}{n}}{\sqrt{\left[\sum X^2 - \dfrac{(\sum X)^2}{n}\right]\left[\sum Y^2 - \dfrac{(\sum Y)^2}{n}\right]}} =$$

$$r = \frac{1,130,483 - \dfrac{(6,087)(1,050)}{9}}{\sqrt{\left[6,796,149 - \dfrac{(6,087)^2}{9}\right]\left[194,526 - \dfrac{(1,050)^2}{9}\right]}} =$$

$$r = \frac{420,333}{\sqrt{(2,679,308)(72,026)}} = \frac{420,333}{439,294.705} = \mathbf{.957}$$

12.53

X	Y
5	8
7	9
3	11
16	27
12	15
9	13

$\Sigma X = 52$ $\Sigma X^2 = 564$

$\Sigma Y = 83$ $\Sigma Y^2 = 1,389$ $b_1 = 1.2853$

$\Sigma XY = 865$ $n = 6$ $b_0 = 2.6941$

a) $\hat{Y} = 2.6941 + 1.2853\ X$

b)

$\hat{Y}$ (Predicted Values)	(Y-$\hat{Y}$) residuals
9.1206	-1.1206
11.6912	-2.6912
6.5500	4.4500
23.2588	3.7412
18.1176	-3.1176
14.2618	-1.2618

c) $\dfrac{(Y-\hat{Y})^2}{}$

  1.2557
  7.2426
  19.8025
  13.9966
  9.7194
  1.5921

SSE $= 53.6089$

$$S_e = \sqrt{\dfrac{SSE}{n-2}} = \sqrt{\dfrac{53.6089}{4}} = \mathbf{3.661}$$

d) $r^2 = 1 - \dfrac{SSE}{\sum Y^2 - \dfrac{(\sum Y)^2}{n}} = 1 - \dfrac{53.6089}{1{,}389 - \dfrac{(83)^2}{6}} = \mathbf{.777}$

e) H_o: $\beta = 0$ $\alpha = .01$
   H_a: $\beta \neq 0$

   Two-tailed test, $\alpha/2 = .005$ df $= n - 2 = 6 - 2 = 4$

   $t_{.005,4} = \pm 4.604$

   $$S_b = \dfrac{S_e}{\sqrt{\sum X^2 - \dfrac{(\sum X)^2}{n}}} = \dfrac{3.661}{\sqrt{564 - \dfrac{(52)^2}{6}}} = .34389$$

   $$t = \dfrac{b_1 - \beta_1}{S_b} = \dfrac{1.2853 - 0}{.34389} = \mathbf{3.74}$$

   Since the observed t $= 3.74 < t_{.005,4} = 4.604$, the decision is to **fail to reject the null hypothesis**.

f) The $R^2 = 77.74\%$ is modest. There appears to be some prediction with this model. The slope of the regression line is not significantly different from zero using $= .01$. However, for $= .05$, the null hypothesis of a zero slope is rejected. The standard error of the estimate, $S_e = 3.661$ is not particularly small given the range of values for Y (11 - 3 = 8).

12.55 $\Sigma X = 1,263$ $\Sigma X^2 = 268,295$
         $\Sigma Y = 417$ $\Sigma Y^2 = 29,135$
         $\Sigma XY = 88,288$ $n = 6$

$$r = \frac{\sum XY - \dfrac{\sum X \sum Y}{n}}{\sqrt{\left[\sum X^2 - \dfrac{(\sum X)^2}{n}\right]\left[\sum Y^2 - \dfrac{(\sum Y)^2}{n}\right]}} =$$

$$r = \frac{88,288 - \dfrac{(1,263)(417)}{6}}{\sqrt{\left[268,295 - \dfrac{(1,263)^2}{6}\right]\left[29,135 - \dfrac{(417)^2}{6}\right]}} =$$

$$r = \frac{509.5}{\sqrt{(2,433.5)(153.5)}} = \frac{509.5}{611.18} = .834$$

Coefficient of determination = r^2 = **.695**

12.57 $\Sigma X = 36$ $\Sigma X^2 = 256$
         $\Sigma Y = 44$ $\Sigma Y^2 = 300$
         $\Sigma XY = 188$ $n = 7$

$$r = \frac{\sum XY - \dfrac{\sum X \sum Y}{n}}{\sqrt{\left[\sum X^2 - \dfrac{(\sum X)^2}{n}\right]\left[\sum Y^2 - \dfrac{(\sum Y)^2}{n}\right]}} =$$

$$r = \frac{188 - \dfrac{(36)(44)}{7}}{\sqrt{\left[256 - \dfrac{(36)^2}{7}\right]\left[300 - \dfrac{(44)^2}{7}\right]}} =$$

$$r = \frac{-38.2857}{\sqrt{(70.8571)(23.42857)}} = \frac{-38.2857}{40.7441} = -.940$$

12.59 n = 12 ΣX = 548 ΣX^2 = 26,592
ΣY = 5940 ΣY^2 = 3,211,546 ΣXY = 287,908

b_1 = 10.626383 b_0 = 9.728511

$\hat{Y}$ = **9.728511 + 10.626383 X**

SSE = $\Sigma Y^2 - b_0 \Sigma Y - b_1 \Sigma XY$ =

3,211,546 - (9.728511)(5940) - (10.626383)(287,908) = 94337.9762

$$S_e = \sqrt{\frac{SSE}{n-2}} = \sqrt{\frac{94,337.9762}{10}} = \textbf{97.1277}$$

$$r^2 = 1 - \frac{SSE}{\Sigma Y^2 - \frac{(\Sigma Y)^2}{n}} = 1 - \frac{94,337.9762}{271,246} = \textbf{.652}$$

$$t = \frac{\dfrac{10.626383 - 0}{97.1277}}{\sqrt{26,592 - \dfrac{(548)^2}{12}}} = \textbf{4.33}$$

If = .01, then $t_{.005,10}$ = 3.169. Since the observed t = 4.33 > $t_{.005,10}$ = 3.169, the decision is to **reject the null hypothesis**.

12.61   <u>1977</u>   <u>1997</u>

581   642
213   242
668   729
345   269
1476   1497
1776   6129

ΣX = 5059 ΣY = 9508 ΣX^2 = 6,280,931
ΣY^2 = 40,880,180 ΣXY = 14,099,001   n = 6

a) $r = \dfrac{\sum XY - \dfrac{\sum X \sum Y}{n}}{\sqrt{\left[\sum X^2 - \dfrac{(\sum X)^2}{n}\right]\left[\sum Y^2 - \dfrac{(\sum Y)^2}{n}\right]}} = $

$r = \dfrac{14{,}099{,}001 - \dfrac{(5059)(9508)}{6}}{\sqrt{\left[6{,}280{,}931 - \dfrac{(5059)^2}{6}\right]\left[40{,}880{,}180 - \dfrac{(9508)^2}{6}\right]}} = .8433$

b) $b_1 = \dfrac{SS_{XY}}{SS_X} = \dfrac{\sum XY - \dfrac{\sum X \sum Y}{n}}{\sum X^2 - \dfrac{(\sum X)^2}{n}} = \dfrac{14{,}099{,}001 - \dfrac{(5059)(9508)}{6}}{6{,}280{,}931 - \dfrac{(5059)^2}{6}} = 3.01792$

$b_0 = \dfrac{\sum Y}{n} - b_1 \dfrac{\sum X}{n} = \dfrac{9508}{6} - (3.01792)\dfrac{5059}{6} = -959.94487$

$\hat{Y} = \mathbf{-959.94487 + 3.01792\ X}$

for X = 700:

$\hat{Y} = 1152.6008$

$\hat{Y} \pm t_{\alpha/2,n-2} S_e \sqrt{\dfrac{1}{n} + \dfrac{(X_0 - \overline{X})^2}{\sum X^2 - \dfrac{(\sum X)^2}{n}}}$

$\alpha = .05, \quad t_{.025,4} = 2.776$

$X_0 = 700, n = 6$

$\overline{X} = 843.167$

$SSE = \sum Y^2 - b_0 \sum Y - b_1 \sum XY =$

$40{,}880{,}180 - (-959.9448)(9508) - (3.01792)(14{,}099{,}001) = 7{,}457{,}678.726$

$$S_e = \sqrt{\frac{SSE}{n-2}} = \sqrt{\frac{7,457,678.726}{4}} = 1365.4375$$

Confidence Interval =

$$1152.6008 \pm (2.776)(1365.4375)\sqrt{\frac{1}{6} + \frac{(700 - 843.167)^2}{6,280,931 - \frac{(5059)^2}{6}}} =$$

$$1152.6008 \pm 1593.9616$$

-441.3608 to 2746.5624

H_0: $\beta_1 = 0$
H_a: $\beta_1 \neq 0$

$\alpha = .05$ df = 4

Table $t_{.025,4} = 2.132$

$$t = \frac{b_1 - 0}{S_b} = \frac{3.01792 - 0}{\frac{1365.4375}{\sqrt{2,015,350.833}}} = \frac{3.01792}{.961826} = \mathbf{3.138}$$

Since the observed t = 3.138 > $t_{.025,4}$ = 2.132, the decision is to **reject the null hypothesis**.

12.63 $\Sigma X = 44,754$ $\Sigma Y = 17,314$ $\Sigma X^2 = 167,540,610$

$\Sigma Y^2 = 24,646,062$ $n = 13$ $\Sigma XY = 59,852,571$

a) $b_1 = \dfrac{SS_{XY}}{SS_X} = \dfrac{\sum XY - \dfrac{\sum X \sum Y}{n}}{\sum X^2 - \dfrac{(\sum X)^2}{n}} = \dfrac{59,852,571 - \dfrac{(44,754)(17,314)}{13}}{167,540,610 - \dfrac{(44,754)^2}{13}} = .01835$

$b_0 = \dfrac{\sum Y}{n} - b_1 \dfrac{\sum X}{n} = \dfrac{17,314}{13} - (.01835)\dfrac{44,754}{13} = 1268.685$

$\hat{Y} = \mathbf{1268.685 + .01835\ X}$

b) $r = \dfrac{\sum XY - \dfrac{\sum X \sum Y}{n}}{\sqrt{\left[\sum X^2 - \dfrac{(\sum X)^2}{n}\right]\left[\sum Y^2 - \dfrac{(\sum Y)^2}{n}\right]}} =$

$r = \dfrac{59,852,571 - \dfrac{(44,754)(17,314)}{13}}{\sqrt{\left[167,540,610 - \dfrac{(44,754)^2}{13}\right]\left[24,646,062 - \dfrac{(17,314)^2}{13}\right]}} = \mathbf{.0535}$

12.65 $\Sigma X = 323.3$ $\Sigma Y = 676.8$
$\Sigma X^2 = 29,629.13$ $\Sigma Y^2 = 7,583,144.64$
$\Sigma XY = 339,342.76$ $n = 7$

$b_1 = \dfrac{SS_{XY}}{SS_X} = \dfrac{\sum XY - \dfrac{\sum X \sum Y}{n}}{\sum X^2 - \dfrac{(\sum X)^2}{n}} = \dfrac{339,342.76 - \dfrac{(323.3)(676.8)}{7}}{29,629.13 - \dfrac{(323.3)^2}{7}} = 1.82751$

$b_0 = \dfrac{\sum Y}{n} - b_1 \dfrac{\sum X}{n} = \dfrac{676.8}{7} - (1.82751)\dfrac{323.3}{7} = 882.138$

$\hat{Y} = \mathbf{882.138 + 1.82751\ X}$

$$SSE = \Sigma Y^2 - b_0 \Sigma Y - b_1 \Sigma XY$$

$$= 7,583,144.64 - (882.138)(676.8) - (339,342.76) = 994,623.07$$

$$S_e = \sqrt{\frac{SSE}{n-2}} = \sqrt{\frac{994,623.07}{7}} = \mathbf{446.01}$$

$$r^2 = 1 - \frac{SSE}{\Sigma Y^2 - \frac{(\Sigma Y)^2}{n}} = 1 - \frac{994,623.07}{7,583,144.64 - \frac{(6765.8)^2}{7}} = 1 - .953 = \mathbf{.047}$$

$H_0: \beta = 0$
$H_a: \beta \neq 0$ $\alpha = .05$ $t_{.025,5} = 2.571$

$$SS_{XX} = \Sigma X^2 - \frac{(\Sigma X)^2}{n} = 29,629.13 - \frac{(323.3)^2}{7} = 14,697.29$$

$$t = \frac{b_1 - 0}{\frac{S_e}{\sqrt{SS_{XX}}}} = \frac{1.82751 - 0}{\frac{446.01}{\sqrt{14,697.29}}} = \mathbf{0.50}$$

Since the observed $t = 0.50 < t_{.025,5} = 2.571$, the decision is to **fail to reject the null hypothesis**.

12.67   a) The regression equation is: $\hat{Y} = \mathbf{67.2 - 0.0565\ X}$

b) For every unit of increase in the value of X, the predicted value of Y will decrease by -.0565.

c) The t ratio for the slope is −5.50 with an associated p-value of .000. This is significant at $\alpha = .10$. The t ratio negative because the slope is negative and the numerator of the t ratio formula equals the slope minus zero.

d) r^2 is .627 or 62.7% of the variability of Y is accounted for by X. This is only a modest proportion of predictability. The standard error of the estimate is 10.32. This is best interpreted in light of the data and the magnitude of the data.

e) The F value which tests the overall predictability of the model is 30.25. For simple regression analysis, this equals the value of t^2 which is $(-5.50)^2$.

f) The negative is not a surprise because the slope of the regression line is also negative indicating an inverse relationship between X and Y. In addition, taking the square root of r^2 which is .627 yields .7906 which is the magnitude of the value of r considering rounding error.

12.69 The residuals appear to not be normally distributed. There is evidence of heterogeneity.

Chapter 13
Multiple Regression Analysis and
Model Building

LEARNING OBJECTIVES

This chapter presents the potential of multiple regression analysis as a tool in business decision making and its applications, thereby enabling you to:

1.   Be able to develop a multiple regression model.

2.   Understand and apply techniques that can be used to determine how well a regression model fits the data.

3.   Analyze and interpret nonlinear variables in multiple regression analysis.

4.   Understand the role of qualitative variables and how to use them in multiple regression analysis.

5.   Learn how to build and evaluate multiple regression models.

6.   Work one-way ANOVA problems by regression techniques and interpret the output.

CHAPTER OUTLINE

13.1 The Multiple Regression Model

>> Multiple Regression Model with Two Independent Variables (First-Order)

>> Determining the Multiple Regression Equation

>> A Multiple Regression Model

13.2 Evaluating the Multiple Regression Model

>> Testing the Overall Model

>> Significance Tests of the Regression Coefficients

>> Residuals, SSE, and the Standard Error of the Estimate

>> Coefficient of Multiple Determination (R^2)

>> Adjusted R^2

>> A Reexamination of the Multiple Regression MINITAB Output

13.3 Indicator (Dummy) Variables

13.4 More Complex Regression Models

>> Polynomial Regression

>> Tukey's Ladder of Transformations

>> Regression Models with Interaction

>> Model Transformation

13.5 Model-Building: Search Procedures

>> Search Procedures

>>> All Possible Regressions

>>> Stepwise Regression

>>> Forward Selection

>>> Backward Elimination

13.6 Multicollinearity

13.7 Using Regression to Solve ANOVA Problems

KEY WORDS

Adjusted R^2

All Possible Regressions

Backward Elimination

Coefficient of Multiple Determination (R^2)

Dependent Variable

Dummy Variable

Forward Selection

General Linear Regression Model

Independent Variable

Indicator Variable

Least Squares Analysis

Multicollinearity

Multiple Regression

Outliers

Partial Regression Coefficient

Qualitative Variable

R^2

Residual

Response Plane

Response Surface

Response Variable

Search Procedures

Standard Error of the Estimate

Stepwise Regression

Sum of Squares of Error

Tukey's Four-quadrant Approach

Tukey's Ladder of Transformations

Variance Inflation Factor

STUDY QUESTIONS

1. In multiple regression, an _____ statistic is used to test for the overall effectiveness of the model.

2. The significance of individual regression coefficients in a multiple regression model is tested using a _____ ratio.

3. The value, S_e, represents the _____.

4. The coefficient of multiple determination is denoted by _____.

5. Residuals can sometimes be used to locate _____ or values that are apart from the mainstream of the data.

6. Because R^2 may sometimes yield an inflated figure, statisticians have developed a(n) _____ to take into consideration both the additional information of each new independent variable and the changed degrees of freedom.

7. Examine the computer output below taken from a multiple regression analysis with three independent variables.

The regression equation is: = 28.4 + 1.30 X_1 - 0.25 X_2 + 2.20 X_3

Predictor	Coef	Stdev	t-ratio	p
Constant	28.410	56.520	0.50	0.631
X_1	1.295	2.052	0.63	0.548
X_2	-0.247	1.816	-0.14	0.895
X_3	2.202	.028	0.73	0.491

$S_e = 32.68$ $R^2 = 8.1\%$ $R^2 (adj) = 0.0\%$

Analysis of Variance

Source	df	SS	MS	F	p
Regression	3	659	220	0.21	0.889
Error	7	7474	1068		
Total	10	8134			

The overall test of significance yields _____. This test is (is not) significant _____. The coefficient of multiple determination is _____. The standard error of the estimate is _____. The t-ratios and their associated probabilities indicate that _____ are significant predictor variables. The regression coefficient of the X_3 variable is _____. The value of the adjusted R^2 is _____. This indicates _____.

8. Another name for an indicator variable is a _____ variable. These variables are _____ as opposed to quantitative variables.

9. Indicator variables are coded using _____ and _____.

10. Suppose an indicator variable has four categories. In coding this into variables for multiple regression analysis, there should be _____ variables.

11. Regression models in which the highest power of any predictor variable is one and in which there are no interaction terms are referred to as _____ models.

12. The interaction of two variables can be studied in multiple regression using the _____ terms.

13. Suppose a researcher wants to analyze a set of data using the model: $\hat{Y} = b_0 b_1^x$ The model would be transformed by taking the _____ of both sides of the equation.

14. Perhaps the most widely known and used of the multiple regression search procedures is _____ regression.

15. One multiple regression search procedure is Forward Selection. Forward selection is essentially the same as stepwise regression except that _____.

16. Backward elimination is a step-by-step process that begins with the _____ model.

17. A search procedure that computes all the possible linear multiple regression models from the data using all variables is called _____.

18. When two or more of the independent variables of a multiple regression model are highly correlated it is referred to as _____. This condition causes several other problems to occur including

   (1) difficulty in interpreting _____.

   (2) Inordinately small _____ for the regression coefficients may result.

   (3) The standard deviations of regression coefficients are _____.

   (4) The _____ of estimated regression coefficients may be the opposite of what would be expected for a particular predictor variable.

ANSWERS TO STUDY QUESTIONS

1. F

2. t

3. Standard Error of the Estimate

4. R^2

5. Outliers

6. Adjusted R^2

7. $F = 0.21$ with $p = .889$, not, .081, 32.68, None of the Independent Variables, 2.20, .000, There is Virtually No Predictability in this Model

8. Dummy, Qualitative

9. 0, 1

10. 3

11. First-Order

12. $X_1 \cdot X_2$ or Cross Product

13. Logarithm

14. Stepwise

15. Once a Variable is Entered Into the Process, It is Never Removed

16. Full

17. All Possible Regressions

18. Multicollinearity, the Estimates of the Regression Coefficients, t Values, Overestimated, Algebraic Sign

SOLUTIONS TO ODD-NUMBERED PROBLEMS IN CHAPTER 13

13.1   The regression model is:

$$\hat{Y} = 25.03 - 0.0497 \, X_1 + 1.928 \, X_2$$

Predicted value of Y for $X_1 = 200$ and $X_2 = 7$ is:

$$\hat{Y} = 25.03 - 0.0497(200) + 1.928(7) = 28.586$$

13.3   The regression model is:

$$\hat{Y} = 121.62 - 0.174 \, X_1 + 6.02 \, X_2 + 0.00026 \, X_3 + 0.0041 \, X_4$$

There are **four** independent variables. If X_2, X_3, and X_4 are held constant, the predicted Y will decrease by - 0.174 for every unit increase in X_1. Predicted Y will increase by 6.02 for every unit increase in X_2 is X_1, X_3, and X_4 are held constant. Predicted Y will increase by 0.00026 for every unit increase in X_3 holding X_1, X_2, and X_4 constant. If X_4 is increased by one unit, the predicted Y will increase by 0.0041 if X_1, X_2, and X_3 are held constant.

13.5   The regression model is:

Per Capita = -538 + 0.23368 Paper Consumption +
18.09 Fish Consumption – 0.2116 Gasoline Consumption.

For every unit increase in paper consumption, the predicted per capita consumption increases by 0.23368 if fish and gasoline consumption are held constant. For every unit increase in fish consumption, the predicted per capita consumption increases by 18.09 if paper and gasoline consumption are held constant. For every unit increase in gasoline consumption, the predicted per capita consumption decreases by 0.2116 if paper and fish consumption are held constant.

13.7   There are 9 predictors in this model. The F test for overall significance of the model is 1.99 with a probability of .0825. This model is not significant at $\alpha = .05$. Only one of the t values is statistically significant. Predictor X_1 has a t of 2.73 which has an associated probability of .011 and this is significant at $\alpha = .05$. The standard error of the estimate is 3.503. R^2 is .408 and the adjusted R^2 is only .203. This indicates that there are a lot of insignificant predictors in the model. That is underscored by the fact that eight of the nine predictors have nonsignificant t values.

13.9   The regression model is:

Per Capita Consumption = -538 + 0.23368 Paper Consumption + 18.09 Fish Consumption − 0.2116 Gasoline Consumption

This model yields an F = 24.63 with p = .002. Thus, there is overall significance at $\alpha = .01$. One of the three predictors is significant. Paper Consumption has a t = 5.31 with p = .003. Paper Consumption is statistically significant at $\alpha = .01$. The standard error of the estimate of 2085 indicates that this model predicts within $\pm$ 2085 on Per Capita Consumption about 68% of the time. The entire range of Per Capita for the data is slightly more than 19,000. Relative to this range, the standard error of the estimate is small. $R^2 = .937$ and the adjusted value of R^2 is .899. Overall, this model is strong. The p-values of the t statistics for the other two predictors are insignificant indicating that a model with just Paper Consumption as a single predictor might be nearly as strong.

13.11   The regression model is:

$$\hat{Y} = 3.981 + 0.07322\ X_1 - 0.03232\ X_2 - 0.003886\ X_3$$

The overall F for this model is 100.47 with is significant at $\alpha = .001$. Only one of the predictors, X_1, has a significant t value (t = 3.50, p = .005). The other independent variables have non significant t values (X_2: t = -1.55, p = .15 and X_3: t = -1.01, p = .332). The value of $S_e = 0.2331$, $R^2 = .965$, and adjusted $R^2 = .955$. This is a very strong regression model. However, since X_2 and X_3 are nonsignificant predictors, the researcher should consider the using a simple regression model with only X_1 as a predictor. The R^2 would drop some but the model would be much more parsimonious.

13.13   There are **3 predictors in this model and 15 observations**.

The regression equation is:

$$\hat{Y} = 657.0534435 + 5.710310868\ X_1 - 0.416916682\ X_2 - 3.471481072\ X_3$$

$R^2 = .842$, adjusted $R^2 = .630$, $S_e = 109.43$,
$F = 8.96$ with a p-value of .0027
X_1 is significant at $= .01$ ($t = 3.187$, $p = .009$)
X_3 is significant at $= .05$ ($t = -2.406$, $p = .035$)

The model is significant overall. The R^2 is relatively
high but the adjusted R^2 is more than 20% lower indicating
an inflated value of R^2. The model is not as strong as the
$R^2 = .842$ might indicate.

13.15   The regression equation is:

$$\hat{Y} = 13.619 - 0.01201\ X_1 + 2.998\ X_2$$

The overall $F = 8.43$ is significant at $\alpha = .01$ ($p = .009$).

$S_e = 1.245$, $R^2 = .652$, adjusted $R^2 = .575$

The t ratio for the X_1 variable is only t = -0.14 with p = .893. However the t ratio for the
dummy variable, X_2 is t = 3.88 with p = .004. The indicator variable is the significant
predictor in this regression model which has some predictability (adjusted $R^2 = .575$).

13.17   This regression model has relatively strong predictability as indicated by $R^2 = .795$. Of
the three predictor variables, only X_1 and X_2 have significant t ratios (using $\alpha = .05$). X_3
(a non indicator variable) is not a significant predictor. X_1, the indicator variable, plays a
significant role in this model along with X_2.

13.19 The regression equation is:

Price = 7.066 - 0.0855 Hours + 9.614 ProbSeat + 10.507 FQ

The overall $F = 6.80$ with $p = .009$ which is significant at $\alpha = .01$. $S_e = 4.02$, $R^2 = .671$, and adjusted $R^2 = .573$. The difference between R^2 and adjusted R^2 indicates that there are some non significant predictors in the model. The t ratios, $t = -0.56$ with $p = .587$ and $t = 1.37$ with $p = .202$, of Hours and Probability of Being Seated are non significant at $\alpha = .05$. The only significant predictor is the dummy variable, French Quarter or not, which has a t ratio of 3.97 with $p = .003$ which is significant at $\alpha = .01$. The positive coefficient on this variable indicates that being in the French Quarter adds to the price of a meal.

13.21 Simple Regression Model:

$$\hat{Y} = -147.27 + 27.128 X$$

$F = 229.67$ with $p = .000$, $S_e = 27.27$, $R^2 = .97$, adjusted $R^2 = .966$, and $t = 15.15$ with $p = .000$. This is a very strong simple regression model.

Quadratic Model (Using both X and X^2):

$$\hat{Y} = -22.01 + 3.385 X + 0.9373 X^2$$

$F = 578.76$ with $p = .000$, $S_e = 12.3$, $R^2 = .995$, adjusted $R^2 = .993$, for X: $t = 0.75$ with $p = .483$, and for X^2: $t = 5.33$ with $p = .002$. The quadratic model is also very strong with an even higher R^2 value. However, in this model only the X^2 term is a significant predictor.

13.23   The model is:

$$\hat{Y} = b_0 b_1{}^x$$

Using logs: $\log Y = \log b_0 + X \log b_1$

The regression model is solved for in the computer using the values of X and the values of log Y. The resulting regression equation is:

$\log Y = 0.5797 + 0.82096\ X$

$F = 68.83$ with $p = .000$, $S_e = 0.1261$, $R^2 = .852$, and adjusted $R^2 = .839$. This model has relatively strong predictability.

13.25   The model is:

$$\hat{Y} = b_0 b_1{}^x$$

Using logs: $\log Y = \log b_0 + X \log b_1$

The regression model is solved for in the computer using the values of X and the values of log Y where X is failures and Y is liabilities. The resulting regression equation is:

$\log$ liabilities $= 3.1256 + 0.012846$ failures

$F = 19.98$ with $p = .001$, $S_e = 0.2862$, $R^2 = .666$, and adjusted $R^2 = .633$. This model has modest predictability.

13.27   Stepwise Regression:

Step 1: X_2 enters the model, $t = -7.35$ and $R^2 = .794$
                 The model is $= 36.15 - 0.146\ X_2$

Step 2: X_3 enters the model and X_2 remains in the model.
                 t for X_2 is -4.60, t for X_3 is 2.93. $R^2 = .876$.
                 The model is $\hat{Y} = 26.40 - 0.101\ X_2 + 0.116\ X_3$

The variable, X_1, never enters the procedure.

13.29   The output shows that the final model had four predictor variables, C4, C2, C5, and C7. C1 was the dependent variable, Y. The variables, C3 and C6 did not enter the stepwise analysis. The procedure took four steps. The final model was:

$$C1 = -5.00\ C4 + 3.22\ C2 + 1.78\ C5 + 1.56\ C7$$

The R^2 for this model was .5929, S_e was 3.36. The t ratios were:
$t_{C4} = 3.07$, $t_{C2} = 2.05$, $t_{C5} = 2.02$, and $t_{C7} = 1.98$.

13.31   The output indicates that the procedure went through two steps. At step 1, dividends entered the process yielding an R^2 of .833 by itself. The t value was 6.69 and the model was $= -11.062 + 61.1\ C3$. At step 2, net income entered the procedure and dividends remained in the model. The R^2 for this two predictor model was .897 which is a modest increase from the simple regression model shown in step one.   The step 2 model was:

Premiums earned $= -3.726 + 45.2$ dividends $+ 3.6$ net income

For step 2, $t_{dividends} = 4.36$ and $t_{net\ income} = 2.24$.

13.33   Y X_1 X_2 X_3

Y   -   -.653   -.891   .821

X_1 -.653   -   .650   -.615

X_2 -.891   .650   -   -.688

X_3 .821   -.615   -.688   -

There appears to be some correlation between all pairs of the predictor variables, X_1, X_2, and X_3. All pairwise correlations between independent variables are in the .600 to .700 range.

13.35   The stepwise regression analysis of problem 13.27 resulted in two of the three predictor variables being included in the model. The simple regression model yielded an R^2 of .833 jumping to .897 with the two predictors. The predictor intercorrelations are:

	Net Income	Dividends	Gain/Loss
Net Income	-	.682	.092
Dividends	.682	-	-.522
Gain/Loss	.092	-.522	-

An examination of the predictor intercorrelations reveals that Gain/Loss and Net Income have very little correlation, but Net Income and Dividends have a correlation of .682 and Dividends and Gain/Loss have a correlation of -.522. These correlations might suggest multicollinearity.

13.37 F from regression = **39.71**
F from Demonstration Problem 11.1 = **39.80**

Regression equation:

$$\hat{Y} = 24.8 + 3.40\ X_1 + 7.20\ X_2$$

$X_1 = 24.8 + 3.40(1) + 7.20(0) = \mathbf{28.2}$
$X_2 = 24.8 + 3.40(0) + 7.20(1) = \mathbf{32}$
$X_3 = 24.8 + 3.40(0) + 7.20(0) = \mathbf{24.8}$

13.39 $F = \mathbf{15.82}$ with a p-value = .000. There is a significant difference in treatment levels at $\alpha = .001$. There are 5 treatment levels. The means are:

$X_1 = 13 - .6667 = \mathbf{12.3333}$
$X_2 = 13 - 3 = \mathbf{10}$
$X_3 = 13 - 1 = \mathbf{12}$
$X_4 = 13 + 3 = \mathbf{16}$
$X_5 = \mathbf{13}$

13.41   The regression model is:

$$\hat{Y} = 564 - 27.99\ X_1 - 6.155\ X_2 - 15.90\ X_3$$

F = 11.32 with p = .003, S_e = 42.88, R^2 = .809, adjusted R^2 = .738. For X_1, t = -0.92 with p = .384, for X_2, t = -4.34 with p = .002, for X_3, t = -0.71 with p = .497. Thus, only one of the three predictors, X_2, is a significant predictor in this model. This model has very good predictability (R^2 = .809). The gap between R^2 and adjusted R^2 underscores the fact that there are two nonsignificant predictors in this model. X_1 is a nonsignificant indicator variable.

13.43   In this model with X_1 and the log of X_1 as predictors, only the log X_1 was a significant predictor of Y. The stepwise procedure only went to step 1. The regression model was:

$$\hat{Y} = -13.20 + 11.64\ Log\ X_1.\quad R^2 = .9617\ \text{and the t ratio of Log } X_1 \text{ was } 17.36.$$ This model has very strong predictability using only the log of the X_1 variable.

13.45   The stepwise regression procedure only used two steps. At step 1, Silver was the lone predictor. The value of R^2 was .5244. At step 2, Aluminum entered the model and Silver remained in the model. However, the R^2 jumped to .8204. The final model at step 2 was:

Gold = - 50.19 + 18.9 Silver +3.59 Aluminum.

The t values were: t_{Silver} = 5.43 and $t_{Aluminum}$ = 3.85.

Copper did not enter into the process at all.

13.47   There were four predictor variables. The stepwise regression procedure went three steps. The predictor, apparel, never entered in the stepwise process. At step 1, food entered the procedure producing a model with an R^2 of .84. At step 2, fuel oil entered and food remained. The R^2 increased to .95. At step 3, shelter entered the procedure and both fuel oil and food remained in the model. The R^2 at this step was .96. The final model was:

All = -1.0615 + 0.474 Food + 0.269 Fuel Oil + 0.249 Shelter

The t ratios were: t_{food} = 8.32, $t_{fuel\ oil}$ = 2.81, $t_{shelter}$ = 2.56.

13.49   The stepwise regression process with these two independent variables only went one step. At step 1, Soybeans entered in producing the model,
Corn = - 2,962 + 5.4 Soybeans. The R^2 for this model was .7868.
The t ratio for Soybeans was 5.43. Wheat did not enter in to the analysis.

13.51 F = 11.76 with a p-value of .001. This analysis is significant at α = .001. The regression equation is:

$$\hat{Y} = 5.83 + 1.77\ X_1 + 3.02\ X_2$$

The means are solved for as:

$$\overline{X}_1 = 5.83 + 1.77(1) + 3.02(0) = 7.60$$

$$\overline{X}_2 = 5.83 + 1.77(0) + 3.02(1) = 8.85$$

$$\overline{X}_3 = 5.83 + 1.77(0) + 3.02(0) = 5.83$$

There is a significant difference in the means of these three groups.

13.53   The output suggests that the procedure only went two steps.

At step 1, X_1 entered the model yielding an R^2 of .7539. At step 2, X_2 entered the model and X_1 remained. The procedure stopped here with a final model of:

$$\hat{Y} = 124.5 - 43.4\,X_1 + 1.36\,X_2$$

The R^2 for this model was .8059 which indicates relatively strong predictability with two independent variables. Since there were four predictor variables, two of the variables did not enter the stepwise process.

13.55   The R^2 for the full model is .321. After dropping out variable, X_3, the R^2 is still .321. Variable X_3 added virtually no information to the model. This is underscored by the fact that the p-value for the t test of the slope for X_3 is .878 indicating that there is no significance. The standard error f the estimate actually drops slightly after X_3 is removed from the model.

Chapter 14
Index Numbers

LEARNING OBJECTIVES

This chapter discusses the role of index numbers in business, thereby enabling you to:

1. Understand the importance and usefulness of index numbers to business decision makers.

2. Compute and interpret simple index numbers.

3. Compute and interpret simple aggregate price indexes.

4. Compute and interpret weighted price indexes, including Laspeyres price index, Paasche price index, and Fisher's ideal price index.

5. Become aware of some important index numbers used in business.

CHAPTER OUTLINE

14.1   Simple Index Numbers and Unweighted Aggregate Price Indexes

Unweighted Aggregate Price Index Numbers

14.2   Weighted Aggregate Price Index Numbers

Laspeyres Price Index

Paasche Price Index

Fisher's Ideal Price Index

14.3   Other Important Indexes

Quantity Indexes

Consumer Price Index

Producer Price Index

Dow Jones Indexes

Other Indexes

Base Period

KEY WORDS

Consumer Price Index
Dow Jones Indexes
Fisher's Ideal Price Index
Index Number
Laspeyres Price Index
Paasche Price Index

Producer Price Index
Simple Index Numbers
Unweighted Aggregate Price Index
 Numbers
Weighted Aggregate Price Index
 Numbers

STUDY GUIDE QUESTIONS

1. Examine the price figures shown below for various years.

Year	Price
1996	23.8
1997	47.3
1998	49.1
1999	55.6
2000	53.0

   The simple index number for 1999 using 1996 as a base year is _____.
   The simple index number for 2000 using 1997 as a base year is _____.

2. Examine the price figures given below for four commodities.

	Year			
Item	1997	1998	1999	2000
1	1.89	1.90	1.87	1.84
2	.41	.48	.55	.69
3	.76	.73	.79	.82

   The unweighted aggregate price index for 1998 using 1997 as a base year is
   _____.   The unweighted aggregate price index for 1999 using 1997 as
   a base year is _____.   The unweighted aggregate price index for 2000 using
   1997 as a base year is _____.

3. Weighted aggregate price indexes that are computed by using the quantities for the
   year of interest rather than the base year are called _____
   price indexes.

4. Weighted aggregate price indexes that are computed by using the quantities for the
   base year are called _____ price indexes.

5. A weighted aggregate price index that is computed by using both indexes discussed n
   questions 3 and 4 is called _____ price index.

6. Examine the data below.

Item	Quantity 1999	Quantity 2000	Price 1999	Price 2000
1	23	27	1.33	1.45
2	8	6	5.10	4.89
3	61	72	.27	.29
4	17	24	1.88	2.11

Using 1999 as the base year

The Laspeyres price index for 2000 is _____.
The Paasche price index for 2000 is _____.
Fisher's ideal price indexfor 2000 is _____.

7. A popular measure of consumer purchasing power that is based on the relative measure of the cost of a market basket of goods and services is the

_____.

8. A price index that was formerly called the wholesale price index is the

_____.

9. The index based on 3100 commodities and the price of the first large-volume commercial transaction for each commodity is called the

_____.

10. There are actually _____ Dow Jones averages. The Dow Jones average that is most well-known is based on _____ industrials.

ANSWERS TO STUDY QUESTIONS

1. 233.6, 112.05

2. 101.6, 104.9, 109.5

3. Paasche

4. Laspeyres

5. Fisher's Ideal

6. 105.18, 106.82, 106.0

7. Consumer Price Index

8. Producer Price Index

9. Producer Price Index

10. 4, 30

SOLUTIONS TO ODD-NUMBERED PROBLEMS IN CHAPTER 14

14.1

Year	Price	a.) Index$_{1950}$	b.) Index$_{1980}$
1950	22.45	100.0	32.2
1955	31.40	139.9	45.0
1960	32.33	144.0	46.4
1965	36.50	162.6	52.3
1970	44.90	200.0	64.4
1975	61.24	272.8	87.8
1980	69.75	310.7	100.0
1985	73.44	327.1	105.3
1990	80.05	356.6	114.8
1995	84.61	376.9	121.3
2000	87.28	388.8	125.1

14.3

Year	Patents	Index
1980	66.2	93.2
1981	71.0	100.0
1982	63.3	89.2
1983	62.0	87.3
1984	72.7	102.4
1985	77.2	108.7
1986	76.9	108.3
1987	89.4	125.9
1988	84.3	118.7
1989	102.5	144.4
1990	99.2	139.7
1991	106.8	150.4
1992	107.4	151.3
1993	109.7	154.5
1994	124.1	174.8
1995	114.4	161.1
1996	122.6	172.7
1997	125.5	176.8

14.5   Year

	1985	1992	1997
	1.31	1.53	1.40
	1.99	2.21	2.15
	2.14	1.92	2.68
	2.89	3.38	3.10
Totals	8.33	9.04	9.33

$$\text{Index}_{1987} = \frac{8.33}{8.33}(100) = \textbf{100.0}$$

$$\text{Index}_{1992} = \frac{9.04}{8.33}(100) = \textbf{108.5}$$

$$\text{Index}_{1995} = \frac{9.33}{8.33}(100) = \textbf{112.0}$$

14.7

Item	Quantity 1990	Price 1990	Price 1997	Price 1998	Price 1999
1	21	0.50	0.67	0.68	0.71
2	6	1.23	1.85	1.90	1.91
3	17	0.84	0.75	0.75	0.80
4	43	0.15	0.21	0.25	0.25

	$P_{1990}Q_{1990}$	$P_{1997}Q_{1990}$	$P_{1998}Q_{1990}$	$P_{1999}Q_{1990}$
	10.50	14.07	14.28	14.91
	7.38	11.10	11.40	11.46
	14.28	12.75	12.75	13.60
	6.45	9.03	10.75	10.75
Totals	38.61	46.95	49.18	50.72

$$\text{Index}_{1997} = \frac{\sum P_{1997}Q_{1990}}{\sum P_{1990}Q_{1990}}(100) = \frac{46.95}{38.61}(100) = \textbf{121.6}$$

$$\text{Index}_{1998} = \frac{\sum P_{1998}Q_{1990}}{\sum P_{1990}Q_{1990}}(100) = \frac{49.18}{38.61}(100) = \textbf{127.4}$$

$$\text{Index}_{1999} = \frac{\sum P_{1999}Q_{1990}}{\sum P_{1990}Q_{1990}}(100) = \frac{50.72}{38.61}(100) = \textbf{131.4}$$

14.9

Item	Price 1980	Quantity 1980	Price 1995	Quantity 1995	Price 2000	Quantity 2000
1	1.75	55	1.90	43	2.10	41
2	0.65	12	0.70	14	1.95	15
3	3.45	6	3.60	8	3.65	8
4	0.90	67	1.15	61	1.28	57
5	14.35	3	13.90	5	12.60	6

a.)

$P_{1980}Q_{1980}$	$P_{1995}Q_{1980}$	$P_{2000}Q_{1980}$
96.25	104.50	115.50
7.80	8.40	23.40
20.70	21.60	21.90
60.30	77.05	85.76
43.05	41.70	37.80

Totals   228.10   253.25   284.36

$$\text{Index}_{1980} = \frac{\sum P_{1980}Q_{1980}}{\sum P_{1980}Q_{1980}}(100) = \frac{228.10}{228.10}(100) = \textbf{100.0}$$

$$\text{Index}_{1995} = \frac{\sum P_{1995}Q_{1980}}{\sum P_{1980}Q_{1980}}(100) = \frac{253.25}{228.10}(100) = \textbf{111.0}$$

$$\text{Index}_{2000} = \frac{\sum P_{2000}Q_{1980}}{\sum P_{1980}Q_{1980}}(100) = \frac{284.36}{228.10}(100) = \textbf{124.7}$$

b.)

$P_{1980}Q_{1995}$	$P_{1980}Q_{2000}$	$P_{1995}Q_{1995}$	$P_{2000}Q_{2000}$
75.25	71.75	81.70	86.10
9.10	9.75	9.80	29.25
27.60	27.60	28.80	29.20
54.90	51.30	70.15	72.96
71.75	86.10	69.50	75.60
Totals 238.60	246.50	259.95	293.11

$$\text{Index}_{1995} = \frac{\sum P_{1995}Q_{1995}}{\sum P_{1980}Q_{1995}}(100) = \frac{259.95}{238.60}(100) = \mathbf{108.9}$$

$$\text{Index}_{2000} = \frac{\sum P_{2000}Q_{2000}}{\sum P_{1980}Q_{2000}}(100) = \frac{293.11}{246.50}(100) = \mathbf{118.9}$$

c.)   For 1995: $I_F = \sqrt{I_L I_P} = \sqrt{(111.0)(108.9)} = \mathbf{109.9}$

For 2000: $I_F = \sqrt{I_L I_P} = \sqrt{(124.7)(118.9)} = \mathbf{121.8}$

d.)   For 2000, Laspeyres index was largest at 124.7, Paasche index was smallest at 118.9, and Fisher's was in between. Laspeyres was computed using 1980 quantities and Paasche was computed using 2000.

14.11

Item	Price 1987	Quantity 1987	Price 1992	Quantity 1992	Price 1997	Quantity 1997
Beef	1.31	175	1.53	126	1.40	115
Sausage	1.99	8	2.21	6	2.15	5
Bacon	2.14	24	1.92	16	2.68	17
Steak	2.89	35	3.38	23	3.10	14

$P_{1987}Q_{1987}$	$P_{1992}Q_{1987}$	$P_{1997}Q_{1987}$
229.25	267.75	245.00
15.92	17.68	17.20
51.36	46.08	64.32
101.15	118.30	108.50

| Totals | 397.68 | 449.81 | 435.02 |

Laspeyres:

$$\text{Index}_{1987} = \frac{\sum P_{1987}Q_{1987}}{\sum P_{1987}Q_{1987}}(100) = \frac{397.68}{397.68}(100) = \textbf{100.0}$$

$$\text{Index}_{1992} = \frac{\sum P_{1992}Q_{1987}}{\sum P_{1987}Q_{1987}}(100) = \frac{449.81}{397.68}(100) = \textbf{113.1}$$

$$\text{Index}_{1997} = \frac{\sum P_{1997}Q_{1987}}{\sum P_{1987}Q_{1987}}(100) = \frac{435.02}{397.68}(100) = \textbf{109.4}$$

14.13   Fisher's:

$$\text{Index}_{1992} = \sqrt{I_L I_P} = \sqrt{(113.1)(113.2)} = \textbf{113.15}$$

$$\text{Index}_{1997} = \sqrt{I_L I_P} = \sqrt{(109.4)(109.8)} = \textbf{109.6}$$

14.15

Item	1996		1997		1998		1999	
	P	Q	P	Q	P	Q	P	Q
1	2.75	12	2.98	9	3.10	9	3.21	11
2	0.85	47	0.89	52	0.95	61	0.98	66
3	1.33	20	1.32	28	1.36	25	1.40	32

Laspeyres$_{1998}$:

	$P_{1996}Q_{1996}$	$P_{1998}Q_{1996}$
	33.00	37.20
	39.95	44.65
	26.60	27.20
Totals	99.55	109.05

$$\text{Laspeyres Index}_{1998} = \frac{\sum P_{1998}Q_{1996}}{\sum P_{1996}Q_{1996}}(100) = \frac{109.05}{99.55}(100) = \mathbf{109.5}$$

Paasche$_{1997}$:

	$P_{1996}Q_{1997}$	$P_{1997}Q_{1997}$
	24.75	26.82
	44.20	46.28
	37.24	36.96
Totals	106.19	110.06

$$\text{Paasche Index}_{1997} = \frac{\sum P_{1997}Q_{1997}}{\sum P_{1996}Q_{1997}}(100) = \frac{110.06}{106.19}(100) = \mathbf{103.6}$$

Fisher's$_{1999}$:

	$P_{1996}Q_{1996}$	$P_{1999}Q_{1996}$	$P_{1999}Q_{1999}$	$P_{1996}Q_{1999}$
	33.00	38.52	35.31	30.25
	39.95	46.06	64.68	56.10
	26.60	28.00	44.80	42.56
Totals	99.55	112.58	144.79	128.91

$$\text{Index}_{L1999} = \frac{\sum P_{1999}Q_{1996}}{\sum P_{1996}Q_{1996}}(100) = \frac{112.58}{99.55}(100) = \mathbf{113.1}$$

$$\text{Index}_{P1999} = \frac{\sum P_{1999}Q_{1999}}{\sum P_{1996}Q_{1999}}(100) = \frac{144.79}{128.91}(100) = \mathbf{112.3}$$

$$I_F = \sqrt{I_L I_P} = \sqrt{(113.1)(112.7)} = \mathbf{112.7}$$

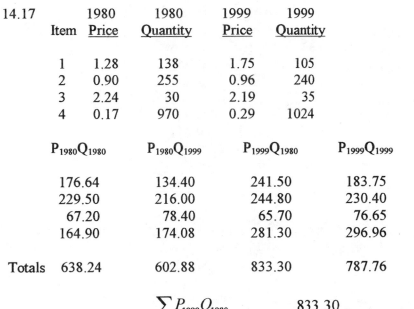

14.17

Item	1980 Price	1980 Quantity	1999 Price	1999 Quantity
1	1.28	138	1.75	105
2	0.90	255	0.96	240
3	2.24	30	2.19	35
4	0.17	970	0.29	1024

$P_{1980}Q_{1980}$	$P_{1980}Q_{1999}$	$P_{1999}Q_{1980}$	$P_{1999}Q_{1999}$
176.64	134.40	241.50	183.75
229.50	216.00	244.80	230.40
67.20	78.40	65.70	76.65
164.90	174.08	281.30	296.96
Totals 638.24	602.88	833.30	787.76

a.) $\text{Index}_{\text{Laspeyres99}} = \dfrac{\sum P_{1999}Q_{1980}}{\sum P_{1980}Q_{1980}}(100) = \dfrac{833.30}{638.24}(100) = \mathbf{130.6}$

b.) $\text{Index}_{\text{Paasche99}} = \dfrac{\sum P_{1999}Q_{1999}}{\sum P_{1980}Q_{1999}}(100) = \dfrac{787.76}{602.88}(100) = \mathbf{130.7}$

c.) $\text{Index}_{\text{Fishers}} = \sqrt{I_L I_P} = \sqrt{(130.6)(130.7)} = \mathbf{130.65}$

14.19

Item	1995	1996	1997	1998	1999
1	3.21	3.37	3.80	3.73	3.65
2	0.51	0.55	0.68	0.62	0.59
3	0.83	0.90	0.91	1.02	1.06
4	1.30	1.32	1.33	1.32	1.30
5	1.67	1.72	1.90	1.99	1.98
6	0.62	0.67	0.70	0.72	0.71
Totals	8.14	8.53	9.32	9.40	9.29

$$\text{Index}_{1995} = \frac{\sum P_{1995}}{\sum P_{1995}}(100) = \frac{8.14}{8.14}(100) = \mathbf{100.0}$$

$$\text{Index}_{1996} = \frac{\sum P_{1996}}{\sum P_{1995}}(100) = \frac{8.53}{8.14}(100) = \mathbf{104.8}$$

$$\text{Index}_{1997} = \frac{\sum P_{1997}}{\sum P_{1995}}(100) = \frac{9.32}{8.14}(100) = \mathbf{114.5}$$

$$\text{Index}_{1998} = \frac{\sum P_{1998}}{\sum P_{1995}}(100) = \frac{9.40}{8.14}(100) = \mathbf{115.5}$$

$$\text{Index}_{1999} = \frac{\sum P_{1999}}{\sum P_{1995}}(100) = \frac{9.29}{8.14}(100) = \mathbf{114.1}$$

14.21

	1995		1996		1997	
Item	P	Q	P	Q	P	Q
Marg.	0.83	21	0.81	23	0.83	22
Short.	0.89	5	0.87	3	0.87	4
Milk	1.43	70	1.56	68	1.59	65
Coffee	1.05	12	1.02	13	1.01	11
Chips	3.01	27	3.06	29	3.13	28
Total	7.21		7.32		7.43	

$$\text{Index}_{1995} = \frac{\sum P_{1995}}{\sum P_{1995}}(100) = \frac{7.21}{7.21}(100) = \mathbf{100.0}$$

$$\text{Index}_{1996} = \frac{\sum P_{1996}}{\sum P_{1995}}(100) = \frac{7.32}{7.21}(100) = \mathbf{101.5}$$

$$\text{Index}_{1997} = \frac{\sum P_{1997}}{\sum P_{1995}}(100) = \frac{7.43}{7.21}(100) = \mathbf{103.05}$$

14.23

Year	Cattle	Index(1900)	Index(1960)
1900	59,739	100.0	62.1
1910	58,993	98.8	61.3
1920	70,400	117.8	73.2
1930	61,003	102.1	63.4
1940	68,309	114.3	71.0
1950	77,963	130.5	81.0
1960	96,236	161.1	100.0
1970	112,369	188.1	116.8
1980	111,242	186.2	115.6
1985	109,582	183.4	113.9
1990	98,162	164.3	102.0
1991	98,896	165.5	102.8
1992	99,559	166.7	103.5
1993	99,176	166.0	103.1
1994	100,974	169.0	104.9
1995	102,785	172.1	106.8
1996	103,548	173.3	107.6
1997	101,656	170.2	105.6
1998	99,744	167.0	103.6

14.25 For Laspeyres:

$P_{1980}Q_{1980}$	$P_{1985}Q_{1980}$	$P_{1990}Q_{1980}$	$P_{1995}Q_{1980}$
24.38	28.09	39.75	37.10
36.54	44.37	50.46	56.55
44.10	70.35	89.25	109.20
15.82	18.08	36.16	45.20
Total 120.84	160.89	215.62	248.05

$$\text{Index}_{1985} = \frac{\sum P_{1985}Q_{1980}}{\sum P_{1980}Q_{1980}}(100) = \frac{160.89}{120.84}(100) = \mathbf{133.1}$$

$$\text{Index}_{1990} = \frac{\sum P_{1990}Q_{1980}}{\sum P_{1980}Q_{1980}}(100) = \frac{215.62}{120.84}(100) = \mathbf{178.4}$$

$$\text{Index}_{1995} = \frac{\sum P_{1995}Q_{1980}}{\sum P_{1980}Q_{1980}}(100) = \frac{248.05}{120.84}(100) = \mathbf{205.3}$$

For Paasche:

	$P_{1980}Q_{1985}$	$P_{1980}Q_{1990}$	$P_{1980}Q_{1995}$
	26.22	28.06	28.52
	39.48	40.32	42.42
	40.74	43.26	44.52
	14.28	13.72	13.58
Total	120.72	125.36	129.04

	$P_{1985}Q_{1985}$	$P_{1990}Q_{1990}$	$P_{1995}Q_{1995}$
	30.21	45.75	43.40
	47.94	55.68	65.65
	64.99	87.55	110.24
	16.32	31.36	38.80
Total	159.46	220.34	258.09

$$\text{Index}_{1985} = \frac{\sum P_{1985}Q_{1985}}{\sum P_{1980}Q_{1985}}(100) = \frac{159.46}{120.72}(100) = \mathbf{132.1}$$

$$\text{Index}_{1990} = \frac{\sum P_{1990}Q_{1990}}{\sum P_{1980}Q_{1990}}(100) = \frac{220.34}{125.36}(100) = \mathbf{175.8}$$

$$\text{Index}_{1995} = \frac{\sum P_{1995}Q_{1995}}{\sum P_{1980}Q_{1995}}(100) = \frac{258.09}{129.04}(100) = \mathbf{200.0}$$

For Fisher's:

$$\text{Index}_{1985} = \sqrt{I_L I_P} = \sqrt{(133.1)(132.1)} = \mathbf{132.6}$$

$$\text{Index}_{1990} = \sqrt{I_L I_P} = \sqrt{(178.4)(175.8)} = \mathbf{177.1}$$

$$\text{Index}_{1995} = \sqrt{I_L I_P} = \sqrt{(205.3)(200.0)} = \mathbf{202.6}$$

Chapter 15
Forecasting and Time Series

LEARNING OBJECTIVES

This chapter discusses the general use of forecasting in business, several tools that are available for making business forecasts, and the nature of time series data, thereby enabling you to:

1. Gain a general understanding of regression-based forecasting techniques and time series forecasting techniques and the difference between the two.

2. Become aware of several ways to measure forecasting error.

3. Understand how regression models are used in trend analysis.

4. Learn how to decompose time series data into their various elements and to forecast by using decomposition techniques.

5. Understand several time series forecasting techniques, including averaging models and exponential smoothing models.

6. Understand the nature of autocorrelation and how to test for it.

7. Understand autoregression in forecasting.

CHAPTER OUTLINE

15.1 The Measurement of Forecasting Error

> Error

> Mean Error (ME)

> Mean Absolute Deviation (MAD)

> Mean Square Error (MSE)

> Mean Percentage Error (MPE)

> Mean Absolute Percentage Error (MAPE)

15.2 Using Regression for Trend Analysis

> Time Series Data

> Determining Trend by Using Regression (No Seasonal Effects Present)

15.3 Time Series: Decomposition

> Seasonal Effects

> Trend Effects

> Cyclical Effects

> Forecasting by Using Decomposition

> Using the Computer to Do Decomposition

15.4 Introduction to Time Series Forecasting Techniques

> Naive Forecasting Models

> Averaging Models

>> Simple Averages

>> Moving Averages

>> Weighted Moving Averages

> Exponential Smoothing

> Advanced Exponential Smoothing

15.5 Autocorrelation and Autoregression

Autocorrelation

Ways to Overcome the Autocorrelation Problem

Addition of Independent Variables

Transforming Variables

Autoregression

KEY TERMS

Autocorrelation
Autoregression
Averaging Models
Cyclical Effects
Decomposition
Deseasonalized Data
Durbin-Watson Test
Error of an Individual
  Forecast
Exponential Smoothing
First-Difference Approach
Forecasting
Forecasting Error
Irregular Fluctuations
Mean Absolute Deviation (MAD)
Mean Absolute Percentage
  Error (MAPE)

Mean Error (ME)
Mean Percentage Error (MPE)
Mean Squared Error (MSE)
Moving Average
Naive Forecasting Methods
Percentage Error (PE)
Quadratic Regression Model
Regression-based Forecasting
  Techniques
Seasonal Effects
Serial Correlation
Simple Average
Simple Average Model
Time Series Data
Trend
Weighted Moving Average

STUDY QUESTIONS

1. Shown below are the forecast values and actual values for six months of data:

Month	Actual Values	Forecast Values
June	29	40
July	51	37
Aug.	60	49
Sept.	57	55
Oct.	48	56
Nov.	53	52

    The mean error for these data is _____. The mean absolute deviation of forecasts for these data is _____. The mean square error is _____. The mean percentage error is _____. The mean absolute percentage error is _____.

2. Data gathered on a given characteristic over a period of time at regular intervals are referred to as _____.

3. Time series data are thought to contain four elements: _____, _____, _____, and _____.

4. Patterns of data behavior that occur in periods of time of less than 1 year are called _____ effects.

5. Long-term time series effects are usually referred to as _____.

6. Patterns of data behavior that occur in periods of time of more than 1 years are called _____ effects.

7. Consider the time series data below. The equation of the trend line to fit these data is _____.

Year	Sales
1990	28
1991	31
1992	39
1993	50
1994	55
1995	58
1996	66
1997	72
1998	78
1999	90
2000	97

8. Time series data are deseasonalized by dividing the each data value by its associated value of _____.

9. Perhaps the simplest of the time series forecasting techniques are _____ models in which it is assumed that more recent time periods of data represent the best predictions.

10. Consider the time-series data shown below:

Month	Volume
Jan.	1230
Feb.	1211
Mar.	1204
Apr.	1189
May	1195

The forecast volumes for April, May, and June are _____, _____, and _____ using a three-month moving average on the data shown above and starting in January. Suppose a three-month moving average is used to predict volume figures for April, May, and June. The weights on the moving average are 3 for the most current month, 2 for the month before, and 1 for the other month. The forecasts for April, May, and June are _____, _____, and _____._ using a three-month moving average starting in January.

11. Consider the data below:

Month	Volume
Jan.	1230
Feb.	1211
Mar.	1204
Apr.	1189
May	1195

If exponential smoothing is used to forecast the Volume for May using $\alpha = .2$ and using the January actual figure as the forecast for February, the forecast is _____. If $\alpha = .5$ is used, the forecast is _____. If $\alpha = .7$ is used, the forecast is _____. The alpha value of _____ produced the smallest error of forecast.

12. _____ occurs when the error terms of a regression forecasting model are correlated. Another name for this is _____.

13. The Durbin-Watson statistic is used to test for _____.

14. Examine the data given below.

Year	Y	X
1985	126	34
1986	203	51
1987	211	60
1988	223	57
1989	238	64
1990	255	66
1991	269	80
1992	271	93
1993	276	92
1994	286	97
1995	289	101
1996	294	108
1997	305	110
1998	311	107
1999	324	109
2000	338	116

The simple regression forecasting model developed from this data is
_____. The value of R^2 for this model is _____. The
Durbin-Watson D statistic for this model is _____. The critical value of
d_L for this model using = .05 is _____ and the critical value of d_U for this
model is _____. This model (does, does not, inconclusive) _____
contain significant autocorrelation.

15. One way to overcome the autocorrelation problem is to add _____
to the analysis. Another way to overcome the autocorrelation problem is to transform
variables. One such method is the _____ approach.

16. A forecasting technique that takes advantage of the relationship of values to previous period
values is _____. This technique is a multiple regression
technique where the independent variables are time-lagged versions of the dependent
variable.

ANSWERS TO STUDY QUESTIONS

1. 1.5, 7.83, 84.5, - 0.57, 17.63

2. Time Series Data

3. Seasonal, Cyclical, Trend, Irregular

4. Seasonal

5. Trend

6. Cyclical

7. $\hat{Y} = 19.29091 + 6.84545X$

8. S

9. Naive Forecasting

10. 1215, 1201.3, 1196, 1210.7, 1197.7, 1194.5

11. 1215.21, 1200.63, 1194.64, .7

12. Autocorrelation, Serial Correlation

13. Autocorrelation

14. $\hat{Y} = 93.602 + 2.023X$, .916, 1.004, 1.10, 1.37, Does

15. Independent Variables, First-Differences

16. Autoregression

SOLUTIONS TO ODD-NUMBERED PROBLEMS IN CHAPTER 15

15.1

Period	e	$|e|$	e^2
1	2.30	2.30	5.29
2	1.60	1.60	2.56
3	-1.40	1.40	1.96
4	1.10	1.10	1.21
5	0.30	0.30	0.09
6	-0.90	0.90	0.81
7	-1.90	1.90	3.61
8	-2.10	2.10	4.41
9	0.70	0.70	0.49
Total	-0.30	12.30	20.43

$$\text{ME} = \frac{\sum e}{no.\,forecasts} = \frac{-0.30}{9} = \textbf{-0.033}$$

$$\text{MAD} = \frac{\sum |e|}{no.\,forecasts} = \frac{12.30}{9} = \textbf{1.367}$$

$$\text{MSE} = \frac{\sum e^2}{no.\,forecasts} = \frac{20.43}{9} = \textbf{2.27}$$

15.3

Period	Value	F	e	$|e|$	e^2	PE	APE
1	19.4	16.6	2.8	2.8	7.84	14.43	14.43
2	23.6	19.1	4.5	4.5	20.25	19.07	19.07
3	24.0	22.0	2.0	2.0	4.00	8.33	8.33
4	26.8	24.8	2.0	2.0	4.00	7.46	7.46
5	29.2	25.9	3.3	3.3	10.89	11.30	11.30
6	35.5	28.6	6.9	6.9	47.61	19.45	19.45
Total			21.5	21.5	94.59	80.04	80.04

$$ME = \frac{\sum e}{no.\,forecasts} = \frac{21.5}{4} = \mathbf{5.375}$$

$$MAD = \frac{\sum |e|}{no.\,forecasts} = \frac{21.5}{4} = \mathbf{5.375}$$

$$MSE = \frac{\sum e^2}{no.\,forecasts} = \frac{94.59}{4} = \mathbf{23.65}$$

$$MPE = \frac{\sum \left(\frac{e}{X} \cdot 100 \right)}{no.\,forecasts} = \frac{80.04}{4} = \mathbf{20.01}$$

$$MAPE = \frac{\sum \left(\frac{|e|}{X} \cdot 100 \right)}{no.\,forecasts} = \frac{80.04}{4} = \mathbf{20.01}$$

15.5 Simple Regression Trend Model:

$\hat{Y} = 37{,}969 + 9899.1 \text{ Period}$

$F = 1603.11$ (p = .000), $R^2 = .988$, adjusted $R^2 = .988$,
S_e 6,861, t = 40.04 (p = .000)

Quadratic Regression Trend Model:

$\hat{Y} = 35{,}769 + 10{,}473 \text{ Period} - 26.08 \text{ Period}^2$

$F = 772.71$ (p = .000), $R^2 = .988$, adjusted $R^2 = .987$
S_e 6,988, $t_{period} = 9.91$ (p = .000), $t_{periodsq} = -0.56$ (p = .583)

The simple linear regression trend model is superior, the period^2 variable is not a significant addition to the model.

15.7

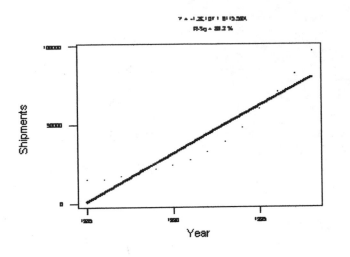

Shipments (y-axis)

Year (x-axis)

Trend Model:

Shipments = -12,138,725 + 6115.6 Year

$R^2 = 88.2$ adjusted $R^2 = 87.3$ $S_e = 9725$
t = 9.49 (p = .000)   F = 89.97 (p = .000)

Quadratic Model:

Shipments = 2,434,939,619 – 2,451,417 Year + 617.01 Year^2

$R^2 = 99.7$ adjusted $R^2 = 99.7$ $S_e = 1544$
t_{year} = -21.51 (p = .000)
t_{yearsq} = 21.56 (p = .000)
F = 2016.66 (p = .000)

The graph indicates a quadratic fit rather than a linear fit. The quadratic model produced an $R^2 = 99.7$ compared to $R^2 = 88.2$ for linear trend indicating a better fit for the quadratic model.

15.9

Month	Ship	12m tot	2yr tot	TC	SI	TCI	T	C
Jan(Yr1)	1891					1968.64	2047.09	
Feb	1986					1971.49	2054.11	
Mar	1987					1945.22	2061.12	
Apr	1987					1977.97	2068.14	
May	2000					1977.85	2075.16	
June	2082					1963.24	2082.18	
		23822						
July	1878		47689	1987.04	94.51	1969.94	2089.19	95.11
		23867						
Aug	2074		47852	1993.83	104.02	2020.52	2096.21	95.11
		23985						
Sept	2086		48109	2004.54	104.06	2006.76	2103.23	95.31
		24124						
Oct	2045		48392	2016.33	101.42	1978.71	2110.25	95.55
		24268						
Nov	1945		48699	2029.13	95.85	2042.25	2117.27	95.84
		24431						
Dec	1861		49126	2046.92	90.92	2002.94	2124.28	96.36
		24695						
Jan(Yr2)	1936		49621	2067.54	93.64	2015.49	2131.30	97.01
		24926						
Feb	2104		49989	2082.88	101.01	2088.63	2138.32	97.41
		25063						
Mar	2126		50308	2096.17	101.42	2081.3	2145.34	97.71
		25245						
Apr	2131		50730	2113.75	100.82	2121.32	2152.35	98.21
		25485						
May	2163		51132	2130.50	101.53	2139.04	2159.37	98.66
		25647						
June	2346		51510	2146.25	109.31	2212.18	2166.39	99.07
		25863						
July	2109		51973	2165.54	97.39	2212.25	2173.41	99.64
		26110						
Aug	2211		52346	2181.08	101.37	2153.99	2180.43	100.03
		26236						
Sept	2268		52568	2190.33	103.55	2181.85	2187.44	100.13
		26332						
Oct	2285		52852	2202.17	103.76	2210.93	2194.46	100.35
		26520						

Nov	2107		53246	2218.58	94.97	2212.35	2201.48	100.78
		26726						
Dec	2077		53635	2234.79	92.94	2235.42	2208.50	101.19
		26909						
Jan(Yr3)	2183		53976	2249.00	97.07	2272.63	2215.51	101.51
		27067						
Feb	2230		54380	2265.83	98.42	2213.71	2222.53	101.95
		27313						
Mar	2222		54882	2286.75	97.17	2175.28	2229.55	102.56
		27569						
Apr	2319		55355	2306.46	100.54	2308.46	2236.57	103.12
		27786						
May	2369		55779	2324.13	101.93	2342.76	2243.59	103.59
		27993						
June	2529		56186	2341.08	108.03	2384.75	2250.60	104.02
		28193						
July	2267		56539	2355.79	96.23	2377.98	2257.62	104.35
		28346						
Aug	2457		56936	2372.33	103.57	2393.65	2264.64	104.76
		28590						
Sept	2524		57504	2396.00	105.34	2428.12	2271.66	105.47
		28914						
Oct	2502		58075	2419.79	103.40	2420.90	2278.68	106.19
		29161						
Nov	2314		58426	2434.42	95.05	2429.70	2285.69	106.51
		29265						
Dec	2277		58573	2440.54	93.30	2450.67	2292.71	106.45
		29308						
Jan(Yr4)	2336		58685	2445.21	95.53	2431.91	2299.73	106.33
		29377						
Feb	2474		58815	2450.63	100.95	2455.93	2306.75	106.24
		29438						
Mar	2546		58806	2450.25	103.91	2492.47	2313.76	105.90
		29368						
Apr	2566		58793	2449.71	104.75	2554.34	2320.78	105.56
		29425						
May	2473		58920	2455.00	100.73	2445.61	2327.80	105.46
		29495						
June	2572		59018	2459.08	104.59	2425.29	2334.82	105.32
		29523						
July	2336		59099	2462.46	94.86	2450.36	2341.84	105.15
		29576						
Aug	2518		59141	2464.21	102.18	2453.08	2348.85	104.91
		29565						
Sept	2454		59106	2462.75	99.64	2360.78	2355.87	104.54
		29541						
Oct	2559		58933	2455.54	104.21	2476.05	2362.89	103.92
		29392						
Nov	2384		58779	2449.13	97.34	2503.20	2369.91	103.34

		29387					
Dec	2305		58694	2445.58	94.25	2480.81	2376.92	-102.89
		29307					
Jan(Yr5)	2389		58582	2440.92	97.87	2487.08	2383.94	102.39
		29275					
Feb	2463		58543	2439.29	100.97	2445.01	2390.96	102.02
		29268					
Mar	2522		58576	2440.67	103.33	2468.97	2397.98	101.78
		29308					
Apr	2417		58587	2441.13	99.01	2406.02	2405.00	101.50
		29279					
May	2468		58555	2439.79	101.16	2440.66	2412.01	101.15
		29276					
June	2492		58458	2435.75	102.31	2349.86	2419.03	100.69
		29182					
July	2304		58352	2431.33	94.76	2417.63	2468.16	98.51
		29170					
Aug	2511		58258	2427.42	103.44	2435.74	2475.17	98.07
		29088					
Sept	2494		57922	2413.42	103.34	2401.31	2482.19	97.23
		28834					
Oct	2530		57658	2402.42	105.31	2436.91	2489.21	96.51
		28824					
Nov	2381		57547	2397.79	99.30	2478.40	2496.23	96.06
		28723					
Dec	2211		57400	2391.67	92.45	2379.47	2503.24	95.54
		28677					
Jan(Yr6)	2377		57391	2391.29	99.40	2454.31	2510.26	95.26
		28714					
Feb	2381		57408	2392.00	99.54	2368.68	2517.28	95.02
		28694					
Mar	2268		57346	2389.42	94.92	2252.91	2524.30	94.66
		28652					
Apr	2407		57335	2388.96	100.76	2389.32	2531.32	94.38
		28683					
May	2367		57362	2390.08	99.03	2339.63	2538.33	94.16
		28679					
June	2446		57424	2392.67	102.23	2329.30	2545.35	94.00
		28745					
July	2341						
Aug	2491						
Sept	2452						
Oct	2561						
Nov	2377						
Dec	2277						

Seasonal Indexing:

Month	Year1	Year2	Year3	Year4	Year5	Year6	Index
Jan		93.64	97.07	95.53	97.87	99.40	96.82
Feb	101.01	98.42	100.95	100.97	99.54	100.49	
Mar		101.42	97.17	103.91	103.33	94.92	100.64
Apr		100.82	100.54	104.75	99.01	100.76	100.71
May		101.53	101.93	100.73	101.16	99.03	101.14
June		109.31	108.03	104.59	102.31	102.23	104.98
July	94.51	97.39	96.23	94.86	94.76		95.28
Aug	104.02	101.37	103.57	102.18	103.44		103.06
Sept	104.60	103.55	105.34	99.64	103.34		103.83
Oct	101.42	103.76	103.40	104.21	105.31		103.79
Nov	95.85	94.97	95.05	97.24	99.30		96.05
Dec	90.92	92.94	93.30	94.25	92.45		92.90

Total		1199.69

Adjust each seasonal index by 1.0002584

Final Seasonal Indexes:

Month	Index
Jan	96.85
Feb	100.52
Mar	100.67
Apr	100.74
May	101.17
June	105.01
July	95.30
Aug	103.09
Sept	103.86
Oct	103.82
Nov	96.07
Dec	92.92

Regression Output for Trend Line: $\hat{Y} = 2035.58 + 7.1481\,X$
$R^2 = .682,\ S_e = 102.9$

15.11

Period	Value	F(=.1)	Error	F(=.8)	Error	Difference
1	211					
2	228	211				
3	236	213	23	225	11	12
4	241	215	26	234	7	19
5	242	218	24	240	2	22
6	227	220	7	242	-15	22
7	217	221	-4	230	-13	9
8	203	220	-17	220	-17	0

Using alpha of .1 produced forecasting errors that were larger than those using alpha = .8 for the first three forecasts. For the next two forecasts (periods 6 and 7), the forecasts using alpha = .1 produced smaller errors. Each exponential smoothing model produced the same amount of error in forecasting the value for period 8. There is no strong argument in favor of either model.

15.13

Year	Orders	(a) F(a)	(c) e(a)	(b) F(b)	(c) e(b)
1987	2512.7				
1988	2739.9				
1989	2874.9				
1990	2934.1				
1991	2865.7				
1992	2978.5	2785.46	193.04	2852.36	126.14
1993	3092.4	2878.62	213.78	2915.49	176.91
1994	3356.8	2949.12	407.68	3000.63	356.17
1995	3607.6	3045.50	562.10	3161.94	445.66
1996	3749.3	3180.20	569.10	3364.41	384.89
1997	3952.0	3356.92	595.08	3550.76	401.24

15.15   Regression Analysis

The regression equation is: Food = 0.7542 + 0.6788 Shelter

Predictor	Coef	Stdev	t-ratio	p
Constant	0.7542	0.8379	0.90	0.378
Shelter	0.6788	0.1128	6.02	0.000

S = 2.098   R-sq = 62.2%   R-sq(adj) = 60.5%

Food	Shelter	$\hat{Y}$	e	e^2
14.3	9.6	7.2711	7.02888	49.4052
8.5	9.9	7.4748	1.02523	1.0511
3.0	5.5	4.4879	-1.48785	2.2137
6.3	6.6	5.2346	1.06542	1.1351
9.9	10.2	7.6784	2.22157	4.9354
11.0	13.9	10.1902	0.80985	0.6559
8.6	17.6	12.7019	-4.10188	16.8254
7.8	11.7	8.6967	-0.89669	0.8041
4.1	7.1	5.5740	-1.47401	2.1727
2.1	2.3	2.3155	-0.21555	0.0465
3.8	4.9	4.0805	-0.28055	0.0787
2.3	5.6	4.5557	-2.25574	5.0884
3.2	5.5	4.4879	-1.28785	1.6586
4.1	4.7	3.9448	0.15522	0.0241
4.1	4.8	4.0127	0.08734	0.0076
5.8	4.5	3.8090	1.99099	3.9640
5.8	5.4	4.4200	1.38003	1.9045
2.9	4.5	3.8090	-0.90901	0.8263
1.2	3.3	2.9944	-1.79439	3.2199
2.2	3.0	2.7907	-0.59074	0.3490
2.4	3.1	2.8586	-0.45863	0.2103
2.8	3.2	2.9265	-0.12651	0.0160
3.3	3.2	2.9265	0.37349	0.1395
2.6	3.1	2.8586	-0.25863	0.0669

$\sum(e_t - e_{t-1})^2 = 36.044 + 6.316 + 6.519 + 1.337 + 1.993 + 24.125 + 10.273 + $

$\qquad\qquad 0.333 + 1.584 + 0.004 + 3.901 + 0.937 + 2.082 + 0.005 + $

$\qquad\qquad 3.624 + 0.373 + 5.240 + 0.784 + 1.449 + 0.017 + 0.110 + 0.25 + $

$\qquad\qquad 0.40 = 107.7$

$$D = \frac{\sum(e_t - e_{t-1})^2}{\sum e^2} = \frac{107.7}{96.799} = 1.11$$

Since D = 1.11 is less than d_L, the decision is to reject the null hypothesis. **There is significant autocorrelation**.

15.17   The regression equation is:

Failed Bank Assets = 1,379 + 136.68 Number of Failures

for X = 150: $\hat{Y}$ = 21,881 (million $)

R^2 = 37.9%   adjusted R^2 = 34.1% S_e = 13,833   F = 9.78, p = .006

The Durbin Watson statistic for this model is:

D = 2.49

The critical table values for k = 1 and n = 18 are d_L = 1.16 and d_U = 1.39. Since the observed value of D = 2.49 is above d_U, the decision is to fail to reject the null hypothesis. There is no significant autocorrelation.

Failed Bank Assets	Number of Failures	$\hat{Y}$	e	e^2
8,189	11	2,882.8	5,306.2	28,155,356
104	7	2,336.1	-2,232.1	4,982,296
1,862	34	6,026.5	-4,164.5	17,343,453
4,137	45	7,530.1	-3,393.1	11,512,859
36,394	79	12,177.3	24,216.7	586,449,390
3,034	118	17,507.9	-14,473.9	209,494,371
7,609	144	21,061.7	-13,452.7	180,974,565
7,538	201	28,852.6	-21,314.6	454,312,622
56,620	221	31,586.3	25,033.7	626,687,597
28,507	206	29,536.0	- 1,029.0	1,058,894
10,739	159	23,111.9	-12,372.9	153,089,247
43,552	108	16,141.1	27,410.9	751,357,974
16,915	100	15,047.6	1,867.4	3,487,085
2,588	42	7,120.0	- 4,532.0	20,539,127
825	11	2,882.8	- 2,057.8	4,234,697
753	6	2,199.4	- 1,446.4	2,092,139
186	5	2,062.7	- 1,876.7	3,522,152
27	1	1,516.0	- 1,489.0	2,217,144

15.19

Starts	lag1	lag2
311	*	*
486	311	*
527	486	311
429	527	486
285	429	527
275	285	429
400	275	285
538	400	275
545	538	400
470	545	538
306	470	545
240	306	470
205	240	306
382	205	240
436	382	205
468	436	382
483	468	436
420	483	468
404	420	483
396	404	420
329	396	404
254	329	396
288	254	329
302	288	254
351	302	288
331	351	302
361	331	351
364	361	331

The model with 1 lag:

Housing Starts = 158 + 0.589 lag 1

$F = 13.66$ $p = .001$ $R^2 = 35.3\%$ adjusted $R^2 = 32.7\%$ $S_e = 77.55$

The model with 2 lags:

Housing Starts = 401 - 0.065 lag 2

$F = 0.11$ $p = .744$ $R^2 = 0.5\%$ adjusted $R^2 = 0.0\%$ $S_e = 95.73$

The model with 1 lag is the best model with a very modest R^2 32.7%. The model with 2 lags has no predictive ability.

15.21   a) The linear model: Yield = 9.96 - 0.14 Month

$F = 219.24$ $p = .000$ $R^2 = 90.9\%$ $S_e = .3212$

The quadratic model: Yield = 10.4 - 0.252 Month + .00445 Month^2

$F = 176.21$ $p = .000$ $R^2 = 94.4\%$ $S_e = .2582$

Both t ratios are significant, for X,
$t = -7.93, p = .000$ and for $X, t = 3.61, p = .002$

The linear model is a strong model. The quadratic term adds some
predictability but has a smaller t ratio than does the linear term.

b)

X	F	$\lvert e \rvert$
10.08	-	-
10.05	-	-
9.24	-	-
9.23	-	-
9.69	9.65	.04
9.55	9.55	.00
9.37	9.43	.06
8.55	9.46	.91
8.36	9.29	.93
8.59	8.96	.37
7.99	8.72	.73
8.12	8.37	.25
7.91	8.27	.36
7.73	8.15	.42
7.39	7.94	.55
7.48	7.79	.31
7.52	7.63	.11
7.48	7.53	.05
7.35	7.47	.12
7.04	7.46	.42
6.88	7.35	.47
6.88	7.19	.31
7.17	7.04	.13
7.22	6.99	.23

$$\sum \lvert e \rvert = 6.77$$

$$\text{MAD} = \frac{6.77}{20} = \mathbf{.3385}$$

c)

	α = .3		α = .7	
X	F	$\|e\|$	F	$\|e\|$
10.08	-	-	-	-
10.05	10.08	.03	10.08	.03
9.24	10.07	.83	10.06	.82
9.23	9.82	.59	9.49	.26
9.69	9.64	.05	9.31	.38
9.55	9.66	.11	9.58	.03
9.37	9.63	.26	9.56	.19
8.55	9.55	1.00	9.43	.88
8.36	9.25	.89	8.81	.45
8.59	8.98	.39	8.50	.09
7.99	8.86	.87	8.56	.57
8.12	8.60	.48	8.16	.04
7.91	8.46	.55	8.13	.22
7.73	8.30	.57	7.98	.25
7.39	8.13	.74	7.81	.42
7.48	7.91	.43	7.52	.04
7.52	7.78	.26	7.49	.03
7.48	7.70	.22	7.51	.03
7.35	7.63	.28	7.49	.14
7.04	7.55	.51	7.39	.35
6.88	7.40	.52	7.15	.27
6.88	7.24	.36	6.96	.08
7.17	7.13	.04	6.90	.27
7.22	7.14	.08	7.09	.13

$$\sum\left|e\right| = 10.06 \qquad \sum\left|e\right| = 5.97$$

$$\text{MAD}_{\alpha=.3} = \frac{10.06}{23} = \textbf{.4374} \qquad\qquad \text{MAD}_{\alpha=.7} = \frac{5.97}{23} = \textbf{.2596}$$

α = .7 produces better forecasts based on MAD.

d) MAD for b) .3385, c) .4374 and .2596. Exponential smoothing with α = .7 produces the lowest error (.2596 from part c).

e)

TCSI	4 period moving tots	8 period moving tots	TC	SI
10.08				
10.05				
	38.60			
9.24		76.81	9.60	96.25
	38.21			
9.23		75.92	9.49	97.26
	37.71			
9.69		75.55	9.44	102.65
	37.84			
9.55		75.00	9.38	101.81
	37.16			
9.37		72.99	9.12	102.74
	35.83			
8.55		70.70	8.84	96.72
	34.87			
8.36		68.36	8.55	97.78
	33.49			
8.59		66.55	8.32	103.25
	33.06			
7.99		65.67	8.21	97.32
	32.61			
8.12		64.36	8.05	100.87
	31.75			
7.91		62.90	7.86	100.64
	31.15			
7.73		61.66	7.71	100.26
	30.51			
7.39		60.63	7.58	97.49
	30.12			
7.48		59.99	7.50	99.73
	29.87			
7.52		59.70	7.46	100.80
	29.83			
7.48		59.22	7.40	101.08
	29.39			
7.35		58.14	7.27	101.10
	28.75			
7.04		56.90	7.11	99.02
	28.15			
6.88		56.12	7.02	98.01
	27.97			
6.88		56.12	7.02	98.01
	28.15			
7.17				
7.22				

1st Period	<u>102.65</u>	<u>97.78</u>	100.64	100.80	98.01
2nd Period	101.81	<u>103.25</u>	100.26	101.08	<u>98.01</u>
3rd Period	<u>96.25</u>	<u>102.74</u>	97.32	97.49	101.10
4th Period	97.26	<u>96.72</u>	<u>100.87</u>	99.73	99.02

The highs and lows of each period (underlined) are eliminated and the others are averaged resulting in:

Seasonal Indexes:
       1st 99.82
       2nd 101.05
       3rd 98.64
       4th <u>98.67</u>
   total 398.18

Since the total is not 400, adjust each seasonal index by multiplying by $\dfrac{400}{398.18}$ = 1.004571 resulting in the final seasonal indexes of:

       1st 100.28
       2nd 101.51
       3rd 99.09
       4th 99.12

The trend line developed using MINITAB on the deseasonalized data is:

$Y_t = 9.9374 - 0.138961\ t$

The trend (linear only) and cyclical effects are:

Period	TCSI	TCI	T	CI
1	10.08	10.05	9.80	102.55
2	10.05	9.90	9.66	102.48
3	9.24	9.32	9.52	97.90
4	9.23	9.31	9.38	99.25
5	9.69	9.66	9.24	104.55
6	9.55	9.41	9.10	103.41
7	9.37	9.46	8.96	105.58
8	8.55	8.63	8.83	97.73
9	8.36	8.34	8.69	95.97
10	8.59	8.46	8.55	98.95
11	7.99	8.06	8.41	95.84
12	8.12	8.19	8.27	99.03
13	7.91	7.89	8.13	97.05
14	7.73	7.62	7.99	95.37
15	7.39	7.46	7.85	95.03
16	7.48	7.55	7.71	97.92
17	7.52	7.50	7.58	98.94
18	7.48	7.32	7.44	98.39
19	7.35	7.42	7.30	101.64
20	7.04	7.10	7.16	99.16
21	6.88	6.86	7.02	97.72
22	6.88	6.78	6.88	98.55
23	7.17	7.24	6.74	107.42
24	7.22	7.28	6.60	110.30

15.23-15.25

Month	Chem	12m tot	2yr tot	TC	SI	TCI	T	C
Jan(91)	23.701							
Feb	24.189							
Mar	24.200							
Apr	24.971							
May	24.560							
June	24.992							
		288.00						
July	22.566		575.65	23.985	94.08	23.872	23.917	99.81
		287.65						
Aug	24.037		575.23	23.968	100.29	24.134	23.919	100.90
		287.58						
Sept	25.047		576.24	24.010	104.32	24.047	23.921	100.52
		288.66						
Oct	24.115		577.78	24.074	100.17	24.851	23.924	103.87
		289.12						
Nov	23.034		578.86	24.119	95.50	24.056	23.926	100.55
		289.74						
Dec	22.590		580.98	24.208	93.32	23.731	23.928	99.18
		291.24						
Jan(92)	23.347		584.00	24.333	95.95	24.486	23.931	102.32
		292.76						
Feb	24.122		586.15	24.423	98.77	24.197	23.933	101.10
		293.39						
Mar	25.282		587.81	24.492	103.23	23.683	23.936	98.95
		294.42						
Apr	25.426		589.05	24.544	103.59	24.450	23.938	102.14
		294.63						
May	25.185		590.05	24.585	102.44	24.938	23.940	104.17
		295.42						
June	26.486		592.63	24.693	107.26	24.763	23.943	103.42
		297.21						
July	24.088		595.28	24.803	97.12	25.482	23.945	106.42
		298.07						
Aug	24.672		597.79	24.908	99.05	24.771	23.947	103.44
		299.72						
Sept	26.072		601.75	25.073	103.98	25.031	23.950	104.51
		302.03						
Oct	24.328		605.59	25.233	96.41	25.070	23.952	104.67
		303.56						
Nov	23.826		607.85	25.327	94.07	24.884	23.955	103.88
		304.29						
Dec	24.373		610.56	25.440	95.81	25.605	23.957	106.88
		306.27						
Jan(93)	24.207		613.27	25.553	94.73	25.388	23.959	105.96
		307.00						

Feb	25.772		614.89	25.620	100.59	25.852	23.962	107.89
		307.89						
Mar	27.591		616.92	25.705	107.34	25.846	23.964	107.86
		309.03						
Apr	26.958		619.39	25.808	104.46	25.924	23.966	108.17
		310.36						
May	25.920		622.48	25.937	99.93	25.666	23.969	107.08
		312.12						
June	28.460		625.24	26.052	109.24	26.608	23.971	111.00
		313.12						
July	24.821		627.35	26.140	94.95	26.257	23.974	109.53
		314.23						
Aug	25.560		629.12	26.213	97.51	25.663	23.976	107.04
		314.89						
Sept	27.218		631.53	26.314	103.44	26.131	23.978	108.98
		316.64						
Oct	25.650		635.31	26.471	96.90	26.432	23.981	110.22
		318.67						
Nov	25.589		639.84	26.660	95.98	26.725	23.983	111.43
		321.17						
Dec	25.370		644.03	26.835	94.54	26.652	23.985	111.12
		322.86						
Jan(94)	25.316		647.65	26.985	93.82	26.551	23.988	110.68
		324.79						
Feb	26.435		652.98	27.208	97.16	26.517	23.990	110.53
		328.19						
Mar	29.346		659.95	27.498	106.72	27.490	23.992	114.58
		331.76						
Apr	28.983		666.46	27.769	104.37	27.871	23.995	116.15
		334.70						
May	28.424		672.57	28.024	101.43	28.145	23.997	117.29
		337.87						
June	30.149		679.39	28.308	106.50	28.187	24.000	117.45
		341.52						
July	26.746		686.66	28.611	93.48	28.294	24.002	117.88
		345.14						
Aug	28.966		694.30	28.929	100.13	29.082	24.004	121.16
		349.16						
Sept	30.783		701.34	29.223	105.34	29.554	24.007	123.11
		352.18						
Oct	28.594		706.29	29.429	97.16	29.466	24.009	122.73
		354.11						
Nov	28.762		710.54	29.606	97.14	30.039	24.011	125.10
		356.43						
Dec	29.018		715.50	29.813	97.33	30.484	24.014	126.95
		359.07						
Jan(95)	28.931		720.74	30.031	96.34	30.342	24.016	126.34
		361.67						
Feb	30.456		725.14	30.214	100.80	30.551	24.019	127.20
		363.47						

Mar	32.372		727.79	30.325	106.75	30.325	24.021	126.25
		364.32						
Apr	30.905		730.25	30.427	101.57	29.719	24.023	123.71
		365.93						
May	30.743		733.94	30.581	100.53	30.442	24.026	126.71
		368.01						
June	32.794		738.09	30.754	106.63	30.660	24.028	127.60
		370.08						
July	29.342							
Aug	30.765							
Sept	31.637							
Oct	30.206							
Nov	30.842							
Dec	31.090							

Seasonal Indexing:

Month	1991	1992	1993	1994	1995	Index
Jan	95.95	94.73	93.82	96.34	95.34	
Feb		98.77	100.59	97.16	100.80	99.68
Mar		103.23	107.34	106.72	106.75	106.74
Apr		103.59	104.46	104.37	101.57	103.98
May		102.44	99.93	101.43	100.53	100.98
June		107.26	109.24	106.50	106.63	106.96
July	94.08	97.12	94.95	93.48		94.52
Aug	100.29	99.05	97.51	100.13		99.59
Sept	104.32	103.98	103.44	105.34		104.15
Oct	100.17	96.41	96.90	97.16		97.03
Nov	95.50	94.07	95.98	97.14		95.74
Dec	93.32	95.81	94.54	97.33		95.18
Total						1199.88

Adjust each seasonal index by 1200/1199.88 = 1.0001

Final Seasonal Indexes:

Month	Index
Jan	95.35
Feb	99.69
Mar	106.75
Apr	103.99
May	100.99
June	106.96
July	94.53
Aug	99.60
Sept	104.16
Oct	97.04
Nov	95.75
Dec	95.19

Regression Output for Trend Line:

$$\hat{Y} = 22.4233 + 0.144974\ X$$

$$R^2 = .913$$

Regression Output for Quadratic Trend:

$$\hat{Y} = 23.8158 + 0.01554\ X + .000247\ X^2$$

$$R^2 = .964$$

In this model, the linear term yields a $t = 0.66$ with $p = .513$ but the squared term predictor yields a $t = 8.94$ with $p = .000$.

Regression Output when using only the squared predictor term:

$$\hat{Y} = 23.9339 + 0.00236647\ X^2$$

$$R^2 = .964$$

Note: The trend model derived using only the squared predictor was used in computing T (trend) in the decomposition process.

15.27 $\hat{Y} = -5,997,939 + 1,032,214\ X$

$\hat{Y}(55) = 50,773,831$

$R^2 = 99.6\%$ $F = 4829.65,\ p = .000$

$S_e = 1,243,142$

15.29   n = 22   k = 1   α = .05

D = 0.16

d_L = 1.24 and d_U = 1.43

Since D = 0.16 < d_L = 1.24, the decision is to **reject the null hypothesis. There is significant autocorrelation**.

15.31 $\hat{Y}$ = 81 + 0.849 X

R^2 = 55.8%   F = 8.83 with p = .021

S_e = 50.18

This model with a lag of one year has modest predictability. The overall F is significant at α = .05 but not at α = .01.

15.32-15.35:

Qtr	TSCI	4qrtot	8qrtot	TC	SI	TCI	T	C
Year1 1	54.019							
2	56.495							
		213.574						
3	50.169		425.044	53.131	94.43	51.699	53.722	96.23
		211.470						
4	52.891		421.546	52.693	100.38	52.341	55.945	93.56
		210.076						
Year2 1	51.915		423.402	52.925	98.09	52.937	58.274	90.84
		213.326						
2	55.101		430.997	53.875	102.28	53.063	60.709	87.41
		217.671						
3	53.419		440.490	55.061	97.02	55.048	63.249	87.04
		222.819						
4	57.236		453.025	56.628	101.07	56.641	65.895	85.96

			230.206						
Year3	1	57.063		467.366	58.421	97.68	58.186	68.646	84.76
			237.160						
	2	62.488		480.418	60.052	104.06	60.177	71.503	84.16
			243.258						
	3	60.373		492.176	61.522	98.13	62.215	74.466	83.55
			248.918						
	4	63.334		503.728	62.966	100.58	62.676	77.534	80.84
			254.810						
Year4	1	62.723		512.503	64.063	97.91	63.957	80.708	79.25
			257.693						
	2	68.380		518.498	64.812	105.51	65.851	83.988	78.41
			260.805						
	3	63.256		524.332	65.542	96.51	65.185	87.373	74.61
			263.527						
	4	66.446		526.685	65.836	100.93	65.756	90.864	72.37
			263.158						
Year5	1	65.445		526.305	65.788	99.48	66.733	94.461	70.65
			263.147						
	2	68.011		526.720	65.840	103.30	65.496	98.163	66.72
			263.573						
	3	63.245		521.415	65.177	97.04	65.174	101.971	63.91
			257.842						
	4	66.872		511.263	63.908	104.64	66.177	105.885	62.50
			253.421						
Year6	1	59.714		501.685	62.711	95.22	60.889	109.904	55.40
			248.264						
	2	63.590		491.099	61.387	103.59	61.238	114.029	53.70
	3	58.088							
	4	61.443							

Quarter	Year1	Year2	Year3	Year4	Year5	Year6	Index
1		98.09	97.68	97.91	99.48	95.22	97.89
2		102.28	104.06	105.51	103.30	103.59	103.65
3	94.43	97.02	98.13	96.51	97.04		96.86
4	100.38	101.07	100.58	100.93	104.64		100.86

Total   399.26

Adjust the seasonal indexes by: $\dfrac{400}{399.26} = 1.00185343$

Adjusted Seasonal Indexes:

Quarter	Index
1	98.07
2	103.84
3	97.04
4	101.05
Total	400.00

15.37

		$\alpha = .1$		$\alpha = .5$		$\alpha = .8$	
Year	PurPwr	F	$|PE|$	F	$|PE|$	F	$|PE|$
1980	6.04						
1981	5.92	6.04	2.03	6.04	2.03	6.04	2.03
1982	5.57	6.03	8.26	5.98	7.36	5.94	6.64
1983	5.40	5.98	10.73	5.78	7.04	5.64	4.44
1984	5.17	5.92	14.51	5.59	8.12	5.45	5.42
1985	5.00	5.85	17.00	5.38	7.60	5.23	4.60
1986	4.91	5.77	17.52	5.19	5.70	5.05	2.85
1987	4.73	5.68	20.08	5.05	6.77	4.94	4.44
1988	4.55	5.59	22.86	4.89	7.47	4.77	4.84
1989	4.34	5.49	26.50	4.72	8.76	4.59	5.76
1990	4.67	5.38	15.20	4.53	3.00	4.39	6.00
1991	5.01	5.31	5.99	4.60	8.18	4.61	7.98
1992	4.86	5.28	8.64	4.81	1.03	4.93	1.44
1993	4.72	5.24	11.02	4.84	2.54	4.87	3.18
1994	4.60	5.19	12.83	4.78	3.91	4.75	3.26
1995	4.48	5.13	14.51	4.69	4.69	4.63	3.35
1996	4.86	5.07	4.32	4.59	5.56	4.51	7.20
1997	5.15	5.05	1.94	4.73	8.16	4.79	6.99

$$\sum |PE| = 213.95 \qquad \sum |PE| = 97.92 \qquad \sum |PE| = 80.42$$

$$\text{MAPE} = \textbf{12.59} \qquad \text{MAPE} = \textbf{5.76} \qquad \text{MAPE} = \textbf{4.73}$$

The smallest mean absolute percentage error is produced using $\alpha = .8$.

The forecast for 1998 is:

$$F(1998) = (.8)(5.15 + (.2)(4.79) = \textbf{5.08}$$

Chapter 16
Chi-Square and Other Nonparametric Statistics

LEARNING OBJECTIVES

This chapter presents several nonparametric statistics that can be used to analyze data enabling you to:

1. Recognize the advantages and disadvantages of nonparametric statistics.

2. Understand the chi-square goodness-of-fit test and how to use it.

3. Analyze data using the chi-square test of independence.

4. Understand how to use the runs test to test for randomness.

5. Know when and how to use the Mann-Whitney U Test, the Wilcoxon matched-pairs signed rank test, the Kruskal-Wallis test, and the Friedman test.

6. Learn when and how to measure correlation using Spearman's rank correlation measurement.

CHAPTER OUTLINE

16.1   Chi-Square Goodness-of-Fit Test

        Testing a Population Proportion Using the Chi-square Goodness-of-Fit Test as an Alternative Technique to the Z Test

16.2   Contingency Analysis: Chi-Square Test of Independence

16.3   Runs Test

        Small-Sample Runs Test

        Large-Sample Runs Test

16.4   Mann-Whitney U Test

        Small-Sample Case

        Large-Sample Case

16.5   Wilcoxon Matched-Pairs Signed Rank Test

        Small-Sample Case ($n \leq 15$)

        Large-Sample Case ($n > 15$)

16.6   Kruskal-Wallis Test

16.7   Friedman Test

16.8   Spearman's Rank Correlation

KEY WORDS

Chi-Square Distribution
Chi-Square Goodness-of-Fit Test
Chi-Square Test of Independence
Contingency Analysis
Contingency Table
Friedman Test
Kruskal-Wallis Test

Mann-Whitney U Test
Nonparametric Statistics
Parametric Statistics
Runs Test
Spearman's Rank Correlation
Wilcoxon Matched-Pairs Signed
  Rank Test

STUDY QUESTIONS

1. Statistical techniques based on assumptions about the population from which the sample data are selected are called _____ statistics.

2. Statistical techniques based on fewer assumptions about the population and the parameters are called _____ statistics.

3. A chi-square goodness-of-fit test is being used to determine if the observed frequencies from seven categories are significantly different from the expected frequencies from the seven categories. The degrees of freedom for this test are _____.

4. A value of alpha = .05 is used to conduct the test described in question 3. The critical table chi-square value is _____.

5. A variable contains five categories. It is expected that data are uniformly distributed across these five categories. To test this, a sample of observed data is gathered on this variable resulting in frequencies of 27, 30, 29, 21, 24. A value of .01 is specified for alpha. The degrees of freedom for this test are _____.

6. The critical table chi-square value of the problem presented in question 5 is

   _____.

7. The calculated chi-square value for the problem presented in question five is
   _____. Based on this value and the critical chi-square value, a researcher would decide to _____ the null hypothesis.

8. A researcher believes that a variable is Poisson distributed across six categories. To test this, a random sample of observations is made for the variable resulting in the following data:

Number of arrivals	Observed
0	47
1	56
2	38
3	23
4	15
5	12

   Suppose alpha is .10, the critical table chi-square value used to conduct this chi-square goodness-of-fit test is _____.

9. The value of the calculated chi-square for the data presented in question 8 is

   _____.

   Based on this value and the critical value determined in question 8, the decision of the researcher is to _____ the null hypothesis.

10. The degrees of freedom used in conducting a chi-square goodness-of-fit test to determine if a distribution is normally distributed are _____.

11. In using the chi-square goodness-of-fit test, a statistician needs to make certain that none of the expected values are less than _____.

12. Suppose we want to test the following hypotheses using a chi-square goodness-of-fit test.

H_0: $P = .20$ and H_a: $P \neq .20$

A sample of 150 data values is taken resulting in 37 items that possess the characteristic of interest. Let $= .05$. The degrees of freedom for this test are _____. The critical chi-square value is _____.

13. The calculated value of chi-square for question 12 is _____. The decision is to _____.

14. The chi-square _____ is used to analyze frequencies of two variables with multiple categories.

15. A two-way frequency table is sometimes referred to as a _____ table.

16. Suppose a researcher wants to use the data below and the chi-square test of independence to determine if variable one is independent of variable two.

Variable One

		A	B	C
Variable	D	25	40	60
Two	E	10	15	20

The expected value for the cell of D and B is _____.

17. The degrees of freedom for the problem presented in question 16 are _____.

18. If alpha is .05, the critical chi-square value for the problem presented in question 16 is _____.

19. The calculated value of chi-square for the problem presented in question 16 is _____. Based on this calculated value of chi-square and the critical chi-square value determined in question 18, the researcher should decide to _____ the null hypothesis that the two variables are independent.

20. A researcher wants to statistically determine if variable three is independent of variable four using the observed data given below:

		Variable Three	
		A	B
Variable	C	92	70
Four	D	112	145

If alpha is .01, the critical chi-square table value for this problem is _____.

21. The calculated chi-square value for the problem presented in question 20 is

_____.

Based on this value and the critical value determined in question 20, the researcher should decide to _____ the null hypothesis.

22. The nonparametric test for the randomness of a sequence of numbers is called the _____ test.

23. Suppose the following sequence of outcomes is obtained using a random sampling process:

XXXYYYYXXXXXX

Testing to determine if this pattern is random, we obtain a critical value of _____ for the lower tail at α = .025 (for each tail). Based on this critical value and the observed sequence, we would conclude that the data are (random, nonrandom) _____?

24. Suppose we are attempting to randomly sample males and females in a study. The sequence shown below is obtained:

MMFFFFFMFMMFMMFFFMMMMMMFFFFMFMFFMFFMMMFMFMMFF

The value of μ_R for these data is _____. The value of σ_R is _____.
The value of R is _____. Suppose = .05 for this test. The critical value of Z is _____. The observed value of Z is _____. The decision is to _____ the null hypothesis. The conclusion is that the data are (random, not random)

_____.

25. The nonparametric counterpart of the t test to compare the means of two independent populations is called _____.

26. A researcher wants to determine if the values obtained for population two are greater than those for population one. To test this, the researcher randomly samples six scores from population one (designated as group one) and six scores from population two (designated as group two) shown below. The sampled groups are independent. Using the Mann-Whitney U test, the values of W_1 and W_2 are _____ and _____. The values of U_1 and U_2 are _____ and _____. This is a _____ tailed test. The p-value obtained from the table in the appendix of the text for this problem is _____. Assuming that $\alpha = .05$, the decision for this problem is to _____ the null hypothesis.

Group 1	Group 2
124	129
131	138
128	136
126	137
132	142
141	139

27. Suppose a Mann-Whitney U test is being used to test to determine if two populations are different or not. A value of alpha = .05 is used. Random samples of size 16 are gathered from each population and the resulting data are given below:

Sample 1: 19, 27, 23, 29, 22, 20, 29, 31, 25, 17, 26, 23, 18, 28, 28, 33

Sample 2: 27, 35, 33, 28, 24, 33, 30, 31, 38, 39, 29, 41, 33, 34, 36, 34

The critical table value of Z for this problem is _____.

28. In the problem presented in question 27 if sample one is designated as group one, the value of W is _____.

29. In the problem presented in question 27, the value of U is _____.

30. For the problem presented in question 27, the calculated value of Z is _____. Based on this value and the critical value determined in question 27, the decision should be to _____ the null hypothesis.

31. The nonparametric alternative to the t test for two related samples or matched-pairs is

_____.

32. A researcher conducts a before/after study in which she believes that scores will decrease after the treatment. A sample of seven people are used in the study. The resulting scores are shown below. Using = .05, the critical table T value for this problem is _____. The observed value of T is _____. The decision is to _____ the null hypothesis.

Before	After
29	18
34	32
17	21
39	30
51	46
64	40
21	18

33. The Wilcoxon matched-pairs signed rank test for large samples uses a _____ statistic to analyze the data.

34. Suppose the following samples of paired data are gathered and the Wilcoxon matched-pairs signed is used to determine if there is a significant difference in the two populations from which the samples are were gathered.

Sample 1	Sample 2
109	98
103	100
111	107
98	102
105	99
108	96
101	100
102	104
100	93
97	98
106	100
112	108
104	105
105	101
109	101

Let alpha be .10. The critical value of Z for this problem is _____.

35. The value of T for the problem presented in question 34 is _____.

36. The mean value of T for the sample size of the problem presented in question 34 is

_____.

The standard deviation of T for this sample size is _____.

37. The calculated Z value for the problem presented in question 34 is _____.
Based on the critical value determined in question 34 and the calculated value of Z, a
statistician would decide to _____ the null hypothesis.

38. The nonparametric alternative to the one-way analysis of variance is the
_____ test.

39. The value of K computed in the Kruskal-Wallis test is distributed approximately as a
_____ value.

40. Suppose a researcher desires to analyze the data below using a Kruskal-Wallis test to
determine if there is a significant difference in the populations from which the four samples
were taken.

Sample 1	Sample 2	Sample 3	Sample 4
113	97	105	109
124	99	108	106
117	98	100	105
118	101	98	108
122		103	110

The degrees of freedom associated with the Kruskal-Wallis test of this data are _____.

41. The critical value of chi-square used to test the data for the problem in question 40 using
$\alpha = .05$ is _____.

42. The calculated value of chi-square for the data of the problem in question 40 is _____.
Using this value and the critical value determined in question 41, a researcher would decide
to _____ the null hypothesis.

43. The nonparametric equivalent to the randomized block design is the _____.

44. A randomized block design is set up for a research study. However, the data are considered
to be only ordinal measurements. Therefore, the data are analyzed using a Friedman test.
The design and data are shown below. In analyzing these data, the sum of the squared ranks
is _____. Using $\alpha = .05$, the critical value of χ^2 is _____. The value of
χ^2_r is _____. Based on these statistics, the decision is to _____ the
null hypothesis.

Block	Treatment				
	A	B	C	D	E
1	105	97	99	112	101
2	106	98	96	109	105
3	110	105	94	104	98
4	108	104	93	106	105

45. A nonparametric alternative to Pearson's product-moment correlation coefficient, r, is

_____.

46. The data below have been gathered in pairs from two variables:

X: 12, 19, 21, 34, 50, 69, 70
Y: 8, 17, 15, 29, 31, 45, 39

The value of Spearman's rank correlation for this data is _____.

47. The data below have been gathered in pairs from two variables:

X: 29, 13, 11,   9,   5, -1, -3, -4, -11
Y: -12, -13, -16, -25, -26, -18, -20, -44, -90

The value of Spearman's correlation for this data is _____.

48. The data below have been gathered in pairs from two variables:

X: 230, 221, 190, 130, 124, 109
Y: 107, 150, 134, 138, 166, 178

The value of Spearman's rank correlation for this data is _____.

49. If the value of Spearman's rank correlation is near -1, the two variables have
_____ correlation. If the value of a Spearman's rank correlation is near 0, the
two variables have _____ correlation.

ANSWERS TO STUDY QUESTIONS

1. Parametric Statistics

2. Nonparametric Statistics

3. 6

4. 12.5916

5. 4

6. 13.2767

7. 2.091, Fail to Reject

8. 7.77944

9. 16.4, Reject

10. $K - 3$

11. 5

12. 1, 3.8416

13. 2.041, Fail to Reject

14. Test of Independence

15. Contingency

16. 40.44

17. 2

18. 5.99147

19. .19, Fail to Reject

20. 6.6349

21. 6.945, Reject

22. Runs

23. 3, nonrandom

24. 23.489, 3.314, 32, ± 1.96, -0.45
    Fail to Reject, Random

25. Mann-Whitney U Test

26. 28, 50, 29, 7, One, .0465, Reject

27. ± 1.96

28. 164.5

29. 227.5

30. 3.75, Reject

31. Wilcoxon Matched-Pairs Signed Rank Test

32. 4, 3, Reject

33. Z

34. ± 1.645

35. 15.5

36. 60, 17.61

37. $- 2.53$, Reject

38. Kruskal-Wallis test

39. Chi-square

40. 3

41. 7.81473

42. 15.11, Reject

43. Friedman Test

44. 840, 9.48773, 12, Reject

45. Spearman's Rank Correlation

46. .929

47. .867

48. -.829

49. High Negative, Little or No

SOLUTIONS TO ODD-NUMBERED PROBLEMS IN CHAPTER 16

16.1

f_0	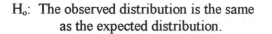 $\dfrac{(f_0 - f_e)^2}{f_0}$	f_e
53	68	3.309
37	42	0.595
32	33	0.030
28	22	1.636
18	10	6.400
15	8	6.125

H_o: The observed distribution is the same
      as the expected distribution.

H_a: The observed distribution is not the same
      as the expected distribution.

Observed $\chi^2 = \sum \dfrac{(f_0 - f_e)^2}{f_e}$ = **18.095**

$df = k - 1 = 6 - 1 = 5, \quad \alpha = .05$

$\chi^2_{.05,5} = 11.07$

Since the observed $\chi^2 = 18.095 > \chi^2_{.05,5} = 11.07$, the decision is to **reject the null hypothesis**.

The observed frequencies are not distributed the same as the expected frequencies.

16.3

Number	f_0	(Number)(f_0)
0	28	0
1	17	17
2	11	22
3	5	15
		54

H_o: The frequency distribution is Poisson.
H_a: The frequency distribution is not Poisson.

$$\lambda = \frac{54}{61} = 0.9$$

Number	Expected Probability	Expected Frequency
0	.4066	24.803
1	.3659	22.312
2	.1647	10.047
≥ 3	.0628	3.831

Since f_e for ≥ 3 is less than 5, collapse categories 2 and ≥ 3:

Number	f_o	f_e	$\dfrac{(f_0 - f_e)^2}{f_0}$
0	28	24.803	0.412
1	17	22.312	1.265
≥ 2	16	13.878	0.324
	61	60.993	2.001

$df = k - 2 = 3 - 2 = 1,$ $\alpha = .05$

$\chi^2_{.05,1} = 3.84146$

Calculated $\chi^2 = \sum \dfrac{(f_0 - f_e)^2}{f_e} = \mathbf{2.001}$

Since the observed $\chi^2 = 2.001 < \chi^2_{.05,1} = 3.84146$, the decision is to **fail to reject the null hypothesis**.

There is insufficient evidence to reject the distribution as Poisson distributed. The conclusion is that the distribution is Poisson distributed.

16.5	Definition	f_o	Exp.Prop.	f_e	$\dfrac{(f_o - f_e)^2}{f_o}$
	Happiness	42	.39	227(.39)= 88.53	24.46
	Sales/Profit	95	.12	227(.12)= 27.24	168.55
	Helping Others	27	.18	40.86	4.70
	Achievement/				
	Challenge	63	.31	70.34	0.77
		227			198.48

H_o: The observed frequencies are distributed the same as the expected frequencies.

H_a: The observed frequencies are not distributed the same as the expected frequencies.

Observed $\chi^2 = \textbf{198.48}$

$df = k - 1 = 4 - 1 = 3, \quad \alpha = .05$

$\chi^2_{.05,3} = 7.81473$

Since the observed $\chi^2 = 198.48 > \chi^2_{.05,3} = 7.81473$, the decision is to **reject the null hypothesis**.

The observed frequencies for men are not distributed the same as the expected frequencies which are based on the responses of women.

16.7

Age	f_o	M	fM	fM^2
10-20	16	15	240	3,600
20-30	44	25	1,100	27,500
30-40	61	35	2,135	74,725
40-50	56	45	2,520	113,400
50-60	35	55	1,925	105,875
60-70	19	65	1,235	80,275
	231		$\Sigma fM = 9,155$	$\Sigma fM^2 = 405,375$

$$\overline{X} = \frac{\sum fM}{n} = \frac{9,155}{231} = 39.63$$

$$S = \sqrt{\frac{\sum fM^2 - \frac{\left(\sum fM\right)^2}{n}}{n-1}} = \sqrt{\frac{405,375 - \frac{(9,155)^2}{231}}{230}} = 13.6$$

H_o: The observed frequencies are normally distributed.
H_a: The observed frequencies are not normally distributed.

For Category 10-20	P

$$Z = \frac{10 - 39.63}{13.6} = -2.18 \qquad .4854$$

$$Z = \frac{20 - 39.63}{13.6} = -1.44 \qquad \underline{-.4251}$$

Expected prob. .0603

For Category 20-30	P

for X = 20, Z = -1.44 $\qquad$ .4251

$$Z = \frac{30 - 39.63}{13.6} = -0.71 \qquad \underline{-.2611}$$

Expected prob. .1640

For Category 30-40	P

for X = 30, Z = -0.71 $\qquad$ .2611

$$Z = \frac{40 - 39.63}{13.6} = 0.03 \qquad \underline{+.0120}$$

Expected prob. .2731

For Category 40-50	P

$$Z = \frac{50 - 39.63}{13.6} = 0.76$$ .2764

for X = 40, Z = 0.03 $\underline{-.0120}$

Expected prob.   .2644

For Category 50-60	P

$$Z = \frac{60 - 39.63}{13.6} = 1.50$$ .4332

for X = 50, Z = 0.76 $\underline{-.2764}$

Expected prob.   .1568

For Category 60-70	P

$$Z = \frac{70 - 39.63}{13.6} = 2.23$$ .4871

for X = 60, Z = 1.50 $\underline{-.4332}$

Expected prob.   .0539

For < 10:
Probability between 10 and the mean = .0603 + .1640 + .2611 = .4854
Probability < 10 = .5000 - .4854 = .0146

For > 70:
Probability between 70 and the mean = .0120 + .2644 + .1568 + .0539 = .4871
Probability > 70 = .5000 - .4871 = .0129

Age	Probability	f_e
< 10	.0146	(.0146)(231) = 3.37
10-20	.0603	(.0603)(231) = 13.93
20-30	.1640	37.88
30-40	.2731	63.09
40-50	.2644	61.08
50-60	.1568	36.22
60-70	.0539	12.45
> 70	.0129	2.98

Categories < 10 and > 70 are less than 5.
Collapse the < 10 into 10-20 and > 70 into 60-70.

Age	f_o	f_e	$\dfrac{(f_0 - f_e)^2}{f_0}$
10-20	16	17.30	0.10
20-30	44	37.88	0.99
30-40	61	63.09	0.07
40-50	56	61.08	0.42
50-60	35	36.22	0.04
60-70	19	15.43	0.83
			2.45

df = k - 3 = 6 - 3 = 3, α = .05

$\chi^2_{.05,3}$ = 7.81473

Observed χ^2 = **2.45**

Since the observed $\chi^2 < \chi^2_{.05,3}$ = 7.81473, the decision is to **fail to reject the null hypothesis**.

There is no reason to reject that the observed frequencies are normally distributed.

16.9 H_0: P = .28   n = 270   X = 62
        H_a: P ≠ .28

	f_o	f_e	$\dfrac{(f_0 - f_e)^2}{f_0}$
Spend More	62	270(.28) = 75.6	2.44656
Don't Spend More	208	270(.72) = 194.4	0.95144
Total	270	270.0	3.39800

The observed value of χ^2 is **3.398**

α = .05 and α/2 = .025   df = k - 1 = 2 - 1 = 1

$\chi^2_{.025,1}$ = 5.02389

Since the observed χ^2 = 3.398 < $\chi^2_{.025,1}$ = 5.02389, the decision is to **fail to reject the null hypothesis**.

16.11

	Variable Two		
Variable One	24	59	83
	13	43	56
	20	35	55
	57	137	194

H_o: Variable one is independent of Variable Two.
H_a: Variable one is not independent of Variable Two.

$$e_{11} = \frac{(83)(57)}{194} = 24.39 \qquad e_{12} = \frac{(83)(13)}{194} = 58.61$$

$$e_{21} = \frac{(56)(57)}{194} = 16.45 \qquad e_{22} = \frac{(56)(137)}{194} = 39.55$$

$$e_{31} = \frac{(55)(57)}{194} = 16.16 \qquad e_{32} = \frac{(55)(137)}{194} = 38.84$$

	Variable Two		
Variable One	(24.39) 24	(58.61) 59	83
	(16.45) 13	(39.55) 43	56
	(16.16) 20	(38.84) 35	55
	57	137	194

$$\chi^2 = \frac{(24-24.39)^2}{24.39} + \frac{(59-58.61)^2}{58.61} + \frac{(13-16.45)^2}{16.45} + \frac{(43-39.55)^2}{39.55} +$$

$$\frac{(20-16.16)^2}{16.16} + \frac{(35-38.84)^2}{38.84} = .01 + .00 + .72 + .30 + .91 + .38 = \mathbf{2.32}$$

$\alpha = .05, \ df = (c-1)(r-1) = (2-1)(3-1) = 2$

$\chi^2_{.05,2} = 5.99147$

Since the observed $\chi^2 = 2.32 < \chi^2_{.05,2} = 5.99147$, the decision is to **fail to reject the null hypothesis**.

Variable One is independent of Variable Two.

16.13

	Variable Two				
Variable One	24	13	47	58	142
	93	59	187	244	583
	117	72	234	302	725

H_o: Variable One is independent of Variable Two.
H_a: Variable One is not independent of Variable Two.

$$e_{11} = \frac{(142)(117)}{725} = 22.92 \qquad e_{12} = \frac{(142)(72)}{725} = 14.10$$

$$e_{13} = \frac{(142)(234)}{725} = 45.83 \qquad e_{14} = \frac{(142)(302)}{725} = 59.15$$

$$e_{21} = \frac{(583)(117)}{725} = 94.08 \qquad e_{22} = \frac{(583)(72)}{725} = 57.90$$

$$e_{23} = \frac{(583)(234)}{725} = 188.17 \qquad e_{24} = \frac{(583)(302)}{725} = 242.85$$

	Variable Two				
Variable One	(22.92) 24	(14.10) 13	(45.83) 47	(59.15) 58	142
	(94.08) 93	(57.90) 59	(188.17) 187	(242.85) 244	583
	117	72	234	302	725

$$\chi^2 = \frac{(24-22.92)^2}{22.92} + \frac{(13-14.10)^2}{14.10} + \frac{(47-45.83)^2}{45.83} + \frac{(58-59.15)^2}{59.15} +$$

$$\frac{(93-94.08)^2}{94.08} + \frac{(59-57.90)^2}{57.90} + \frac{(188-188.17)^2}{188.17} + \frac{(244-242.85)^2}{242.85} =$$

$.05 + .09 + .03 + .02 + .01 + .02 + .01 + .01 = \mathbf{0.24}$

$\alpha = .01, \ df = (c\text{-}1)(r\text{-}1) = (4\text{-}1)(2\text{-}1) = 3$

$\chi^2_{.01,3} = 11.3449$

Since the observed $\chi^2 = 0.24 < \chi^2_{.01,3} = 11.3449$, the decision is to **fail to reject the null hypothesis**.

Variable One is independent of Variable Two.

16.15

		Type of Music Preferred				
		R	R&B	Coun	Clssic	
Region	NE	140	32	5	18	195
	S	134	41	52	8	235
	W	154	27	8	13	202
		428	100	65	39	632

H_o: Type of music preferred is independent of region.
H_a: Type of music preferred is not independent of region.

$e_{11} = \dfrac{(195)(428)}{632} = 132.6$

$e_{23} = \dfrac{(235)(65)}{632} = 24.17$

$e_{12} = \dfrac{(195)(100)}{632} = 30.85$

$e_{24} = \dfrac{(235)(39)}{632} = 14.50$

$e_{13} = \dfrac{(195)(65)}{632} = 20.06$

$e_{31} = \dfrac{(202)(428)}{632} = 136.80$

$$e_{14} = \frac{(195)(39)}{632} = 12.03 \qquad\qquad e_{32} = \frac{(202)(100)}{632} = 31.96$$

$$e_{21} = \frac{(235)(428)}{632} = 159.15 \qquad\qquad e_{33} = \frac{(202)(65)}{632} = 20.78$$

$$e_{22} = \frac{(235)(100)}{632} = 37.18 \qquad\qquad e_{34} = \frac{(202)(39)}{632} = 12.47$$

		\multicolumn{4}{c}{Type of Music Preferred}	
		R	R&B	Coun	Clssic	
Region	NE	(132.06)	(30.85)	(20.06)	(12.03)	195
		140	32	5	18	235
	S	(159.15)	(37.18)	(24.17)	(14.50)	202
		134	41	52	8	632
	W	(136.80)	(31.96)	(20.78)	(12.47)	
		154	27	8	13	
		428	100	65	39	

$$\chi^2 = \frac{(141-132.06)^2}{132.06} + \frac{(32-30.85)^2}{30.85} + \frac{(5-20.06)^2}{20.06} + \frac{(18-12.03)^2}{12.03} +$$

$$\frac{(134-159.15)^2}{159.15} + \frac{(41-37.18)^2}{37.18} + \frac{(52-24.17)^2}{24.17} + \frac{(8-14.50)^2}{14.50} +$$

$$\frac{(154-136.80)^2}{136.80} + \frac{(27-31.96)^2}{31.96} + \frac{(8-20.78)^2}{20.78} + \frac{(13-12.47)^2}{12.47} =$$

$$.48 + .04 + 11.31 + 2.96 + 3.97 + .39 + 32.04 + 2.91 + 2.16 + .77 +$$

$$7.86 + .02 = \mathbf{64.91}$$

$\alpha = .01, \quad df = (c-1)(r-1) = (4-1)(3-1) = 6$

$\chi^2_{.01,6} = 16.8119$

Since the observed $\chi^2 = 64.91 > \chi^2_{.01,6} = 16.8119$, the decision is to **reject the null hypothesis**.

Type of music preferred is not independent of region of the country.

16.17

		Number of Bedrooms			
		≤ 2	3	≥ 4	
Number of	1	116	101	57	274
Stories	2	90	325	160	575
		206	426	217	849

H_0: Number of Stories is independent of number of bedrooms.

H_a: Number of Stories is not independent of number of bedrooms.

$$e_{11} = \frac{(274)(206)}{849} = 66.48 \qquad e_{21} = \frac{(575)(206)}{849} = 139.52$$

$$e_{12} = \frac{(274)(426)}{849} = 137.48 \qquad e_{22} = \frac{(575)(426)}{849} = 288.52$$

$$e_{13} = \frac{(274)(217)}{849} = 70.03 \qquad e_{23} = \frac{(575)(217)}{849} = 146.97$$

$$\chi^2 = \frac{(90-139.52)^2}{139.52} + \frac{(101-137.48)^2}{137.48} + \frac{(57-70.03)^2}{70.03} + \frac{(90-139.52)^2}{139.52} +$$

$$\frac{(325-288.52)^2}{288.52} + \frac{(160-146.97)^2}{146.97} =$$

$$\chi^2 = 36.89 + 9.68 + 2.42 + 17.58 + 4.61 + 1.16 = \mathbf{72.34}$$

$\alpha = .10 \qquad df = (c-1)(r-1) = (3-1)(2-1) = 2$

$\chi^2_{.10,2} = 4.60517$

Since the observed $\chi^2 = 72.34 > \chi^2_{.10,2} = 4.60517$, the decision is to **reject the null hypothesis**.

Number of stories is not independent of number of bedrooms.

16.19 H_o: The observations in the sample are randomly generated.
        H_a: The observations in the sample are not randomly generated.

This is a small sample runs test since n_1, $n_2 \leq 20$

$\alpha = .05$, The lower tail critical value is 6 and the upper tail critical value is 16

$n_1 = 10$ $n_2 = 10$

R = 11

Since R = 11 is between the two critical values, the decision is to **fail to reject the null hypothesis.**

The data are random.

16.21 $n_1 = 8$ $n_2 = 52$ $\alpha = .05$

This is a two-tailed test and $\alpha/2 = .025$. **The p-value from the printout is .0264**.
Since the p-value is the lowest value of "alpha" for which the null hypothesis can
be rejected, the decision is to **fail to reject the null hypothesis**
(p-value = .0264 > .025). There is not enough evidence to reject that the data are
randomly generated.

16.23

H_o: The observations in the sample are randomly generated.

H_a: The observations in the sample are not randomly generated.

Since n_1, $n_2 > 20$, use large sample runs test

$\alpha = .05$ Since this is a two-tailed test, $\alpha/2 = .025$, $Z_{.025} = \pm 1.96$. If the observed value of Z is greater than 1.96 or less than -1.96, the decision is to reject the null hypothesis.

R = 27 $n_1 = 40$ $n_2 = 24$

$$\mu_R = \frac{2n_1 n_2}{n_1 + n_2} + 1 = \frac{2(40)(24)}{64} + 1 = 31$$

$$\sigma_R = \sqrt{\frac{2n_1 n_2 (2n_1 n_2 - n_1 - n_2)}{(n_1 + n_2)^2 (n_1 + n_2 - 1)}} = \sqrt{\frac{2(40)(24)[2(40)(24) - 40 - 24]}{(64)^2 (63)}} = 3.716$$

$$Z = \frac{R - \mu_R}{\sigma_R} = \frac{27 - 31}{3.716} = \textbf{-1.08}$$

Since the observed Z of -1.08 is greater than the critical lower tail Z value of -1.96, the decision is to **fail to reject the null hypothesis**. The data are randomly generated.

16.25 H_o: Group 1 is identical to Group 2

H_a: Group 1 is not identical to Group 2

Use the small sample Mann-Whitney U test since both n_1, $n_2 \leq 10$, $\alpha = .05$. Since this is a two-tailed test, $\alpha/2 = .025$. The p-value is obtained using Table A.13.

Value	Rank	Group
11	1	1
13	2.5	1
13	2.5	2
14	4	2
15	5	1
17	6	1
18	7.5	1
18	7.5	2
21	9.5	1
21	9.5	2
22	11	1
23	12.5	2
23	12.5	2
24	14	2
26	15	1
29	16	1

$n_1 = 8$
$n_2 = 8$

$W_1 = 1 + 2.5 + 5 + 6 + 7.5 + 9.5 + 15 + 16 = 62.5$

$$U = n_1 \cdot n_2 + \frac{n_1(n_1+1)}{2} - W_1 = (8)(8) + \frac{(8)(9)}{2} - 62.5 = 37.5$$

$$U' = n_1 \cdot n_2 - U = 64 - 37.5 = 26.5$$

We use the small U which is 26.5

From Table A.13, the p-value for U = 27 is .3227(2) = **.6454**

Since this p-value is greater than $\alpha/2 = .025$, the decision is to **fail to reject the null hypothesis**.

16.27

Contacts	Rank	Group
6	1	1
8	2	1
9	3.5	1
9	3.5	2
10	5	2
11	6.5	1
11	6.5	1
12	8.5	1
12	8.5	2
13	11	1
13	11	2
13	11	2
14	13	2
15	14	2
16	15	2
17	16	2

$W_1 = 39$

$$U_1 = n_1 \cdot n_2 + \frac{n_1(n_1 + 1)}{2} - W_1 = (7)(9) + \frac{(7)(8)}{2} - 39 = 52$$

$$U_2 = n_1 \cdot n_2 - U_1 = (7)(9) - 52 = 11$$

$$U = 11$$

From Table A.13, the p-value = **.0156**. Since this p-value is greater than $\alpha = .01$, the decision is to **fail to reject the null hypothesis**.

16.29 H_o: Males do not earn more than females
             H_a: Males do earn more than females

Earnings	Rank	Gender
$28,900	1	F
31,400	2	F
36,600	3	F
40,000	4	F
40,500	5	F
41,200	6	F
42,300	7	F
42,500	8	F
44,500	9	F
45,000	10	M
47,500	11	F
47,800	12.5	F
47,800	12.5	M
48,000	14	F
50,100	15	M
51,000	16	M
51,500	17.5	M
51,500	17.5	M
53,850	19	M
55,000	20	M
57,800	21	M
61,100	22	M
63,900	23	M

$n_1 = 11$ $n_2 = 12$

$W_1 = 10 + 12.5 + 15 + 16 + 17.5 + 17.5 + 19 + 20 + 21 + 22 + 23 = 193.5$

$$\mu = \frac{n_1 \cdot n_2}{2} = \frac{(11)(12)}{2} = 66$$

$$\sigma = \sqrt{\frac{n_1 \cdot n_2(n_1 + n_2 + 1)}{12}} = \sqrt{\frac{(11)(12)(24)}{12}} = 16.25$$

$$U = n_1 \cdot n_2 + \frac{n_1(n_1 + 1)}{2} - W_1 = (11)(12) + \frac{(11)(12)}{2} - 193.5 = 4.5$$

$$Z = \frac{U - \mu}{\sigma} = \frac{4.5 - 66}{16.25} = \textbf{-3.78} \qquad\qquad \alpha = .01, \quad Z_{.01} = 2.33$$

Since the observed $Z = 3.78 > Z_{.01} = 2.33$, the decision is to **reject the null hypothesis**.

16.31 H_o: The population differences $= 0$

H_a: The population differences $\neq 0$

1	2	d	Rank
212	179	33	15
234	184	50	16
219	213	6	7.5
199	167	32	13.5
194	189	5	6
206	200	6	7.5
234	212	22	11
225	221	4	5
220	223	-3	- 3.5
218	217	1	1
234	208	26	12
212	215	-3	-3.5
219	187	32	13.5
196	198	-2	-2
178	189	-11	-9
213	201	12	10

$n = 16$

$T_- = 3.5 + 3.5 + 2 + 9 = 18$

$$\mu = \frac{(n)(n+1)}{4} = \frac{(16)(17)}{4} = 68$$

$$\sigma = \sqrt{\frac{n(n+1)(2n+1)}{24}} = \sqrt{\frac{16(17)(33)}{24}} = 19.34$$

$$Z = \frac{T - \mu}{\sigma} = \frac{18 - 68}{19.34} = \textbf{-2.59}$$

$\alpha = .10 \qquad \alpha/2 = .05$

$Z_{.05} = \pm 1.645$

Since the observed $Z = -2.59 < Z_{.05} = -1.645$, the decision is to **reject the null hypothesis**.

16.33 H_o: The population differences $= 0$
         H_a: The population differences < 0

Before	After	d	Rank
10,500	12,600	-2,100	-11
8,870	10,660	-1,790	-9
12,300	11,890	410	3
10,510	14,630	-4,120	-17
5,570	8,580	-3,010	-15
9,150	10,115	-965	-7
11,980	14,320	-2,370	-12
6,740	6,900	-160	-2
7,340	8,890	-1,550	-8
13,400	16,540	-3,140	-16
12,200	11,300	900	6
10,570	13,330	-2,760	-13
9,880	9,990	-110	-1
12,100	14,050	-1,950	-10
9,000	9,500	-500	-4
11,800	12,450	-650	-5
10,500	13,450	-2,950	-14

Since n $= 17$, use the large sample test

$T+ = 3 + 6 = 9$

$T = 9$

$$\mu = \frac{(n)(n+1)}{4} = \frac{(17)(18)}{4} = 76.5$$

$$\sigma = \sqrt{\frac{n(n+1)(2n+1)}{24}} = \sqrt{\frac{17(18)(35)}{24}} = 21.12$$

$$Z = \frac{T-\mu}{\sigma} = \frac{9-76.5}{21.12} = \textbf{-3.20}$$

$\alpha = .05, \quad Z_{.05} = -1.645$

Since the observed $Z = -3.20 < Z_{.05} = -1.645$, the decision is to **reject the null hypothesis**.

16.35 H_o: The population differences $= 0$
        H_a: The population differences < 0

1990	1999	d	Rank
49	54	-5	-7.5
27	38	-11	-15
39	38	1	2
75	80	-5	-7.5
59	53	6	11
67	68	-1	-2
22	43	-21	-20
61	67	-6	-11
58	73	-15	-18
60	55	5	7.5
72	58	14	16.5
62	57	5	7.5
49	63	-14	-16.5
48	49	-1	-2
19	39	-20	-19
32	34	-2	-4.5
60	66	-6	-11
80	90	-10	-13.5
55	57	-2	-4.5
68	58	10	13.5

$n = 20$

$T+ = 2 + 11 + 7.5 + 16.5 + 7.5 + 13.5 = 58$
$T = 58$

$$\mu = \frac{(n)(n+1)}{4} = \frac{(20)(21)}{4} = 105$$

$$\sigma = \sqrt{\frac{n(n+1)(2n+1)}{24}} = \sqrt{\frac{20(21)(41)}{24}} = 26.79$$

$$Z = \frac{T - \mu}{\sigma} = \frac{58 - 105}{26.79} = \mathbf{-1.75}$$

For $\alpha = .10$, $Z_{.10} = -1.28$

Since the observed $Z = -1.75 < Z_{.10} = -1.28$, the decision is to **reject the null hypothesis**.

16.37 H_o: The 5 populations are identical
        H_a: At least one of the 5 populations is different

1	2	3	4	5
157	165	219	286	197
188	197	257	243	215
175	204	243	259	235
174	214	231	250	217
201	183	217	279	240
203		203		233
				213

BY RANKS

	1	2	3	4	5
	1	2	18	29	7.5
	6	7.5	26	23.5	15
	4	12	23.5	27	21
	3	14	19	25	16.5
	9	5	16.5	28	22
	10.5		10.5		20
					13
T_j	33.5	40.5	113.5	132.5	115
n_j	6	5	6	5	7

$$\sum \frac{T_j^2}{n_j} = \frac{(33.5)^2}{6} + \frac{(40.5)^2}{5} + \frac{(113.5)^2}{6} + \frac{(132.5)}{5} + \frac{(115)^2}{7} = 8,062.67$$

$n = 29$

$$K = \frac{12}{n(n+1)} \sum \frac{T_j^2}{n_j} - 3(n+1) = \frac{12}{29(30)}(8,062.67) - 3(30) = \mathbf{21.21}$$

$\alpha = .01 \, df = c - 1 = 5 - 1 = 4$

$\chi^2_{.01,4} = 13.2767$

Since the observed K = 21.21 > $\chi^2_{.01,4}$ = 13.2767, the decision is to **reject the null hypothesis**.

16.39 H_o: The 4 populations are identical

   H_a: At least one of the 4 populations is different

Region 1	Region 2	Region 3	Region 4
$1,200	$225	$ 675	$1,075
450	950	500	1,050
110	100	1,100	750
800	350	310	180
375	275	660	330
200			680
			425

By Ranks

	Region 1	Region 2	Region 3	Region 4
	23	5	15	21
	12	19	13	20
	2	1	22	17
	18	9	7	3
	10	6	14	8
	4			16
				11
T_j	69	40	71	96
n_j	6	5	5	7

$$\sum \frac{T_j^{\,2}}{n_j} = \frac{(69)^2}{6} + \frac{(40)^2}{5} + \frac{(71)^2}{5} + \frac{(96)^2}{7} = 3{,}438.27$$

$n = 23$

$$K = \frac{12}{n(n+1)} \sum \frac{T_j^{\,2}}{n_j} - 3(n+1) = \frac{12}{23(24)}(3{,}428.27) - 3(24) = \mathbf{2.75}$$

$\alpha = .05$ $df = c - 1 = 4 - 1 = 3$

$\chi^2_{.05,3} = 7.81473$

Since the observed K = 2.75 < $\chi^2_{.05,3}$ = 7.81473, the decision is to fail **to reject the null hypothesis**.

16.41 H_o: The 4 populations are identical

H_a: At least one of the 4 populations is different

Amusement Parks	Lake Area	City	National Park
0	3	2	2
1	2	2	4
1	3	3	3
0	5	2	4
2	4	3	3
1	4	2	5
0	3	3	4
	5	3	4
	2	1	
		3	

By Ranks

musement Parks	Lake Area	City	National Park
2	20.5	11.5	11.5
5.5	11.5	11.5	28.5
5.5	20.5	20.5	20.5
2	33	11.5	28.5
11.5	28.5	20.5	20.5
5.5	28.5	11.5	33
2	20.5	20.5	28.5
	33	20.5	28.5
	11.5	5.5	
		20.5	
T_j 34	207.5	154.0	199.5
n_j 7	9	10	8

$$\sum \frac{T_j^{\,2}}{n_j} = \frac{(34)^2}{7} + \frac{(207.5)^2}{9} + \frac{(154)^2}{10} + \frac{(199.5)}{8} = 12,295.80$$

$n = 34$

$$K = \frac{12}{n(n+1)} \sum \frac{T_j^{\,2}}{n_j} - 3(n+1) = \frac{12}{34(35)}(12,295.80) - 3(35) = \mathbf{18.99}$$

$\alpha = .05$ $df = c - 1 = 4 - 1 = 3$

$\chi^2_{.05,3} = 7.81473$

Since the observed K = 18.99 > $\chi^2_{.05,3}$ = 7.81473, the decision is to **reject the null hypothesis**.

16.43 H_o: The treatment populations are equal
       H_a: At least one of the treatment populations yields larger values than at least one
             other treatment population.

Use the Friedman test with $\alpha = .05$

$C = 5$, $b = 5$, $df = C - 1 = 4$, $\chi^2_{.05,4} = 9.48773$

If the observed value of $\chi^2 > 9.48773$, then the decision will be to reject the null
hypothesis.

Shown below are the data ranked by blocks:

	1	2	3	4	5
1	1	4	3	5	2
2	1	3	4	5	2
3	2.5	1	4	5	2.5
4	3	2	4	5	1
5	4	2	3	5	1
R_j	11.5	12	18	25	8.5
R_j^2	132.25	144	324	625	72.25

$\Sigma R_j^2 = 1,297.5$

$$\chi_r^2 = \frac{12}{bC(C+1)}\sum R_j^2 - 3b(C+1) = \frac{12}{(5)(5)(6)}(1,297.5) - 3(5)(6) = \textbf{13.8}$$

Since the observed value of $\chi_r^2 = 13.8 > \chi_{4,.05}^2 = 9.48773$, the decision is to
reject the null hypothesis. At least one treatment population yields larger values than at
least one other treatment population.

16.45　H_o: The treatment populations are equal

H_a: At least one of the treatment populations yields larger values than at least one other treatment population.

Use the Friedman test with $\alpha = .01$

$C = 4$,　$b = 6$,　$df = C - 1 = 3$,　$\chi^2_{.01,3} = 11.3449$

If the observed value of $\chi^2 > 11.3449$, then the decision will be to reject the null hypothesis.

Shown below are the data ranked by blocks:

	1	2	3	4
1	1	4	3	2
2	2	3	4	1
3	1	4	3	2
4	1	3	4	2
5	1	3	4	2
6	2	3	4	1
R_j	8	20	22	10
R_j^2	64	400	484	100

$\sum R_j^2 = 1,048$

$$\chi_r^2 = \frac{12}{bC(C+1)}\sum R_j^2 - 3b(C+1) = \frac{12}{(6)(4)(5)}(1,048) - 3(6)(5) = \mathbf{14.8}$$

Since the observed value of $\chi_r^2 = 14.8 > \chi_{4,.05}^2 = 11.3449$, the decision is to **reject the null hypothesis**. At least one treatment population yields larger values than at least one other treatment population.

16.47   C = 4 treatments   b = 5 blocks

$S = \chi_r^2 = 2.04$ with a p-value of .564.

Since the p-value of .564 > α = .10, .05, or .01, the decision is to **fail to reject the null hypothesis**. There is no significant difference in treatments.

16.49

X	Y	X Ranked	Y Ranked	d	d^2
23	201	3	2	1	1
41	259	10.5	11	-.5	0.25
37	234	8	7	1	1
29	240	6	8	-2	4
25	231	4	6	-2	4
17	209	1	3	-2	4
33	229	7	5	2	4
41	246	10.5	9	1.5	2.25
40	248	9	10	-1	1
28	227	5	4	1	1
19	200	2	1	1	1
					$\Sigma d^2 = 23.5$

n = 11

$$r_s = 1 - \frac{6\sum d^2}{n(n^2-1)} = 1 - \frac{6(23.5)}{11(120)} = .893$$

16.51

X	Y	X Ranked	Y Ranked	d	d^2
99	108	8	2	6	36
67	139	4	5	-1	1
82	117	6	3	3	9
46	168	1	8	-7	49
80	124	5	4	1	1
57	162	3	7	-4	16
49	145	2	6	-4	16
91	102	7	1	6	36
					$\Sigma d^2 = 164$

n = 8

$$r_s = 1 - \frac{6\sum d^2}{n(n^2-1)} = 1 - \frac{6(164)}{8(63)} = -.95$$

16.53

Bank Credit Card	Home Equity Loan	Bank Cr. Cd. Rank	Home Eq. Loan Rank	d	d^2
2.51	2.01	12	1	11	121
2.86	1.95	6.5	2	4.5	20.25
2.33	1.66	13	6	7	49
2.54	1.77	10	3	7	49
2.54	1.51	10	7.5	2.5	6.25
2.18	1.47	14	10	4	16
3.34	1.75	3	4	-1	1
2.86	1.73	6.5	5	1.5	2.25
2.74	1.48	8	9	-1	1
2.54	1.51	10	7.5	2.5	6.25
3.18	1.25	4	14	-10	100
3.53	1.44	1	11	-10	100
3.51	1.38	2	12	-10	100
3.11	1.30	5	13	-8	64
					$\Sigma d^2 = 636$

$n = 14$

$$r_s = 1 - \frac{6\sum d^2}{n(n^2 - 1)} = 1 - \frac{6(636)}{14(14^2 - 1)} = -.3978$$

There is a very modest negative correlation between overdue payments for bank credit cards and home equity loans.

16.55

No. Co. on NYSE	No. Eq. Is. on AMEX	Rank NYSE	Rank AMEX	d	d^2
1774	1063	8	1	7	49
1885	1055	7	2	5	25
2088	943	6	5	1	1
2361	1005	5	3	2	4
2570	981	4	4	0	0
2675	936	3	6	-3	9
2907	896	2	7	-5	25
3047	893	1	8	-7	49
					$\Sigma d^2 = 162$

$n = 8$

$$r_s = 1 - \frac{6\sum d^2}{n(n^2 - 1)} = 1 - \frac{6(162)}{8(8^2 - 1)} = -0.9286$$

There is a strong negative correlation between the number of companies listed on the NYSE and the number of equity issues on the American Stock Exchange.

16.57

	Variable 2			
Variable 1	12	23	21	56
	8	17	20	45
	7	11	18	36
	27	51	59	137

$e_{11} = 11.00$ $e_{12} = 20.85$ $e_{13} = 24.12$

$e_{21} = 8.87$ $e_{22} = 16.75$ $e_{23} = 19.38$

$e_{31} = 7.09$ $e_{32} = 13.40$ $e_{33} = 15.50$

$$\chi^2 = \frac{(12-11.04)^2}{11.04} + \frac{(23-20.85)^2}{20.85} + \frac{(21-24.12)^2}{24.12} + \frac{(8-8.87)^2}{8.87} + $$

$$\frac{(17-16.75)^2}{16.75} + \frac{(20-19.38)^2}{19.38} + \frac{(7-7.09)^2}{7.09} + \frac{(11-13.40)^2}{13.40} + $$

$$\frac{(18-15.50)^2}{15.50} = $$

.084 + .222 + .403 + .085 + .004 + .020 + .001 + .430 + .402 = **1.652**

df = (C-1)(r-1) = (2)(2) = 4 $\alpha = .05$

$\chi^2_{.05,4} = 9.48773$

Since the observed value of $\chi^2 = 1.652 < \chi^2_{.05,4} = 9.48773$, the decision is to **fail to reject the null hypothesis**.

16.59

Sample 1	Sample 2
573	547
532	566
544	551
565	538
540	557
548	560
536	557
523	547

$\alpha = .01$ Since $n_1 = 8$, $n_2 = 8 \leq 10$, use the small sample Mann-Whitney U test.

X	Rank	Group
523	1	1
532	2	1
536	3	1
538	4	2
540	5	1
544	6	1
547	7.5	2
547	7.5	2
548	9	1
551	10	2
557	11.5	2
557	11.5	2
560	13	2
565	14	1
566	15	2
573	16	1

$W_1 = 1 + 2 + 3 + 5 + 6 + 9 + 14 + 16 = 56$

$$U_1 = n_1 \cdot n_2 + \frac{n_1(n_1 + 1)}{2} - W_1 = (8)(8) + \frac{(8)(9)}{2} - 56 = 44$$

$$U_2 = n_1 \cdot n_2 - U_1 = 8(8) - 44 = 20$$

Take the smaller value of U, $U_2 = \mathbf{20}$

From Table A.13, the p-value (1-tailed) is .1172, for 2-tailed, the p-value is **.2344**. Since the p-value is $> \alpha = .05$, the decision is to **fail to reject the null hypothesis**.

16.61 $n_j = 7$, $n = 28$, $C = 4$, df = 3

Group 1	Group 2	Group 3	Group 4
6	4	3	1
11	13	7	4
8	6	7	5
10	8	5	6
13	12	10	9
7	9	8	6
10	8	5	7

By Ranks:

	Group 1	Group 2	Group 3	Group 4
	9.5	3.5	2	1
	25	27.5	13.5	3.5
	17.5	9.5	13.5	6
	23	17.5	6	9.5
	27.5	26	23	20.5
	13.5	20.5	17.5	9.5
	23	17.5	6	13.5
T_j	139	122	81.5	63.5

$$\sum \frac{T_j^2}{n_j} = 2760.14 + 2126.29 + 948.89 + 576.04 = 6411.36$$

$$K = \frac{12}{n(n+1)} \sum \frac{T_j^2}{n_j} - 3(n+1) = \frac{12}{28(29)}(6411.36) - 3(29) = \mathbf{7.75}$$

The critical value of chi-square is: $\chi^2_{3,.01} = 11.3449$.

Since K = 7.75 < $\chi^2_{3,.01}$ = 11.3449, the decision is to **fail to reject the null hypothesis**.

16.63

Ranks

1	2	1	2	d	d^2
101	87	1	7	-6	36
129	89	2	8	-6	36
133	84	3	6	-3	9
147	79	4	5	-1	1
156	70	5	3	2	4
179	64	6	1	5	25
183	67	7	2	5	25
190	71	8	4	4	16

$$\Sigma d^2 = 152$$

$n = 8$

$$r_s = 1 - \frac{6 \sum d^2}{n(n^2 - 1)} = 1 - \frac{6(152)}{8(63)} = \mathbf{-.81}$$

16.65 H_o: The 3 populations are identical
H_a: At least one of the 3 populations is different

1 Gal.	5 Gal.	10 Gal.
1.1	2.9	3.1
1.4	2.5	2.4
1.7	2.6	3.0
1.3	2.2	2.3
1.9	2.1	2.9
1.4	2.0	1.9
2.1	2.7	

By Ranks

1 Gal.	5 Gal.	10 Gal.
1	17.5	20
3.5	14	13
5	15	19
2	11	12
6.5	9.5	17.5
3.5	8	6.5
9.5	16	
T_j 31	91	88

n_j 7   7   6

$$\sum \frac{T_j^{2}}{n_j} = \frac{(31)^2}{7} + \frac{(91)^2}{7} + \frac{(88)^2}{6} = 2,610.95$$

$n = 20$

$$K = \frac{12}{n(n+1)}\sum \frac{T_j^{2}}{n_j} - 3(n+1) = \frac{12}{20(21)}(2,610.95) - 3(21) = \textbf{11.60}$$

$\alpha = .01$ $df = c - 1 = 3 - 1 = 2$

$\chi^2_{.01,2} = 9.21034$

Since the observed K = 11.60 > $\chi^2_{.01,2}$ = 9.21034, the decision is to **reject the null hypothesis**.

16.67 $N = 40$ $n_1 = 24$ $n_2 = 16$ $\alpha = .05$

Use the large sample runs test since both n_1, n_2 are not less than 20.

H_0: The observations are randomly generated
H_a: The observations are not randomly generated

With a two-tailed test, $\alpha/2 = .025$, $Z_{.025} = \pm 1.96$. If the observed $Z > .196$ or < -1.96, the decision will be to reject the null hypothesis.

$R = 19$

$$\mu_R = \frac{2n_1 n_2}{n_1 + n_2} + 1 = \frac{2(24)(16)}{24 + 16} + 1 = 20.2$$

$$\sigma_R = \sqrt{\frac{2n_1 n_2 (2n_1 n_2 - n_1 - n_2)}{(n_1 + n_2)^2 (n_1 + n_2 - 1)}} = \sqrt{\frac{2(24)(16)[2(24)(16) - 24 - 16]}{(40)^2 (39)}} = 2.993$$

$$Z = \frac{R - \mu_R}{\sigma_R} = \frac{19 - 20.2}{2.993} = \textbf{-0.40}$$

Since $Z = -0.40 > Z_{.025} = -1.96$, the decision is to **fail to reject the null hypothesis**.

16.69   Use the Friedman test. Let $\alpha = .05$

H_0: The treatment populations are equal
H_a: The treatment populations are not equal

$C = 3$ and $b = 7$

Operator	Machine 1	Machine 2	Machine 3
1	231	229	234
2	233	232	231
3	229	233	230
4	232	235	231
5	235	228	232
6	234	237	231
7	236	233	230

By ranks:

Operator	Machine 1	Machine 2	Machine 3
1	2	1	1
3	1	3	2
4	2	3	1
5	3	1	2
6	2	3	1
7	3	2	1
R_j	16	15	11
R_j^2	256	225	121

$df = C-1 = 2$ $\chi^2_{.05,2} = 5.99147$.

If the observed $\chi^2_r > 5.99147$, the decision will be to reject the null hypothesis.

$\Sigma R_j^2 = 256 + 225 + 121 = 602$

$$\chi_r^2 = \frac{12}{bC(C+1)}\sum R_j^2 - 3b(C+1) = \frac{12}{(7)(3)(4)}(602) - 3(7)(4) = \mathbf{2}$$

Since $\chi^2_r = 2 < \chi^2_{.05,2} = 5.99147$, the decision is to **fail to reject the null hypothesis**.

16.71

Arrivals	f_o	(f_o)(Arrivals)
0	26	0
1	40	40
2	57	114
3	32	96
4	17	68
5	12	60
6	8	48
	$\Sigma f_o = 192$	$\Sigma(f_o)$(arrivals) $= 426$

$$\lambda = \frac{\sum(f_0)(arrivals)}{\sum f_0} = \frac{426}{192} = 2.2$$

H_o: The observed frequencies are Poisson distributed.
H_a: The observed frequencies are not Poisson distributed.

Arrivals	Probability	f_e
0	.1108	$(.1108)(192) = 21.27$
1	.2438	$(.2438)(192) = 46.81$
2	.2681	51.48
3	.1966	37.75
4	.1082	20.77
5	.0476	9.14
6	.0249	4.78

f_o	f_e	$\dfrac{(f_0 - f_e)^2}{f_0}$
26	21.27	1.05
40	46.81	2.18
57	51.48	0.59
32	37.75	0.88
17	20.77	0.68
12	9.14	0.89
8	4.78	2.17
		8.44

Observed $\chi^2 = \textbf{8.44}$

$\alpha = .05$ $df = k - 2 = 7 - 2 = 5$ $\chi^2_{.05,5} = 11.0705$

Since the observed $\chi^2 = 8.44 < \chi^2_{.05,5} = 11.0705$, the decision is to **fail to reject the null hypothesis**. There is not enough evidence to reject the claim that the observed frequency of arrivals is Poisson distributed.

16.73 H_o: The population differences $= 0$
        H_a: The population differences $\neq 0$

With	Without	d	Rank
1180	1209	-29	-6
874	902	-28	-5
1071	862	209	18
668	503	165	15
889	974	-85	-12.5
724	675	49	9
880	821	59	10
482	567	-85	-12.5
796	602	194	16
1207	1097	110	14
968	962	6	1
1027	1045	-18	-4
1158	896	262	20
670	708	-38	-8
849	642	207	17
559	327	232	19
449	483	-34	-7
992	978	14	3
1046	973	73	11
852	841	11	2

$n = 20$

$T_- = 6 + 5 + 12.5 + 12.5 + 4 + 8 + 7 = 55$
$T = 55$

$$\mu = \frac{(n)(n+1)}{4} = \frac{(20)(21)}{4} = 105$$

$$\sigma = \sqrt{\frac{n(n+1)(2n+1)}{24}} = \sqrt{\frac{20(21)(41)}{24}} = 26.79$$

$$Z = \frac{T - \mu}{\sigma} = \frac{55 - 105}{26.79} = \textbf{-1.87}$$

$\alpha = .01, \quad \alpha/2 = .005 \qquad Z_{.005} = \pm 2.575$

Since the observed $Z = -1.87 > Z_{.005} = -2.575$, the decision is to **fail to reject the null hypothesis**.

16.75 H_0: There is no difference between March and June
          H_a: There is a difference between March and June

GMAT	Rank	Month
300	1	J
380	2	M
410	3	J
420	4	J
440	5	M
450	6	M
460	7	M
470	8	J
480	9.5	M
480	9.5	J
490	11	M
500	12.5	M
500	12.5	J
510	14	M
520	15.5	M
520	15.5	J
540	17	J
550	18	M
560	19	J
580	20	J

$n_1 = 10 \quad n_2 = 10$

$W_1 = 1 + 3 + 4 + 8 + 9.5 + 12.5 + 15.5 + 17 + 19 + 20 = 109.5$

$$U_1 = n_1 \cdot n_2 + \frac{n_1(n_1 + 1)}{2} - W_1 = (10)(10) + \frac{(10)(11)}{2} - 109.5 = 45.5$$

$$U_2 = n_1 \cdot n_2 - U_1 = (10)(10) - 45.5 = 54.5$$

From Table A.13, the p-value for $U = 45$ is .3980 and for 44 is .3697. For a two-tailed test, double the p-value to at least .739. Using $\alpha = .10$, the decision is to **fail to reject the null hypothesis**.

16.77 H_o: The population differences = 0
H_a: The population differences ≠ 0

Box	No Box	d	Rank
185	170	15	11
109	112	-3	-3
92	90	2	2
105	87	18	13.5
60	51	9	7
45	49	-4	-4.5
25	11	14	10
58	40	18	13.5
161	165	-4	-4.5
108	82	26	15.5
89	94	-5	-6
123	139	-16	-12
34	21	13	8.5
68	55	13	8.5
59	60	-1	-1
78	52	26	15.5

n = 16

$T_- = 3 + 4.5 + 4.5 + 6 + 12 + 1 = 31$

T = 31

$$\mu = \frac{(n)(n+1)}{4} = \frac{(16)(17)}{4} = 68$$

$$\sigma = \sqrt{\frac{n(n+1)(2n+1)}{24}} = \sqrt{\frac{16(17)(33)}{24}} = 19.34$$

$$Z = \frac{T - \mu}{\sigma} = \frac{31 - 68}{19.34} = \textbf{-1.91}$$

α = .05,   α/2 = .025 $Z_{.025} = \pm 1.96$

Since the observed Z = -1.91 > $Z_{.025}$ = -1.96, the decision is to **fail to reject the null hypothesis**.

16.79

		Position				
		Manager	Programmer	Operator	Systems Analyst	
Years	0-3	6	37	11	13	67
	4-8	28	16	23	24	91
	> 8	47	10	12	19	88
		81	63	46	56	246

$$e_{11} = \frac{(67)(81)}{246} = 22.06 \qquad e_{23} = \frac{(91)(46)}{246} = 17.02$$

$$e_{12} = \frac{(67)(63)}{246} = 17.16 \qquad e_{24} = \frac{(91)(56)}{246} = 20.72$$

$$e_{13} = \frac{(67)(46)}{246} = 12.53 \qquad e_{31} = \frac{(88)(81)}{246} = 28.98$$

$$e_{14} = \frac{(67)(56)}{246} = 15.25 \qquad e_{32} = \frac{(88)(63)}{246} = 22.54$$

$$e_{21} = \frac{(91)(81)}{246} = 29.96 \qquad e_{33} = \frac{(88)(46)}{246} = 16.46$$

$$e_{22} = \frac{(91)(63)}{246} = 23.30 \qquad e_{34} = \frac{(88)(56)}{246} = 20.03$$

		Position				
		Manager	Programmer	Operator	Systems Analyst	
Years	0-3	(22.06) 6	(17.16) 37	(12.53) 11	(15.25) 13	67
	4-8	(29.96) 28	(23.30) 16	(17.02) 23	(20.72) 24	91
	> 8	(28.98) 47	(22.54) 10	(16.46) 12	(20.03) 19	88
		81	63	46	56	246

$$\chi^2 = \frac{(6-22.06)^2}{22.06} + \frac{(37-17.16)^2}{17.16} + \frac{(11-12.53)^2}{12.53} + \frac{(13-15.25)^2}{15.25} +$$

$$\frac{(28-29.96)^2}{29.96} + \frac{(16-23.30)^2}{23.30} + \frac{(23-17.02)^2}{17.02} + \frac{(24-20.72)^2}{20.72} +$$

$$\frac{(47-28.98)^2}{28.98} + \frac{(10-22.54)^2}{22.54} + \frac{(12-16.46)^2}{16.46} + \frac{(19-20.03)^2}{20.03} =$$

$$11.69 + 22.94 + .19 + .33 + .13 + 2.29 + 2.1 + .52 + 11.2 + 6.98 +$$

$$1.21 + .05 = \textbf{59.63}$$

$\alpha = .01$ \qquad $df = (c-1)(r-1) = (4-1)(3-1) = 6$ \qquad $\chi^2_{.01,6} = 16.8119$

Since the observed $\chi^2 = 59.63 > \chi^2_{.01,6} = 16.8119$, the decision is to **reject the null hypothesis**. Position is not independent of number of years of experience.

16.81 H_0: The population differences $= 0$
   H_a: The population differences < 0

Before	After	d	Rank
430	465	-35	-11
485	475	10	5.5
520	535	-15	- 8.5
360	410	-50	-12
440	425	15	8.5
500	505	-5	-2
425	450	-25	-10
470	480	-10	-5.5
515	520	-5	-2
430	430	0	OMIT
450	460	-10	-5.5
495	500	-5	-2
540	530	10	5.5

$n = 12$

$T+ = 5.5 + 8.5 + 5.5 = 19.5$ \qquad $T = \textbf{19.5}$

From Table A.14, using $n = 12$, the critical T for $\alpha = .01$, one-tailed, is 10.

Since $T = 19.5$ is not less than or equal to the critical $T = 10$, the decision is to **fail to reject the null hypothesis**.

16.83

		Type of College or University			
		Community College	Large University	Small College	
Number of Children	0	25	178	31	234
	1	49	141	12	202
	2	31	54	8	93
	≥3	22	14	6	42
		127	387	57	571

H_o: Number of Children is independent of Type of College or University.
H_a: Number of Children is not independent of Type of College or University.

$$e_{11} = \frac{(234)(127)}{571} = 52.05 \qquad e_{31} = \frac{(93)(127)}{571} = 20.68$$

$$e_{12} = \frac{(234)(387)}{571} = 158.60 \qquad e_{32} = \frac{(193)(387)}{571} = 63.03$$

$$e_{13} = \frac{(234)(57)}{571} = 23.36 \qquad e_{33} = \frac{(93)(57)}{571} = 9.28$$

$$e_{21} = \frac{(202)(127)}{571} = 44.93 \qquad e_{41} = \frac{(42)(127)}{571} = 9.34$$

$$e_{22} = \frac{(202)(387)}{571} = 136.91 \qquad e_{42} = \frac{(42)(387)}{571} = 28.47$$

$$e_{23} = \frac{(202)(57)}{571} = 20.16 \qquad e_{43} = \frac{(42)(57)}{571} = 4.19$$

		Type of College or University			
		Community College	Large University	Small College	
Number of Children	0	(52.05) 25	(158.60) 178	(23.36) 31	234
	1	(44.93) 49	(136.91) 141	(20.16) 12	202
	2	(20.68) 31	(63.03) 54	(9.28) 8	93
	≥3	(9.34) 22	(28.47) 14	(4.19) 6	42
		127	387	57	571

$$\chi^2 = \frac{(25 - 52.05)^2}{52.05} + \frac{(178 - 158.6)^2}{158.6} + \frac{(31 - 23.36)^2}{23.36} + \frac{(49 - 44.93)^2}{44.93} +$$

$$\frac{(141 - 136.91)^2}{136.91} + \frac{(12 - 20.16)^2}{20.16} + \frac{(31 - 20.68)^2}{20.68} + \frac{(54 - 63.03)^2}{63.03} +$$

$$\frac{(8 - 9.28)^2}{9.28} + \frac{(22 - 9.34)^2}{9.34} + \frac{(14 - 28.47)^2}{28.47} + \frac{(6 - 4.19)^2}{4.19} =$$

$$14.06 + 2.37 + 2.50 + 0.37 + 0.12 + 3.30 + 5.15 + 1.29 + 0.18 +$$

$$17.16 + 7.35 + 0.78 = \mathbf{54.63}$$

$\alpha = .05$,   df= $(c - 1)(r - 1) = (3 - 1)(4 - 1) = 6$

$\chi^2_{.05,6} = 12.5916$

Since the observed $\chi^2 = 54.63 > \chi^2_{.05,6} = 12.5916$, the decision is to **reject the null hypothesis**.

Number of children is not independent of type of College or University.

16.85 H_o: Automatic no more productive
H_a: Automatic more productive

Sales	Rank	Type of Dispenser
92	1	M
105	2	M
106	3	M
110	4	A
114	5	M
117	6	M
118	7.5	A
118	7.5	M
125	9	M
126	10	M
128	11	A
129	12	M
137	13	A
143	14	A
144	15	A
152	16	A
153	17	A
168	18	A

$n_1 = 9$ $n_2 = 9$

$W_1 = 4 + 7.5 + 11 + 13 + 14 + 15 + 16 + 17 + 18 = 115.5$

$$U_1 = n_1 \cdot n_2 + \frac{n_1(n_1 + 1)}{2} - W_1 = (9)(9) + \frac{(9)(10)}{2} - 115.5 = 10.5$$

$$U_2 = n_1 \cdot n_2 - U_1 = 81 - 10.5 = 70.5$$

The smaller of the two is $U_1 = 10.5$

$\alpha = .01$

From Table A.13, the p-value = **.0039**. The decision is to **reject the null hypothesis** since the p-value is less than .01.

16.87

Sales	Miles	Ranks Sales	Ranks Miles	d	d^2
150,000	1,500	1	1	0	0
210,000	2,100	2	2	0	0
285,000	3,200	3	7	-4	16
301,000	2,400	4	4	0	0
335,000	2,200	5	3	2	4
390,000	2,500	6	5	1	1
400,000	3,300	7	8	-1	1
425,000	3,100	8	6	2	4
440,000	3,600	9	9	0	0

$$\Sigma d^2 = 26$$

$n = 9$

$$r_s = 1 - \frac{6 \sum d^2}{n(n^2 - 1)} = 1 - \frac{6(26)}{9(80)} = .783$$

16.89 H_o: The population differences $= 0$
           H_a: The population differences < 0

Husbands	Wives	d	Rank
27	35	-8	-12
22	29	-7	-11
28	30	-2	-6.5
19	20	-1	-2.5
28	27	1	2.5
29	31	-2	-6.5
18	22	-4	-9.5
21	19	2	6.5
25	29	-4	-9.5
18	28	-10	-13.5
20	21	-1	-2.5
24	22	2	6.5
23	33	-10	-13.5
25	38	-13	-16.5
22	34	-12	-15
16	31	-15	-18
23	36	-13	-16.5
30	31	-1	-2.5

n = 18

T+ = 2.5 + 6.5 + 6.5 = 15.5

T = 15.51

$$\mu = \frac{(n)(n+1)}{4} = \frac{(18)(19)}{4} = 85.5$$

$$\sigma = \sqrt{\frac{n(n+1)(2n+1)}{24}} = \sqrt{\frac{18(19)(37)}{24}} = 22.96$$

$$Z = \frac{T-\mu}{\sigma} = \frac{15.5 - 85.5}{22.96} = \textbf{-3.05}$$

$\alpha = .01$ $Z_{.01} = -2.33$

Since the observed Z = -3.05 < $Z_{.01}$ = -2.33, the decision is to **reject the null hypothesis**.

16.91   This is a Runs test for randomness. $n_1 = 21$, $n_2 = 29$. Because of the size of the n's, this is a large sample Runs test. There are 28 runs, **R = 28.**

$\mu_R = 25.36$ $\sigma_R = 3.34$

$$Z = \frac{28 - 25.36}{3.34} = \mathbf{0.79}$$

The *p*-value for this statistic is .4387 for a two-tailed test. The decision is to **fail to reject the null hypothesis** at $\alpha = .05$.

16.93   A Kruskal-Wallis test has been used to analyze the data. The null hypothesis is that the four populations are identical; and the alternate hypothesis is that at least one of the four populations is different. The H statistic (same as the K statistic) is 11.28 when adjusted for ties. The *p*-value for this H value is .010 which indicates that there is a significant difference in the four groups at $\alpha = .05$ and marginally so for $\alpha = .01$. An examination of the medians reveals that all group medians are the same (35) except for group 2 which has a median of 25.50. It is likely that it is group 2 that differs from the other groups.

Chapter 17
Statistical Quality Control

LEARNING OBJECTIVES

Chapter 17 presents basic concepts in quality control, with a particular emphasis on statistical quality control techniques, thereby enabling you to:

1. Understand the concepts of quality, quality control, and total quality management.

2. Understand the importance of statistical quality control in total quality management.

3. Learn about process analysis and some process analysis tools, including Pareto charts, fishbone diagrams, and control charts.

4. Learn how to construct $\overline{X}$ charts, R charts, P charts, and c charts.

5. Understand the theory and application of acceptance sampling.

CHAPTER OUTLINE

17.1   Introduction to Quality Control

What is Quality Control?

Total Quality Management

Some Important Quality Concepts

Benchmarking

Just-in-Time Systems

Reengineering

Six Sigma

Team Building

17.2   Process Analysis

Flowcharts

Pareto Analysis

Cause-and-Effect (Fishbone) Diagrams

Control Charts

17.3   Control Charts

Variation

Types of Control Charts

$\overline{X}$ Chart

R Charts

P Charts

c Charts

Interpreting Control Charts

17.4   Acceptance Sampling

`Single Sample Plan

Double-Sample Plan

Multiple-Sample Plan

Determining Error and OC Curves

KEY TERMS

Acceptance Sampling
After-Process Quality Control
Benchmarking
c Chart
Cause-and-Effect Diagram
Centerline
Consumer's Risk
Control Chart
Double-Sample Plan
Fishbone Diagram
Flowchart
In-Process Quality Control
Ishikawa Diagram
Just-in-Time Inventory Systems
Lower Control Limit (LCL)
Manufacturing Quality
Multiple-Sample Plan
Operating Characteristic (OC) Curve

P Chart

Pareto Analysis
Pareto Chart
Process
Producer's Risk
Product Quality
Quality
Quality Circle
Quality Control
R Chart
Reengineering
Single-Sample Plan
Six Sigma
Team Building
Total Quality Management
Transcendent Quality
Upper Control Limit (UCL)
User Quality
Value Quality

$\overline{X}$ Chart

STUDY QUESTIONS

1. The collection of strategies, techniques, and actions taken by an organization to assure themselves that they are producing a quality product is _____.

2. Measuring product attributes at various intervals throughout the manufacturing process in an effort to pinpoint problem areas is referred to as _____ quality control.

3. Inspecting the attributes of a finished product to determine whether the product is acceptable, is in need of rework, or is to be rejected and scrapped is _____ quality control.

4. An inventory system in which no extra raw materials or parts are stored for production is called a _____ system.

5. When a group of employees are organized as an entity to undertake management tasks and perform other functions such as organizing, developing, and overseeing projects, it is referred to as _____.

6. A _____ is a small group of workers, usually from the same department or work area, and their supervisor, who meet regularly to consider quality issues.

7. The complete redesigning of a company's core business process is called _____. This usually involves innovation and is often a complete departure from the company's normal way of doing business.

8. A total quality management approach that measures the capability of a process to perform defect-free work is called _____.

9. A methodology in which a company attempts to develop and establish total quality management from product to process by examining and emulating the best practices and techniques used in their industry is called _____.

10. A graphical method for evaluating whether a process is or is not in a state of statistical control is called a _____.

11. A diagram that is shaped like a fish and displays potential causes of one problem is called a _____ or _____ diagram.

12. A bar chart that displays a quantitative tallying of the numbers and types of defects that occur with a product is called a _____.

13. Two types of control charts for measurements are the _____ chart and the _____ chart. Two types of control charts for attribute compliance are the _____ chart and the _____ chart.

14. An X bar chart is constructed by graphing the _____ of a given measurement computed for a series of small samples on a product over a period of time.

15. An R chart plots the sample _____. The centerline of an R chart is equal to the value of _____.

16. A P chart graphs the proportion of sample items in _____ for multiple samples.   The centerline of a P chart is equal to _____.

17. A c chart displays the number of _____ per item or unit.

18. Normally, an X bar chart is constructed from 20 to 30 samples. However, assume that an X bar chart can be constructed using the four samples of five items shown below:

Sample 1	Sample 2	Sample 3	Sample 4
23	21	19	22
22	18	20	24
21	22	20	18
23	19	21	16
22	19	20	17

The value of A_2 for this control chart is _____.
The centerline value is _____.

The value of $\overline{R}$ is _____.
The value of UCL is _____.
The value of LCL is _____.
The following samples have means that fall outside the outer control limits _____. In constructing an R chart from these data, the value of the centerline is _____. The value of D_3 is _____ and the value of D_4 is _____. The UCL of the R chart is _____ and the value of LCL is _____.
The following samples have ranges that fall outside the outer control limits _____.

19. P charts should be constructed from data gathered from 20 to 30 samples. Suppose, however, that a P chart could be constructed from the data shown below:

Sample	n	Number out of Compliance
1	70	3
2	70	5
3	70	0
4	70	4
5	70	3
6	70	6

The value of the centerline is _____.
The UCL for this P chart is _____.
The LCL for this P chart is _____.
The samples with sample proportions falling outside the outer control limits are

_____.

20. c charts should be constructed using at least 25 items or units. Suppose, however, that a c chart could be constructed from the data shown below:

Item Number	Number of Nonconformities
1	3
2	2
3	2
4	4
5	0
6	3
7	1

The value of the centerline for this c chart is _____.
The value of UCL is _____ and the value of
LCL is _____.

21. A process is considered to be out of control if _____ or more consecutive points occur on one side of the centerline of the control chart.

22. Four possible causes of control chart abnormalities are (at least eight are mentioned in the text) _____, _____, _____, and

_____.

23. Suppose a single sample acceptance sampling plan has a c value of 1, a sample size of 10, a p_0 of .03, and a p_1 of .12. If the supplier really is producing 3% defects, the probability of accepting the lot is _____ and the probability of rejecting the lot is _____. Suppose, on the other hand, the supplier is producing 12% defects. The probability of accepting the lot is _____ and the probability of rejecting the lot is _____.

24. The Type II error in acceptance sampling is sometimes referred to as the _____ risk. The Type I error in acceptance sampling is sometimes referred to as the _____ risk.

25. Using the data from question 22, the producer's risk is _____ and the consumer's risk is _____. Assume that 3% defects is acceptable and 12% defects is not acceptable.

26. Suppose a two-stage acceptance sampling plan is undertaken with $c_1 = 2$, $r_1 = 6$, and $c_2 = 7$. A sample is taken resulting in 4 rejects. A second sample is taken resulting in 2 rejects. The final decision is to _____ the lot.

ANSWERS TO STUDY QUESTIONS

1.   Quality Control

2.   In-Process

3.   After-Process

4.   Just-in-Time

5.   Team Building

6.   Quality Circle

7.   Reengineering

8.   Six Sigma

9.   Benchmarking

10. Control Chart

11. Fishbone, Ishikawa

12. Pareto Chart

13. $\overline{X}$, R, P, c

14. Means

15. Ranges, $\overline{R}$

16. Noncompliance, P (average proportion)

17. Nonconformances

18. 0.577, 20.35, 4.0, 22.658, 18.042, None, 4.0, 0, 2.115, 8.46, 0.00, None

19. .05, .128, .000, None

20. 2.143, 6.535, 0.00

21. 8

22. Changes in the Physical Environment, Worker Fatigue, Worn Tools, Changes in Operators or Machines, Maintenance, Changes in Worker Skills, Changes in Materials, Process Modification

23. .9655, .0345, .6583, .3417

24. Consumer's, Producer's

25. .0345, .6583

26. Accept

SOLUTIONS TO ODD-NUMBERED PROBLEMS IN CHAPTER 17

17.5 $\overline{X}_1 = 4.55$, $\overline{X}_2 = 4.10$, $\overline{X}_3 = 4.80$, $\overline{X}_4 = 4.70$,

      $\overline{X}_5 = 4.30$, $\overline{X}_6 = 4.73$, $\overline{X}_7 = 4.38$

      $R_1 = 1.3$, $R_2 = 1.0$, $R_3 = 1.3$, $R_4 = 0.2$, $R_5 = 1.1$, $R_6 = 0.8$, $R_7 = 0.6$

      $\overline{\overline{X}} = 4.51$ $\overline{R} = 0.90$

For $\overline{X}$ Chart: Since n = 4, $A_2 = 0.729$

Centerline: $\overline{\overline{X}} = 4.51$

UCL: $\overline{\overline{X}} + A_2 \overline{R} = 4.51 + (0.729)(0.90) = 5.17$

LCL: $\overline{\overline{X}} - A_2 \overline{R} = 4.51 - (0.729)(0.90) = 3.85$

For R Chart: Since n = 4, $D_3 = 0$ $D_4 = 2.282$

Centerline: $\overline{R} = 0.90$

UCL: $D_4 \overline{R} = (2.282)(0.90) = 2.05$

LCL: $D_3 \overline{R} = 0$

$\overline{X}$ Chart:

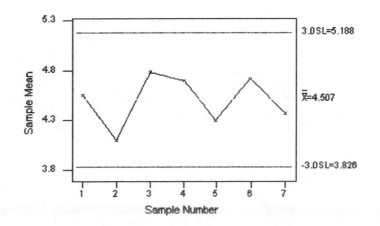

R Chart:

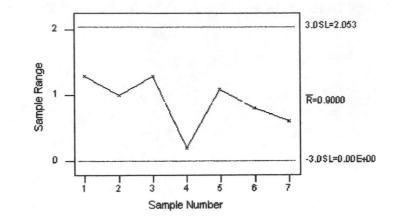

17.7 $\hat{p}_1 = .025,\; \hat{p}_2 = .000,\; \hat{p}_3 = .025,\; \hat{p}_4 = .075,$

$\hat{p}_5 = .05,\; \hat{p}_6 = .125,\; \hat{p}_7 = .05$

P = .050

Centerline: P = .050

UCL: $.05 + 3\sqrt{\dfrac{(.05)(.95)}{100}} \;=\; .05 + .103 \;=\; .153$

LCL: $.05 - 3\sqrt{\dfrac{(.05)(.95)}{100}} \;=\; .05 - .103 \;=\; .000$

P Chart:

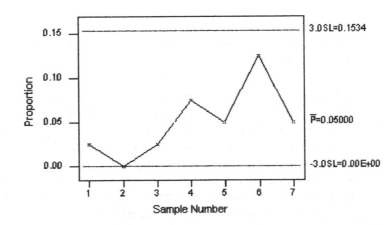

17.9 $\bar{c} = \dfrac{43}{32} = 1.34375$

Centerline: $\bar{c} = 1.34375$

UCL: $\bar{c} + 3\sqrt{c} = 1.34375 + 3\sqrt{1.34375} =$

  $1.34375 + 3.47761 = 4.82136$

LCL: $\bar{c} + 3\sqrt{c} = 1.34375 - 3\sqrt{1.34375} =$

  $1.34375 - 3.47761 = 0.000$

c Chart:

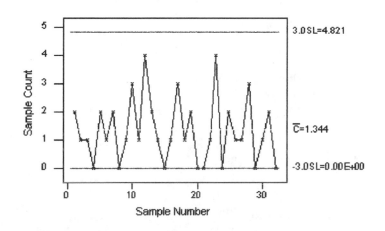

17.11   While there are no points outside the limits, the first chart exhibits some
problems. The chart ends with 9 consecutive points below the centerline.
Of these 9 consecutive points, there are at least 4 out of 5 in the outer 2/3 of the
lower region. The second control chart contains no points outside the control
limit. However, near the end, there are 8 consecutive points above the centerline.
The p chart contains no points outside the upper control limit. Three times, the
chart contains two out of three points in the outer third. However, this occurs in
the lower third where the proportion of noncompliance items approaches zero
and is probably not a problem to be concerned about. Overall, this seems to
display a process that is in control. One concern might be the wide swings in the
proportions at samples 15, 16 and 22 and 23.

17.13 $n = 10$ $c = 0$ $p_0 = .05$

$P(X = 0) = {}_{10}C_0(.05)^0(.95)^{10} = .5987$

$1 - P(X = 0) = 1 - .5987 = .4013$

The producer's risk is **.4013**

$p_1 = .14$

$P(X = 0) = {}_{15}C_0(.14)^0(.86)^{10} =$ **.2213**

The consumer's risk is .2213

17.15 $n = 8$ $c = 0$ $p_0 = .03$ $p_1 = .1$

P	Probability	
.01	.9227	
.02	.8506	
.03	.7837	
.04	.7214	Producer's Risk for ($p_0 = .03$) =
.05	.6634	$1 - .7837 =$ **.2163**
.06	.6096	
.07	.5596	
.08	.5132	Consumer's Risk for ($p_1 = .10$) = **.4305**
.09	.4703	
.10	.4305	
.11	.3937	
.12	.3596	
.13	.3282	
.14	.2992	
.15	.2725	

OC Chart:

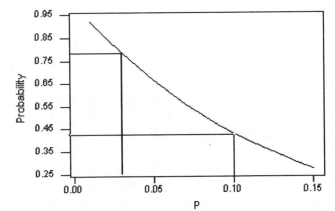

17.17

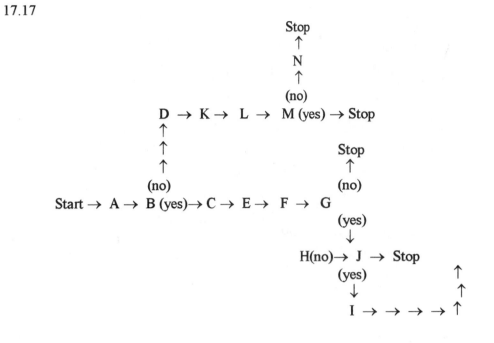

17.19   Fishbone Diagram:

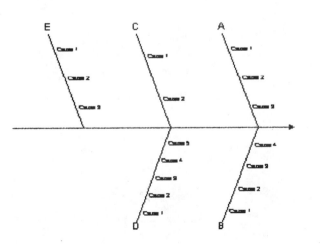

17.21 $\hat{p}_1 = .06, \ \hat{p}_2 = .22, \ \hat{p}_3 = .14, \ \hat{p}_4 = .04, \ \hat{p}_5 = .10,$

$\hat{p}_6 = .16, \ \hat{p}_7 = .00, \ \hat{p}_8 = .18, \ \hat{p}_9 = .02, \ \hat{p}_{10} = .12$

$P = \dfrac{52}{500} = .104$

Centerline: $P = .104$

UCL: $.104 + 3\sqrt{\dfrac{(.104)(.896)}{50}} = .104 + .130 = .234$

LCL: $.104 - 3\sqrt{\dfrac{(.104)(.896)}{50}} = .104 - .130 = .000$

P Chart:

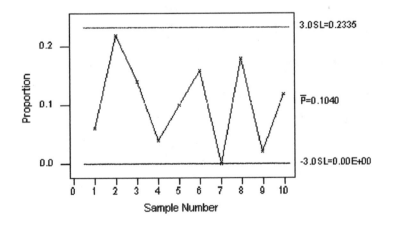

17.23 n = 15, c = 0, p_0 = .02, p_1 = .10

P	Probability
.01	.8601
.02	.7386
.04	.5421
.06	.3953
.08	.2863
.10	.2059
.12	.1470
.14	.1041

Producer's Risk for (p_0 = .02) = 1 - .7386 = **.2614**

Consumer's Risk for (p_1 = .10) = **.2059**

OC Curve:

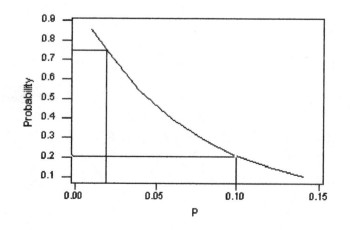

17.25 $\overline{X}_1 = 1.2100, \ \overline{X}_2 = 1.2050, \ \overline{X}_3 = 1.1900, \ \overline{X}_4 = 1.1725,$

$\overline{X}_5 = 1.2075, \ \overline{X}_6 = 1.2025, \ \overline{X}_7 = 1.1950, \ \overline{X}_8 = 1.1950,$

$\overline{X}_9 = 1.1850$

$R_1 = .04, \ R_2 = .02, \ R_3 = .04, \ R_4 = .04, \ R_5 = .06, R_6 = .02,$

$R_7 = .07, \ R_8 = .07, \ R_9 = .06,$

$\overline{\overline{X}} = 1.19583 \qquad \overline{R} = 0.04667$

For $\overline{X}$ Chart: Since n = 9, $A_2 = .337$

Centerline: $\overline{\overline{X}} = 1.19583$

UCL: $\overline{\overline{X}} + A_2\overline{R} = 1.19583 + .337(.04667) =$
$1.19583 + .01573 = 1.21156$

LCL: $\overline{\overline{X}} - A_2\overline{R} = 1.19583 - .337(.04667) =$
$1.19583 - .01573 = 1.18010$

For R Chart: Since n = 9, $D_3 = .184$ $D_4 = 1.816$

Centerline: $\overline{R} = .04667$

UCL: $D_4\overline{R} = (1.816)(.04667) = .08475$

LCL: $D_3\overline{R} = (.184)(.04667) = .00859$

$\overline{X}$ Chart:

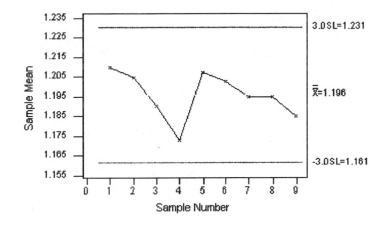

R chart:

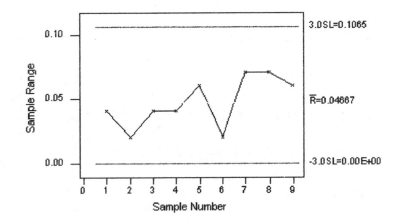

17.27

$\hat{p}_1 = .12, \quad \hat{p}_2 = .04, \quad \hat{p}_3 = .00, \quad \hat{p}_4 = .02667,$

$\hat{p}_5 = .09333, \quad \hat{p}_6 = .18667, \quad \hat{p}_7 = .14667, \quad \hat{p}_8 = .10667,$

$\hat{p}_9 = .06667, \quad \hat{p}_{10} = .05333, \quad \hat{p}_{11} = .0000, \quad \hat{p}_{12} = .09333$

$P = \dfrac{70}{900} = .07778$

Centerline: $P = .07778$

UCL: $.07778 + 3\sqrt{\dfrac{(.07778)(.92222)}{75}} = .07778 + .09278 = .17056$

LCL: $.07778 - 3\sqrt{\dfrac{(.07778)(.92222)}{75}} = .07778 - .09278 = .00000$

P Chart:

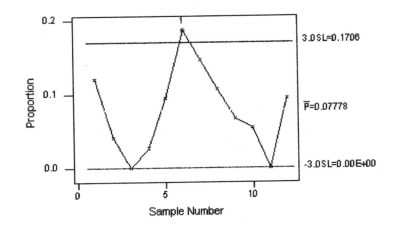

17.29 $n = 10$ $c = 2$ $p_0 = .10$ $p_1 = .30$

P	Probability
.05	.9885
.10	.9298
.15	.8202
.20	.6778
.25	.5256
.30	.3828
.35	.2616
.40	.1673
.45	.0996
.50	.0547

Producer's Risk for ($p_0 = .10$) = 1 - .9298 = **.0702**

Consumer's Risk for ($p_1 = .30$) = **.3828**

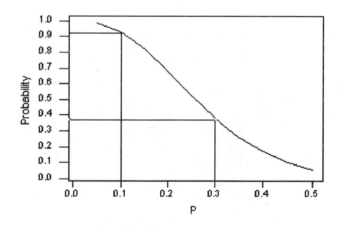

17.31

$$\hat{p}_1 = .05, \quad \hat{p}_2 = .00, \quad \hat{p}_3 = .15, \quad \hat{p}_4 = .075,$$

$$\hat{p}_5 = .025, \quad \hat{p}_6 = .025, \quad \hat{p}_7 = .125, \quad \hat{p}_8 = .00,$$

$$\hat{p}_9 = .10, \quad \hat{p}_{10} = .075, \quad \hat{p}_{11} = .05, \quad \hat{p}_{12} = .05,$$

$$\hat{p}_{13} = .15, \quad \hat{p}_{14} = .025, \quad \hat{p}_{15} = .000$$

$$P = \frac{36}{600} = .06$$

Centerline: $P = .06$

UCL: $.06 + 3\sqrt{\dfrac{(.06)(.94)}{40}} = .06 + .11265 = .17265$

LCL: $.06 - 3\sqrt{\dfrac{(.06)(.94)}{40}} = .06 - .112658 = .00000$

P Chart:

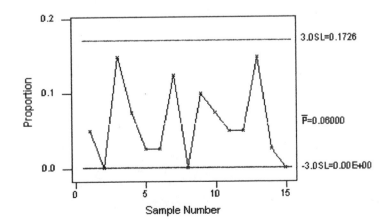

17.33   There are some items to be concerned about with this chart. Only one sample range is above the upper control limit. However, near the beginning of the chart there are eight sample ranges in a row below the centerline. Later in the run, there are nine sample ranges in a row above the centerline. The quality manager or operator might want to determine if there is some systematic reason why there is a string of ranges below the centerline and, perhaps more importantly, why there are a string of ranges above the centerline.

17.35   The centerline of the C chart indicates that the process is averaging 0.74 nonconformances per part. Twenty-five of the fifty sampled items have zero nonconformances. None of the samples exceed the upper control limit for nonconformances. However, the upper control limit is 3.321 nonconformances which, in and of itself, may be too many. Indeed, three of the fifty (6%) samples actually had three nonconformances. An additional six samples (12%) had two nonconformances. One matter of concern may be that there is a run of ten samples in which nine of the samples exceed the centerline (samples 12 through 21). The question raised by this phenomenon is whether or not there is a systematic flaw in the process that produces strings of nonconforming items.

Chapter 18
Decision Analysis

LEARNING OBJECTIVES

Chapter 18 describes how to use decision analysis to improve management decisions, thereby enabling you to:

1. Learn about decision making under certainty, under uncertainty, and under risk.

2. Learn several strategies for decision-making under uncertainty, including expected payoff, expected opportunity loss, maximin, maximax, and minimax regret.

3. Learn how to construct and analyze decision trees.

4. Understand aspects of utility theory.

5. Learn how to revise probabilities with sample information.

CHAPTER OUTLINE

18.1 The Decision Table and Decision Making Under Certainty

   Decision Table

   Decision-Making Under Certainty

18.2 Decision Making Under Uncertainty

   Maximax Criterion

   Maximin Criterion

   Hurwicz Criterion

   Minimax Regret

18.3 Decision Making Under Risk

   Decision Trees

   Expected Monetary Value (EMV)

   Expected Value of Perfect Information

   Utility

18.4 Revising Probabilities in Light of Sample Information

   Expected Value of Sample Information

KEY TERMS

Decision Alternatives
Decision Analysis
Decision Making Under Certainty
Decision Making Under Risk
Decision Making Under Uncertainty
Decision Table
Decision Trees
EMV'er
Expected Monetary Value (EMV)
Expected Value of Perfect Information
Expected Value of Sample Information

Hurwicz Criterion
Maximax Criterion
Maximin Criterion
Minimax Regret
Opportunity Loss Table
Payoffs
Payoff Table
Risk-Avoider
Risk-Taker
States of Nature
Utility

STUDY QUESTIONS

1. In decision analysis, decision-making scenarios are divided into three categories: decision-making under _____, decision-making under _____, and decision-making under _____.

2. Many decision analysis problems can be viewed as having three variables:
    1. _____, 2. _____, and
    3. _____.

3. Occurrences of nature that can happen after a decision has been made that can effect the outcome of the decision and over which the decision-maker has little or no control are called _____. The benefits or rewards that result from selecting a particular decision alternative are called _____. The various choices or options available to the decision-maker in any given problem situation are called _____.

4. Examine the decision table shown below:

		State of Nature			
		1	2	3	4
Decision	1	-50	-25	75	125
Alternative	2	10	15	20	25
	3	-20	-5	10	20

The selected decision alternative using a Maximax criterion is _____ and the optimal payoff is _____.

5. Use the decision table from question 4. The selected decision alternative using a Maximin criterion is _____ and the payoff for this is _____. Suppose Hurwicz criterion is used to select a decision alternative and α is .3. The selected decision alternative is _____ and the payoff is _____. However, if α is .8, the selected decision alternative is _____ and the payoff is _____.

6. Use the decision table from question 4 to construct an Opportunity Loss table. Using this table and a Minimax Regret criterion, the selected decision alternative is _____ and the minimum regret is _____.

7. With decision trees, the decision alternatives are depicted by a _____ node and the states of nature are represented by a _____ node.

8. The decision table presented in question 4 has been reproduced below with probabilities assigned to the states of nature:

		State of Nature 1(.20)	2(.35)	3(.40)	4(.05)
Decision	1	-50	-25	75	125
Alternative	2	10	15	20	25
	3	-20	-5	10	20

The expected monetary value of selecting decision alternative 1 is
_____. The expected monetary value of selecting decision alternative 2
is _____. The expected monetary value of selecting decision alternative
3 is _____.

9. An EMV'er would choose decision alternative _____ based on the results of question 8.

10. The expected value of perfect information for the decision scenario presented in question 8 is _____.

11. The degree of pleasure of displeasure a decision-maker has in being involved in the outcome selection process given the risks and opportunities available is

_____.

12. If it takes more than the expected monetary value to get a player to withdraw from a game, then that person is said to be a _____.

13. Consider the decision table shown below:

		State of Nature X(.40)	Y(.60)
Decision	1	200	500
	2	50	800

The expected monetary value of this decision scenario is _____.
Suppose the decision maker has an opportunity to buy a forecast to assist him/her in
making the decision. When the state of nature is X, the forecaster will predict X 85%
of the time and Y 15% of the time. When the state of nature is Y, the forecaster will
predict Y 95% of the time and will predict X 5% of the time. If the forecast is
purchased and the forecaster predicts that X will occur, then revised probability of X
occurring is _____ and of Y occurring is _____. If the
forecaster predicts that Y will occur, then the revised probability of X occurring is
_____ and of Y occurring is _____. The probability that
the forecaster will predict X is _____. The probability that the forecaster
will predict Y is _____. The expected monetary value with information
is _____. The expected value of sample information is

_____.

ANSWERS TO STUDY QUESTIONS

1. Certainty, Uncertainty, Risk

2. Decision Alternatives, States of Nature, Payoffs

3. States of Nature, Payoffs, Decision Alternatives

4. 1, 125

5. 2, 10, 2, 14.5, 1, 90

6. 1, 60

7. □, ○

8. 17.5, 16.5, -0.75

9. 1

10. 26

11. Utility

12. Risk-taker

13. 500, .9189, .0811, .0952, .9048, .37, .63, .542.02, 42.02

SOLUTIONS TO ODD-NUMBERED PROBLEMS IN CHAPTER 18

18.1

	S_1	S_2	S_3	Max	Min
d_1	250	175	-25	250	-25
d_2	110	100	70	110	70
d_3	390	140	-80	390	-80

a.) Max {250, 110, 390} = **390**   decision: Select d_3

b.) Max {-25, 70, -80} = **70**   decision: Select d_2

c.) For $\alpha = .3$

d_1: .3(250) + .7(-25) = 57.5

d_2: .3(110) + .7(70) = **82**

d_3: .3(390) + .7(-80) = 61

decision: Select d_2

For $\alpha = .8$

d_1: .8(250) + .2(-25) = 195

d_2: .8(110) + .2(70) = 102

d_3: .8(390) + .2(-80) = **296**

decision: Select d_3

Comparing the results for the two different values of alpha, with a more pessimist point-of-view ($\alpha = .3$), the decision is to select d_2 and the payoff is 82. Selecting by using a more optimistic point-of-view ($\alpha = .8$) results in choosing d_3 with a higher payoff of 296.

d.) The opportunity loss table is:

	S_1	S_2	S_3	Max
d_1	140	0	95	140
d_2	280	75	0	280
d_3	0	35	150	150

The minimax regret = min {140, 280, 150} = **140**

Decision: Select d_1 to minimize the regret.

18.3

	R	D	I	Max	Min
A	60	15	-25	60	-25
B	10	25	30	30	10
C	-10	40	15	40	-10
D	20	25	5	25	5

Maximax = Max {60, 30, 40, 25} = **60**

Decision: Select A

Maximin = Max {-25, 10, -10, 5} = **10**

Decision: Select B

18.5

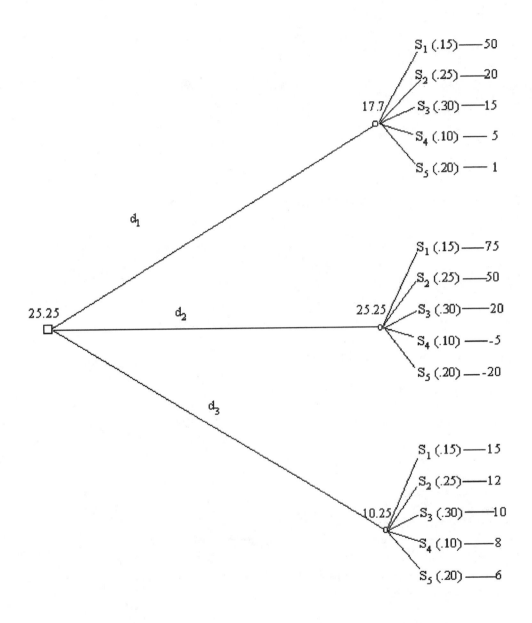

18.7 Expected Payoff with Perfect Information =

5(.15) + 50(.25) + 20(.30) + 8(.10) + 6(.20) = **31.75**

Expected Value of Perfect Information = 31.25 - 25.25 = **6.50**

18.9

	Down(.30)	Up(.65)	No Change(.05)	EMV
Lock-In	-150	200	0	85
No	175	-250	0	-110

Decision: Based on the highest EMV)(85), "Lock-In"

Expected Payoff with Perfect Information =

175(.30) + 200(.65) + 0(.05) = **182.5**

Expected Value of Perfect Information =   182.5 - 85 = **97.5**

18.11   a.) EMV = 200,000(.5) + (-50,000)(.5) = **75,000**

b.) Risk Avoider because the EMV is more than the investment (75,000 > 50,000)

c.) You would have to offer more than 75,000 which is the expected value.

18.13

	Dec(.60)	Inc(.40)	EMV
S	-225	425	35
M	125	-150	15
L	350	-400	50

Decision: Based on EMV = Maximum {35, 15, 50} = **50**

For Forecast (Decrease):

	Prior	Cond.	Joint	Revised
Decrease	.60	.75	.45	.8824
Increase	.40	.15	.06	.1176
			F(Dec) = .51	

For Forecast (Increase):

	Prior	Cond.	Joint	Revised
Decrease	.60	.25	.15	.3061
Increase	.40	.85	.34	.6939
			F(Inc) = .49	

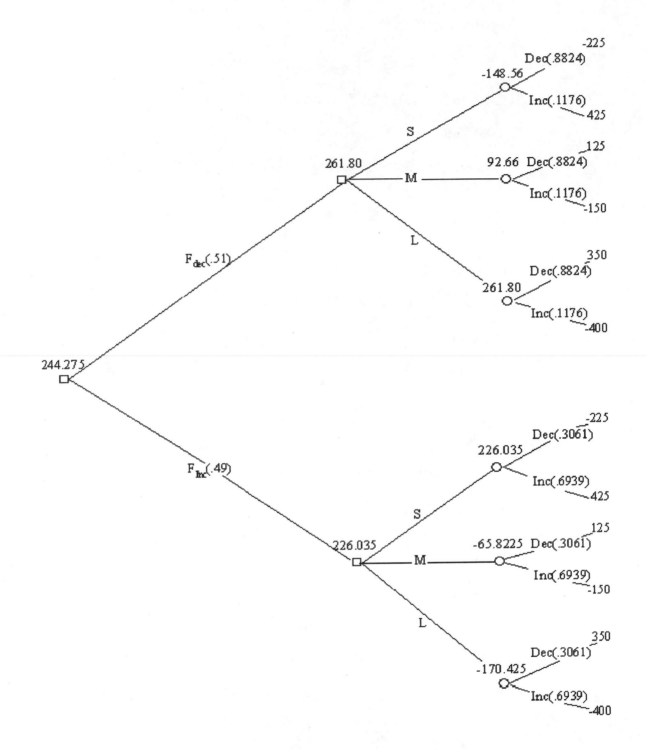

The expected value with sampling is **244.275**

EVSI = EVWS - EMV = 244.275 - 50 = **194.275**

18.15

	Oil(.11)	No Oil(.89)	EMV
Drill	1,000,000	-100,000	21,000
Don't Drill	0	0	0

Decision: The EMV for this problem is Max {21,000, 0} = 21,000. The decision is to Drill.

		Actual	
		Oil	No Oil
Forecast	Oil	.20	.10
	No Oil	.80	.90

Forecast Oil:

State	Prior	Cond.	Joint	Revised
Oil	.11	.20	.022	.1982
No Oil	.89	.10	.089	.8018

$$P(F_{Oil}) = .111$$

Forecast No Oil:

State	Prior	Cond.	Joint	Revised
Oil	.11	.80	.088	.0990
No Oil	.89	.90	.801	.9010

$$P(F_{No\ Oil}) = .889$$

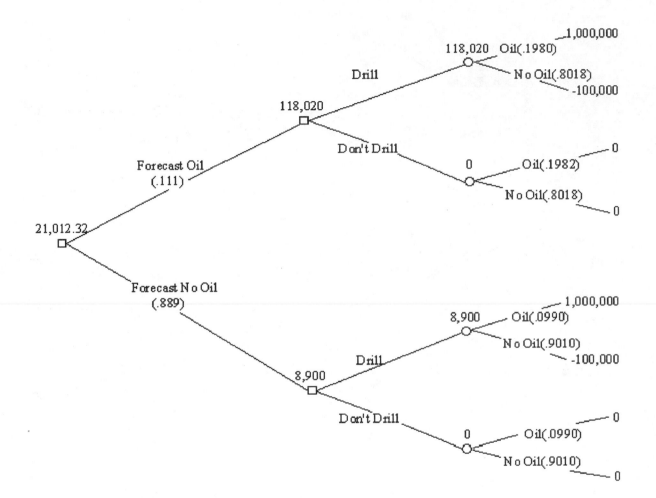

The Expected Value With Sampling Information is **21,012.32**

EVSI = EVWSI - EMV = 21,000 - 21,012.32 = **12.32**

18.17

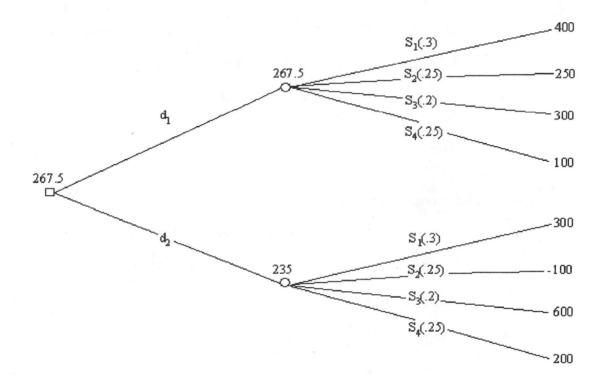

b.) d_1: $400(.3) + 250(.25) + 300(.2) + 100(.25) =$ **267.5**

   d_2: $300(.3) + (-100)(.25) + 600(.2) + 200(.25) = 235$

   Decision: Select d_1

c.) **Expected Payoff of Perfect Information:**

   $400(.3) + 250(.25) + 600(.2) + 200(.25) =$ **352.5**

   Value of Perfect Information = 352.5 - 267.5 = 85

18.19

	Small	Moderate	Large	Min	Max
Small	200	250	300	200	300
Modest	100	300	600	100	600
Large	-300	400	2000	-300	2000

a.) Maximax: Max {300, 600, 2000} = **2000**
Decision: Large Number

Minimax: Max {200, 100, -300} = **200**
Decision: Small Number

b.) Opportunity Loss:

	Small	Moderate	Large	Max
Small	0	150	1700	1700
Modest	100	100	1400	1400
Large	500	0	0	500

Min {1700, 1400, 500} = **500**
Decision: Large Number

c.) Minimax regret criteria leads to the same decision as Maximax.

18.21

	Mild(.75)	Severe(.25)	EMV
Reg.	2000	-2500	875
Weekend	1200	-200	850
Not Open	-300	100	-200

Decision: Based on Max EMV =

Max{875, 850, -200} = **875**, open regular hours.

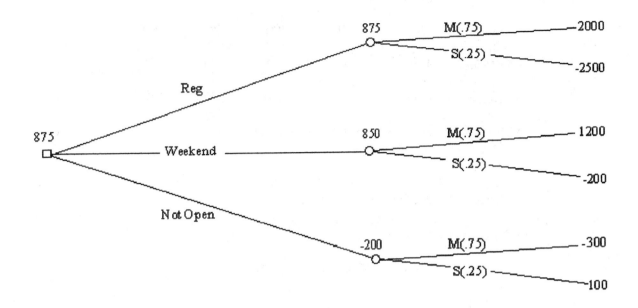

Expected Value with Perfect Information =

2000(.75) + 100(.25) = **1525**

Value of Perfect Information = 1525 - 875 = **650**

18.23

	Red.(.15)	Con.(.35)	Inc.(.50)	EMV
Automate	-40,000	-15,000	60,000	18,750
Do Not	5,000	10,000	-30,000	-10,750

Decision: Based on Max EMV =
Max {18750, -10750} = **18,750**, Select Automate

Forecast Reduction:

State	Prior	Cond.	Joint	Revised
R	.15	.60	.09	.60
C	.35	.10	.035	.2333
I	.50	.05	.025	.1667
			$P(F_{Red}) = .150$	

Forecast Constant:

State	Prior	Cond.	Joint	Revised
R	.15	.30	.045	.10
C	.35	.80	.280	.6222
I	.50	.25	.125	.2778
			$P(F_{Cons}) = .450$	

Forecast Increase:

State	Prior	Cond.	Joint	Revised
R	.15	.10	.015	.0375
C	.35	.10	.035	.0875
I	.50	.70	.350	.8750
			$P(F_{Inc}) = .400$	

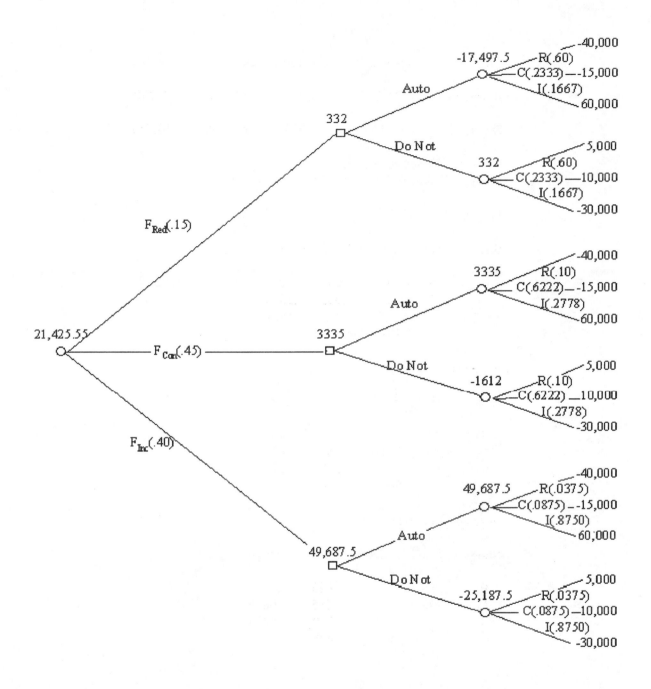

Expected Value With Sample Information = **21,425.55**

EVSI = EVWSI - EMV = 21,425.55 - 18,750 = **2,675.55**

Business Statistics:
Contemporary Decision Making

Third Edition

Ken Black
University of Houston
Clear Lake

SOUTH-WESTERN ™

THOMSON LEARNING

Australia · Canada · Mexico · Singapore · Spain · United Kingdom · United States

Solutions Manual and Study Guide,
Business Statistics: Contemporary Decision Making, 3/e, by Ken Black

Publisher: Dave Shaut
Senior Acquisitions Editor: Charles McCormick, Jr.
Senior Developmental Editor: Alice C. Denny
Senior Marketing Manager: Joseph A. Sabatino
Production Editor: Sandra Gangelhoff
Manufacturing Coordinator: Sandee Milewski
Printer: Globus Printing, Inc.

Printed in the United States of America
1 2 3 4 5 03 02 01 00

For more information contact South-Western College Publishing, 5101 Madison Road, Cincinnati, Ohio, 45227 or find us on the Internet at http://www.swcollege.com

For permission to use material from this text or product, contact us by
• **telephone: 1-800-730-2214**
• **fax: 1-800-730-2215**
• **web: http://www.thomsonrights.com**

ISBN 0-324-00923-2

This book is printed on acid-free paper.